IN THE NAME OF LOVE

IN THE NAME OF LOVE

Women's Narratives of Love and Abuse

Heather Fraser

Women's Press
Toronto

In the Name of Love: Women's Narratives of Love and Abuse
Heather Fraser

First published in 2008 by
Women's Press, an imprint of Canadian Scholars' Press Inc.
180 Bloor Street West, Suite 801
Toronto, Ontario
M5S 2V6

www.womenspress.ca

Copyright © 2008 by Heather Fraser and Canadian Scholars' Press Inc. All rights reserved. No part of this publication may be photocopied, reproduced, stored in a retrieval system, or transmitted in any form or by any means, electronic, mechanical, or otherwise, without the written permission of Canadian Scholars' Press Inc., except for brief passages quoted for review purposes. In the case of photocopying, a licence may be obtained from Access Copyright: One Yonge Street, Suite 1900, Toronto, Ontario, M5E 1E5, (416) 868-1620, fax (416) 868-1621, toll-free 1-800-893-5777, www.accesscopyright.ca.

Every reasonable effort has been made to identify copyright holders. Canadian Scholars' Press Inc. would be pleased to have any errors or omissions brought to its attention.

Canadian Scholars' Press Inc./Women's Press gratefully acknowledge financial support for our publishing activities from the Government of Canada through the Book Publishing Industry Development Program (BPIDP).

Library and Archives Canada Cataloguing in Publication

Fraser, Heather, 1965-
    In the name of love : women's narratives of love and abuse / Heather Fraser.

Includes bibliographical references.
ISBN 978-0-88961-462-8

    1. Sexual abuse victims. 2. Victims of family violence. 3. Abused women.
4. Adult child abuse victims. 5. Love. 6. Social work with women. I. Title.

HV6626.23.C3F73 2008   362.82'92   C2008-900508-2

Book design: Em Dash Design

08 09 10 11 12   5 4 3 2 1

Printed and bound in Canada by Marquis Book Printing Inc.

Canada

Contents

	Acknowledgements	7
Preface:	The Power of Love	9
Chapter 1:	Women, Abuse, and Social Work: What's Love Got to Do with It?	15
Chapter 2:	Dominant Stories about Love: History (Never) Repeats	27
Chapter 3:	Popular Stories about Love: Love, Love Me Do	47
Chapter 4:	First and Second Wave Feminist Stories about Love and Abuse: All's (Not) Fair in Love and War	57
Chapter 5:	Third Wave Feminist Stories about Love and Abuse: Pleasures and Paradoxes	73

Chapter 6: Using a Narrative Feminist Perspective: Analyzing Women's Stories of Love and Abuse 87

Chapter 7: Love and Abuse in Childhood: It's Not All Sugar and Spice 97

Chapter 8: Romance, Love, and Abuse in Early Adulthood: Cinderella's (Un)happy Ending? 121

Chapter 9: Love and Abuse in Adulthood: When Love Is (Not) the Answer 147

Chapter 10: Reviewing the Scripts for Loving: (Not) Losing Hope 171

Chapter 11: Revising the Scripts for Loving: Trying to Move On 191

Chapter 12: Still Wanting Love, But Not Wanting Abuse 203

Chapter 13: Changing Worlds: Future Possibilities for Professional Practice 227

References 253

Acknowledgements

There are many people I would like to thank for helping me to bring this book to life over the last decade or so. First, thanks go to Susan Silva-Wayne for having faith in the proposal and being so encouraging throughout the course of the writing. To the women who so generously allowed me to interview them: Thank you so much. Without exception I learned a great deal from your stories. I also enjoyed the many laughs we had and the latitude you gave me to stumble. Thanks also go to Candace Neufeld and the men with whom I shared some great conversations about love during the "Men and Love" workshop series at the Men's Resource Centre in Winnipeg in late 2004.

To my friends and family who never doubted that I had this book in me, I am indebted. Through your love and support I have had the motivation and confidence to go beyond what I already knew to explore, experiment, and express. Special thanks go to Bernadette Schwerdt, Linda Briskman, Wendy Fraser, Desma and Sid Strong, and Sara Charlesworth.

To the many colleagues, students, and practitioners with whom I have shared all or parts of the book's contents, and who have signalled that the project is interesting and worthwhile, thanks. I am grateful to Ros Thorpe, Jim Ife, and Bob Pease for their work on the early material I produced through the Ph.D. Finally, I want to acknowledge the love and support I got from Bob Mullaly and others in Winnipeg, including Susan Strega, Dori Vanderheyden, Anne MacDiarmid, Helen Fallding, Jo Cowen, Susan Prentice, and Karen Grant.

To someone on the other side of Canada, I want to acknowledge the contributions Art Fisher has made to this book. Through our lengthy conversations in person, over the phone, and in writing, he has been a great and generous source of knowledge and inspiration. Thanks, too, to Ian Gray in Melbourne for the chats we've had about the work he's been doing with men in relation to love and abuse. Last but not least, I want to thank Meg, my Bernese Mountain Dog, for being beside me each step of the way.

*All our lives we have heard stories of various
kinds, many with love as a leitmotif.*
(Sternberg 1998, p. 26)

Preface
THE POWER OF LOVE

I FIND IT IRONIC THAT WHILE LOVE IS THE hallmark of humanity, it is not widely discussed in social work and other related professions. In turn, very little professional knowledge has been developed about love, including its potential connection to abuse. Having spent many years working in the area of abuse (child abuse, domestic violence, and sexual assault), and after hearing so many women tell stories of abuse done in the name of love, I realized that this was quite a gap.

From my own life experience, and women's refuge work I did from the age of 18, I knew that love relationships were sites where power flowed, and not always in equitable and democratic ways. When I undertook my doctoral thesis in the mid-1990s, the politics of love became much clearer. Notably, it was through some of the interviews I had with Australian women that I learned how love and abuse could co-exist. However, I wondered whether I had a skewed view, given my practice background, the small number of women I had interviewed, and my choice of research participants (10 women who had experienced child abuse and had spent some period separated from their birth families when they were young). When I moved to Canada in 2003 I tested this idea by expanding the study and broadening the participant base.

By August 2004 I had interviewed 74 Canadian women, across a wide age range and socio-economic spectrum, for an average of two hours per person. Focusing most on sexualized love relationships, I asked the women to tell me stories about love and I quizzed them about whether they preferred equal love relationships or more traditional ones. From the thousands of stories I heard, I noticed the high priority women gave to loving others. In hindsight this was not surprising given that the women self-selected to participate in a project about women and love. However, what was surprising was the number of women who quite unexpectedly told me stories where the lines between love and abuse were or had been blurred. This came from women who traversed the divides of money, age, culture, religion, and sexual orientation. Among them were the women who made no mention of abuse, but who were open to the idea that love and abuse could converge, once I introduced them to it.

This book introduces ideas about love and social work from academic, popular, and everyday circles. While I am eager to examine connections between love and abuse, I have fore-grounded love to compensate for the lack of attention it usually receives. Similarly, because women carry out most social work, and since "ordinary" women are often constructed not as authors of their own love stories (but audiences to the stories others tell), it is women's experiences of love that capture much of the spotlight.

While there is much to be learned about love, and many ways to approach its study, I take the position that not all studies are equally useful. As Lyotard (1979, p. 488) argued, "It is one thing for an undertaking to be possible and another for it to be just." This is why the focus of this book is on the politics of love, rather than a more simple inquiry into the positive benefits of loving. Read in light of the value of social justice, I concentrate on some of the gendered, classed, and hetero-normative dimensions of women's sexual love relationships. I do this because they are three of the axes onto which oppression is engraved. As such, I do not assume that love is instinctual or genetic, nor do I attempt to provide a precise definition of love so that it can be measured.

Moreover, I reject the claim that particular love styles are "nothing more than common sense" (Lee 1998, p. 39). I also challenge the idea that women's love relationships are inherently pathological; that they are outgrowths of "castration anxiety" or somehow connected to "penis envy" (Freud 1986, p. 408). Because I am cautious about using sweeping generalizations and appreciative of the different love styles possible, I make no attempt to establish whether love relationships, particularly heterosexual ones, either liberate or oppress women (Firestone 1970; Langford 1999). Instead, I theorize the discourses people use to attribute meanings to love in their lives.

Quite simply, I was interested to learn how the people who participated in this study thought and felt about love; how much they invested in their love relationships; and how their beliefs and attitudes about love changed over time. Hearing their experiences of abuse was a central part of the process. Figuring out how social workers and other health and welfare professionals might hear and represent alternative views about love and abuse, without relinquishing their right and responsibility to keep questions of injustice alive, was another part of the process.

Guiding this book are four main questions: (1) How is love represented in Anglo-American-dominated cultures? (2) How does power infiltrate women's love relationships? (3) How do women interact with dominant stories about love and abuse? (4) What can social workers and other health and welfare professionals learn from the love stories that individual women narrate, especially those subjected to abuse, coercion, and brutality?

An Overview of the Chapters

In Chapter 1, I introduce love in relation to women and social work and give reasons for taking love seriously. I provide preliminary reasons for understanding love in relation to abuse. I then point to some of the obstacles social workers and other related health and welfare professionals face as they try to overcome their tendency to repress love and assume that the differences between good and bad relationships are self-evident.

In Chapter 2, I advocate for an interdisciplinary approach to studying love. I examine a selection of philosophical, psychological, and physiological claims made about love, before focusing on some of the historical and sociological dimensions of love. I pay particular attention to heterosexual love conventions because they dominate so many love stories.

In Chapter 3, popular love stories are then inspected. Given the volume of popular love stories, I concentrate on some of the most popular stories in light of the contradictory messages that they contain. I describe the expectation that people should love as the injunction to love.

In Chapter 4, I consider why some feminists claim that love can conquer women. Moving through the three waves of feminism, I explore some of the conflicting views that Western feminists have expressed about love and sexuality. I note that in the first wave, love was often seen as a distraction to more important pursuits, such as women's suffrage. By the second wave, however, heterosexual relationships were charged with eroticizing women's subordination.

In Chapter 5, I consider the stories told about love by third wave feminists. Shying away from polemical (or oppositional) modes of storytelling, I note how much attention is given to the contradictions and paradoxes often apparent when love and gender are performed. I observe that during this wave more optimism has tended to surface about love and its potential to induce happiness in women's lives, including those who identify as heterosexual.

In Chapter 6, I argue that love lives are productively examined through a narrative feminist approach. I talk about how I deployed this approach in the research interviews I conducted with women in Australia and Canada.

Stories about love and abuse during early and late childhood are narratively analyzed in Chapter 7. I inspect the performance of archetypal scripts such as "Mommy Dearest," "Being Daddy's Princess," and "Sibling Rivalry." Since assumptions are often made about women who have suffered abuse and/or a period of separation from their birth families while young, I direct much of my attention to analyzing stories provided by women who grew up in (state) care.

In Chapter 8, I focus on romance, love, and abuse in early adulthood. I argue that a central part of the process for girls to become women is through the formation of (sexual) love relationships. I examine the sexual scripts that have circulated for good girls, bad girls, and modern women. I then consider some of the challenges facing women after sexual abuse. Toward the end, stories about the utility of love are included because they illustrate how many girls hope that love will rescue them from suffering.

Love and abuse in adulthood is the topic for discussion in Chapter 9. I pay attention to the ways women develop, maintain, and terminate their love relationships. I show how many of the women have pursued conventional scripts, with varying degrees of success. While some ended up satisfied, others found their dreams a far cry from their everyday experiences of domestic labour and male privilege. Still others were left wondering why it was that they had sublimated so many personal goals for the good of their relationships.

Trying to effect change is the subject matter of Chapters 10 and 11. In Chapter 10, I look at the social sanctions and material obstacles that can deter women from separating from abusive loved ones. I also consider the hope that change plays in spurring women on to persist with abusive partners. I note that it is usually when all hope is lost that abusive relationships are dissolved.

In Chapter 11, I consider some of the vows the women make to themselves as they try to institute change. Self-help recovery narratives are considered because a sizable group of women survivors of abuse referred to them. Taken-for-granted assumptions about what abuse survivors need to do to move on are also considered. I then explore turning points or epiphanies that lead to change since they were common plots in the women's stories about rebuilding post-separation.

In Chapter 12, a much broader range of women's beliefs about, and hopes for, love are canvassed. I contend that although most women still want sexual love in their lives, they do not want to be abused by others, nor do they want to be abusive toward others. A guide for respectful love ensues using the women's own definitions of love and advice for loving.

Chapter 13 revolves around the theme of changing worlds. I reiterate why it is important for social workers and other health and welfare professionals to study love. I provide examples of projects where love and abuse have already been connected. I then provide a rationale for connecting love with abuse before considering some of the risks of doing so. Drawing on ideas from many of the participants, I remind readers that the socio-political contexts of people's lives are important, particularly post-separation. I note that our structural, cultural, interpersonal, and intrapersonal worlds are changing, often at breakneck speed. I talk about how some of the currents of macro-change have affected, and are affecting policies, programs, and benefits made available to victims/survivors of intimate abuse. Periodically, I use tables to summarize some of the findings already presented and to point to possible ways forward.

Let's talk about love.
(Celine Dion 1998)

I
WOMEN, ABUSE, AND SOCIAL WORK
What's Love Got to Do with It?

IN WESTERN SOCIETIES, INDIVIDUALS ARE exposed to many stories about love. Narratives of ecstasy, euphoria, and happiness achieved through love punctuate many human beings' thoughts and conversations. Stories of betrayal, heartache, loss, grief, abuse, and exploitation can also be heard. These stories are taken up and fed back to us through films, sitcoms, magazines, soap operas, thrillers, novels, theatre performances, poetry, art, dance, music, advertising, and real-life news reports. Inside and beyond universities, research is undertaken and disputes over love's meaning ensue. In a constant series of production, consumption, and reproduction, narratives of the heart preoccupy a large number of people much of the time.

Studying Love

There is so much to say because love has many realities and truths. No amount of talk will settle, once and for all, the many meanings that may be attributed to love. While language is critical to the way love is represented, it cannot be fully captured by words. As this first chapter suggests, the multiplicity of love makes it a phenomenon that is difficult to define and extremely challenging to study, especially from the discipline of social work (also see Fraser 2002, 2003).

Defining Love

As a word, "love" contains many meanings. It is a noun and a verb. It refers to both subjects and objects. We can perform love and we can have (a) love. We may love other humans, as well as animals, gardens, and countries. We may also speak of love when we describe the attachments we have to our homes and our possessions. For some, this love rivals that which they feel toward other humans.

Whether it is for convenience or because of a deep commitment to the ideals of romance, some commentators refer to only one possible subset of love when they use its name. For instance, Baumeister and Wotman (1992, p. 6) declared that they would "use the term 'love' broadly, referring to any strong romantic attraction." Featherstone (1998) did likewise. Mainstream psychologists, however, referred to "romantic love" when they talked about Western relationships of sexual intimacy. Anthropologists, on the other hand, have tended to use the language of "passionate love" to argue for or against the universality of romantic love (see Jankowiak 1995).

As with so many other abstracted words, such as "happiness," "desire," "distress," "crisis," and "loss," definitions of love contain much slippage. According to Fuery (1995), all definitions are transitory, relying heavily on social conventions for their persistence. Love is no exception. This is why I draw upon Snyder's (1992, p. 52) contention that "Love is a metaphor, a kind of shorthand for a complex system of attitudes, beliefs, feelings and behaviours." Yet for me, it is also an emotion or series of emotions, (Jackson 1996); a code of behaviour (Luhmann 1986); a story or series of stories (Sternberg 1998); and an ideology (Lee 1998).

Taking Love Seriously

Despite the attention given to love in popular culture, love has tended to hover uneasily over academia, with many academics treating love as a footnote to other topics deemed to be more credible (Evans 1998; Gray 1993; Lee 1998; Lindholm 1998). For social work in particular, a number of possible arguments can be advanced for not taking love too seriously.

For a start, love may be linked to the concept of divinity, with the love of God appearing as a gift from the heavens (Tarnas 1991). With its magic and mystery, love's affiliation with spirituality makes it an anathema to rational, empirical study. Resistant to definition, measurement, and logic, love can appear chaotic, irrational, and unfathomable. For instance, P. Gray (1993, p. 49) claims that "the more we learn about love, the more preposterous and mysterious it is likely to appear."

Distinguishable from the razor sharp, scientific refinement of Western intellectual thought, love may be conceptualized as a sentimental portrayal of duty and desire—desire that can appear to be soppy and sloppy, embarrassing, and, for the most part, feminine. Because of its proximity to mainstream women's culture and to the broader concept of femininity (Davidson 1992; Evans 1998; French 1985; hooks 2000), love may appear to be too expressive and too nebulous to study. Yet at the same time, heterosexual love may be dismissed as enslaving women, encouraging their dependency on men, and otherwise distracting them from higher pursuits (also see Chapter 4).

Reservations about studying love may be expressed for a range of other reasons. Some people fear that attempts to discover love's secrets will undermine love's magic (Livermore 1993). Others have a jaundiced view of love because they connect it to humanism, which they dismiss for its tendency to assume that humans are naturally good (Seidman 1994). Humanism and associated terms, such as "compassion," "community," and "home," stand in stark contrast to economic conservatism (Ellis 1998). With its greed-is-good, number-crunching bottom lines, economic conservatism tends to be intolerant of that which may be described as impractical, whimsical, exaggerated, and extravagant. Love's emotionally unruly potential makes matters even worse, leading some to view it as a high-risk investment, a gamble, and a possible source of financial and emotional bankruptcy.

Yet at the same time, love is often commodified as a profitable product. In popular culture, love merchandising generates billions of dollars each year. The marketing of love stories may prompt some people to view love as a quick buck-making gimmick of popular culture used to siphon off the spare cash of the masses. Often these love stories appear corny, narcissistic, and naive. As such, they may not seem worthy of "serious study" (Lindholm 1998).

"Serious" scholars may also disparage love, especially sexual love, because they associate it with romance, which they dismiss as frivolous and infantile, and/or too bourgeois since courtly love emerged as a way for the philandering rich to justify extramarital affairs (Luhmann 1986; also see Chapter 2). For others, love is understood as a natural part of life that does not require analysis or explanation. For all or some of these reasons, granting love the same status of inquiry as social problems (such as mental illness, poverty, and unemployment) may seem insulting to researchers who dedicate themselves to "real problems," and whose work promises to improve the practical well-being of people.

On face value these arguments might appear to be plausible, yet they do not constitute a compelling case against the study of love because if the criteria for scholarly concern hinged on studying only that which is rational and secular, amenable to concrete substantiation and measurement, financially profitable, and applicable to every member of the society, then theology would not be studied in the academy, nor would the fine arts. For that matter, much of philosophy, psychology, sociology, and anthropology would be disqualified as well. Certainly a history of football or a sociological analysis of unpaid labour would be seen to have nothing to teach us. Studies that are not categorically designed to solve problems, test formulae, maximize profit, or reduce risk have a place in the academy because they contribute to the body of knowledge that is produced about the world and our lives in it. These bodies of knowledge are important because they contain research that explores how people attribute meaning to their lives (de Certeau 1984; Denzin 1995; Weeks 1998). Often raising more questions than they can answer, research into meaning may raise some of the most vexing questions about human life. Such is the case with love.

Exploring Love's Many Meanings

Love is an important subject to study because it is meaningful to many people. It is so meaningful that it constitutes part of the Western definition of what it means to be human. Imbued with desire and socially regulated but individually expressed, love involves a complex web of emotions, motivations, actions, and explanations. Research can help us to make sense of these complexities, particularly if it helps us to understand more about the ways power infiltrates the intimate spaces of everyday life (also see Fraser 2002, 2003). It is time for social workers to develop knowledge about love and contribute to discussions about love relationships.

Love in Social Work

Just as definitions of love are complicated, so are definitions of social work. As Margolin (1997) pointed out, the term "social work" has always been unclear, signifying a multitude of ideologies, practices, technologies, and interventions. Agreeing that social work has never been a single entity, Ife (1997) noted that all generalizations made about it run the risk of oversimplification.

Social Work's Multiple Identities

Questions remain about how social work might be conceptualized. Is it a profession? Or is it, as Pithouse (1987) argued, an invisible trade? Is it best thought of as a science or an art (England 1986)? Is it largely a technical exercise or is it driven by its values? Is it fundamentally conservative or inherently radical? Is it more about care or control? Is it predominantly rational or emotional? Is it unisex or is it largely women's business? Is it possible that definitions of social work tell us more about those who define it than they do about the nature of social work?

For me, social work is a profession shaped by its values. I value the emotional and artistic elements of social work and do not forget that it is conducted mostly by and for women. Yet these elements are not necessarily promoted by mainstream social workers, nor those who identify as radical. For all their differences, conservatives and radicals still tend to define social work by its problem orientation, an orientation that has a long history in Western social work.

Social Work's Problem Focus

Around the 1890s, the term "social work" emerged in Britain and the United States of America to refer to a specific occupation and a general field of social concern (Camilleri 1996). In the early days Anglo-American social work emerged to deal with the problem of *poverty*, yet the causes of poverty and its associated problems (such as unemployment, violent crime, personal suffering, poor education, substance abuse, and so on) were subject to many debates. At the time, four alternative views of poverty were provided, views that seeded contemporary analyses of poverty.

The Charity Organization Society (COS) presented the first view of poverty. Working within what we now call a "neo-conservative paradigm" (see Mullaly 1997, 2007), they attributed the causes of poverty to the weaknesses and failings of individuals. For them, designing a more systematic way to distribute charity was crucial (Margolin 1997). Casework served this purpose well. By monitoring the poor through casework, and visiting them in their homes, they assessed their level of cleanliness and judged people as deserving or undeserving. COS members were keen to make this distinction because they believed that if charity was given to the "undeserving poor," they would be encouraging mendicity (idle begging). By keeping case files that included notes on the amount and type of charitable funds already allocated, they could also prevent individuals from visiting a number of charitable agencies to double dip (Mullaly 1997). Casework also allowed COS members to advise the poor about matters concerning sobriety, thrift, self-help, and religious redemption.

In contrast to the COS, the Settlement House Movement developed the belief that impoverished neighbourhoods rather than impoverished individuals were the main causes of poverty (Mullaly 2007). Rejecting the moral means test as intrusive and demeaning, the Settlement House Movement tried to ameliorate poverty through the development of local neighbourhoods (Margolin 1997). Using methods now associated with liberalism and liberal forms of community development/organizing, Settlement members moved into poor neighbourhoods. Becoming acquainted with the poor and the living conditions in which they lived, they concentrated on improving the local infrastructure, such as sanitation, health care, housing, education, labour, and race relations (Camilleri 1996). They did, however, stop short of trying to change the social order that produced a relatively small group of people who could enjoy the privileges associated with wealth, and a much larger mass of people who were forced to live in poverty.

The Fabians provided the third way of understanding poverty. Using a more extensive collectivist approach, they promoted the view that poverty was an outcome of an unfair social order, not individual weakness. For them, capitalism's inherent thirst for profit and disregard for human need was at the root of human suffering. Hoping to transform the social order, they looked for ways to move from capitalism to democratic socialism. However, because they were interested in evolutionary (rather than revolutionary) socialism, they tried to effect this transformation by devising social policies that would provide universal programs and benefits to the whole society (Ife 1997; Mullaly 2007). In other words, they wanted to use an expanding array of state programs and benefits to make the transition from capitalism to socialism.

Decades later the fourth response to poverty surfaced. Sharing some commonalities with the Fabians, Marxists believed that poverty and its associated problems were caused by capitalism, yet they contested the idea that state reforms were able to effect a transformation of socio-economic order, which was needed to achieve emancipation (Galper 1975). Skeptical of state benefits and programs, including those that many social workers were providing, some Marxists argued that rather than helping the poor and working classes, they propped up an unfair social order and forestalled the possibility of revolutionary socialism (Galper 1975).

Many decades have passed since these four groups offered Western social work its origins. As I have suggested, traces of these perspectives can still be seen in social work today. While many other perspectives have been spawned, contemporary social work has retained its close proximity to social problems (Camilleri 1996; Margolin 1997; Mullaly 2007). From a psychodynamic perspective to a structural approach, social problems continue to be constituted as the shopfront of social work. Subjects not framed by a problem focus tend to be positioned as either secondary to, or outside of, the parameters of social work. Love is one such subject.

Unlike abuse, which is now a clearly designated social problem, love amounts to more than the sum of its problems. Associated with desire, pleasure, happiness, and joy, love often involves problems but in and of itself, it is not *a* problem. This is one of the reasons why social work has found it difficult to accommodate the study of love in its curriculum. There are, however, many other reasons why social work's treatment of love, especially love affiliated with sexuality, may be characterized as repressive.

The Repression of Love and Sexuality in Social Work

Social work has had a long-standing but uneasy relationship with love. On the one hand, social workers have regularly assumed love's existence; but on the other, they have not recognized love as a subject in its own right. From making case plans to devising social policies, social workers routinely take for granted love's existence, yet few social work texts speak directly to the subject and few, if any, social work courses dedicate any time to its exploration. The relatively small number of social work texts that do attend to love usually do so from the perspective of psychoanalysis, which, as Ireland (1988) explained, tends to define love by its pathologies.

Having said that the main plot of social work is to try to resolve social problems, subplots are evident in the history of social work, and the pursuit of love is one of them. For instance, as much as the COS might be remembered for its casework interventions, it might also be remembered that Christian love—often referred to as agape—was a motivating force for its members (Camilleri 1996). Expressed through charity, Christian love was offered as one of the more palatable reasons for affluent "good Christians" to enter the realms of the "dangerous classes." As a discourse, it encouraged subscribers to serve God by "loving thy neighbour." In its most conservative hue, it is a discourse that still extracts love from sexual desire (Ireland 1988). Armed with the view that love associated with sexual desire (known as "eros" and "amour") was dangerous and sinful, many members of the COS were particularly harsh critics of those who engaged in sexual activities outside the confines of marriage and/or procreation. Yet, through the relationships they formed across the socio-economic divide, some COS members became more understanding and less judgmental of the poor.

Historical accounts of the Settlement House Movement also tend to gloss over the fact that Christian love also inspired many members of this movement toward the more benevolent dispensation of philanthropy. As Camilleri (1996) noted, when the Settlement House Movement first started, there was considerable overlap in volunteers of this movement and the COS. However, by becoming neighbours to the poor, members of this movement developed less punitive attitudes, concentrating their energy on their (albeit limited) program of social reforms.

For Fabians and Marxists, although politics was the ostensible driving force, altruism was never far away. Closely associated with love, altruism inspired many Fabians and Marxists to imagine that a radically different kind of world was possible. Promoting the values of equality, humanitarianism, fellowship, democracy, and self-realization, both the Fabians and Marxists endeavoured to create a world without domination and unfairness (Galper 1975; Ife 1997). Arguably, it is a world that has the potential to produce the optimal conditions in which more democratic forms of love can flourish.

With different forms of love acting as a catalyst for social work, it is significant that social work has historically been construed as "a calling" (Camilleri 1996; Margolin 1997; Parton & Byrne 2000). Apart from being predestined, "a calling" usually involves deferring to a higher good and behaving in ways associated with humility and self-sacrifice. These attributes require one to do things for love rather than for money (also see Chapter 9).

In the process of reconstructing social work from a calling to a profession, social work started to distance itself from love (also see Fraser 2003). As I have argued, love's resistance to scientific measurement and its close association with the feminine have proved troublesome to the academy. Because of the desire to be recognized as a discipline in its own right and as a fully fledged profession, social work increasingly dissociated itself from that which was ascribed to the feminine. This was, however, no easy task. For a start, social work had to overcome the "problem" that it was largely conducted by women, who were expected to demonstrate love in their homes, not the public sphere. Then social work had to manage the idea that it did a lot more than "brighten up" other people's lives (Bosanquet 1901 in Camilleri 1996, p. 23). Thirsty for academic and professional status, social workers may well have avoided any association with love so as to "disavow their image as soft-headed do-gooders and bleeding hearts" (Ricketts & Gochros 1987, p. 2).

Perhaps another challenge that social workers faced in their quest for professional status was the possibility of developing a bad reputation, particularly if their interest in sexuality was seen to exceed the conventional bounds of "feminine decency." It is interesting that given all that social workers bear witness to, that even today many Western social workers are uncomfortable talking openly and explicitly about sex. For many social workers, sexual relations are still seen to be too private to be discussed, and too indelicate to inquire about, particularly if they do not involve some form of abuse. As Margolin (1997) argued, the residual effects of social work's long-standing connection to Christianity are still evident. With its sexually repressive tendencies, Christianity, and its correlating desire to "help people," still motivates many social work students. At the same time, Christian-based organizations continue to offer social work many sites within which it is taught and practised.

To reiterate, social work's professional inclinations and Christian overtones can be implicated in the repression of discourses about love and sexuality. This is problematic because without some space for social work students to explain, defend, and consider revising their beliefs about love, most graduates are left to import un-inspected ideas into their practice. Un-inspected ideas are potentially hazardous because they contain homespun, commonsensical views that bear a close resemblance to those circulating in mainstream culture (Rossiter 1996; Shultz 1987). With so much said about love in popular culture, and with so many of these texts reinforcing traditional expressions of heterosexuality (Laws & Schwartz 1977; Rose 2000; Ussher 1997), social workers risk unwittingly incorporating popular ideas about love into their practice.

Popular love narratives are problematic for social workers because they are usually based on oversimplified polarities such as men/women, good/bad, strong/weak, normal/abnormal. These polarities are played out in a number of ways. First, by assuming that heterosexuality is normal and desirable, stories told by people identifying as gay, lesbian, bisexual, or trans-gendered tend to be drowned out, trivialized, and/or pathologized (Greer 1999; Westlund 1999; Wood 2001). Second, by giving attention to monogamous and publicly committed heterosexual coupledom, popular love narratives usually delegitimize or discredit heterosexual relationships that transgress convention (Schultz 1987). Third, by displaying such strong optimism about the potential for monogamous heterosexual coupledom to produce lasting happiness, popular love narratives tend to underestimate the possibility of abuse in the family (Westlund 1999; Wood 2001).

According to Schultz (1987), social workers are liable to make four rather narrow assumptions: (1) that heterosexuality is the most "natural" expression of sexuality; (2) that sexual relationships should involve more than sex; (3) that intimacy is "good" only if it is long lasting; and (4) that women need to experience trust and romance before they can be sexually satisfied. Two decades have passed, but not a lot seems to have changed (Thompson 1998; Westlund 1999). This is problematic given that many social workers become privy to other people's love lives, including many not well served by dominant discourses and stereotypical assumptions.

Making Connections between Love and Abuse

With other health professionals, many social workers expend a great deal of energy developing knowledge about abuse. This is not surprising given that so many of the people with whom they work experience problems associated with abuse, especially abuse from "loved ones."

Defining Abuse

Like love, abuse is a code word that signifies a complex set of phenomena. For instance, abuse may be defined as acts of domination by one individual or group over another. Often overlapping, abuse may take physical, sexual, emotional, psychological, spiritual, and/or financial forms. It may include coercion, threats, physical force, and/or aggression, along with psychological processes that have the effect of denigrating and devaluing an individual or group of people. Abuse may be overt or covert; deliberate and carefully rationalized or impulsive, random, and/or denied (see Bagshaw et al. 2000).

Abuse frequently involves (1) control, (2) exploitation, (3) deprivation, (4) surveillance, and/or (5) manipulation (see Herman 1992; Ristock 2002). Control may be enacted in a number of ways and may include systematic or more random acts of deprivation, including the deprivation of food, sleep, freedom of movement, money, or other resources (Bagshaw et al. 2000). Exploitation often occurs through the theft or inadequate remuneration for the abused person's labour. It may also involve the theft of property, including the abuser's refusal to recognize contributions (financial, emotional, and domestic) made by the abused toward the accumulation of assets. Surveillance may be used to maintain dominant-subordinate relations. Surveillance regimes may be formal or informal, but often rely on the close scrutiny of the subordinated by those in power. Manipulation is common. Subordinate peoples' perceptions of rights or hopes for the future are often discredited and denied. Feelings may be blocked to the point where victims are denied the right to express any negative emotions at all (see Goldrick Jones 2002).

Abuse can occur at the individual and group level. People can be abused because they are associated with a devalued social group. As Young (1990, 1997) argued, abuse occurs when people are discriminated against on the basis of gender, class, race, sexuality, age, and ability, and blocked from pursuing their needs and interests. Sometimes these experiences are reported through inquiries into human rights abuses (see Ife 2001). Mostly they are not. Ordinarily, "abuse" is defined narrowly and related exclusively to interpersonal acts of aggression, leaving the more systematic, structural forms of abuse to go unnoticed or be hidden from view. Indigenous communities around the world have testified to this.

Debates about Terminology Used to Describe Abuse/Violence

Words chosen to define abuse are important. They are so important that they are a source of debate among those similarly positioned. For instance, some feminists prefer to use the term "abuse" with respect to forms of manipulation, control, and dominance that are not connected to the use of physical violence, reserving the word "violence" for *physical* abuse or threat of physical abuse that occurs between/among intimately involved partners, roommates, or family members. In this instance, "abuse" is applied to situations where other forms of harmful, controlling, and/or degrading acts are undertaken. However, other feminists, including some feminist social workers, deliberately use the term "violence" to refer to *any* kind of dominating act (irrespective of whether it is physical, sexual, emotional, material, or spiritual in nature) in the hope that they will be able to expand the popular understanding of violence and prevent a hierarchy of abuses from forming (also see Department of Justice Canada 2007, Web site http://canada.justice.gc.ca/en/ps/fm/).

The potential slippage of terms and variation in definitions becomes even more pressing once we sort through different types of abuses and consider their uses. Take the terms "domestic violence" and "family violence" as examples. In some circles, "domestic violence" is the preferred term because it is associated with the women's movement and is seen to cover violent situations across a range of relationships beyond the traditional nuclear family. In other circles, "domestic violence" is supplanted with "family violence" precisely because it is associated with feminism (Blagg 2000). In response, some have rejected the notion of "family violence" and reinstated "domestic violence" because they believe "family violence" implicates victims/survivors in the abuse perpetrated against them (see Memmott et al. 2001). Intimate abuse or spousal violence are other linguistic options that point to the potential dangers of sexual intimacy.

Adding a similar degree of confusion, the term "domestic abuse" may be seen as less serious or not as extreme as "domestic violence." Some assume that "abuse" is more long term, leaving "violence" to signify critical incidents. Others adopt terms such as "violent *and controlling behaviours*" to cover acts of domination, including those not stereotypically associated with violence. Alongside these debates are debates about standardizing definitions so that international research can be more meaningfully compared. However, standardizing definitions of abuse and violence runs the risk of denying the politics of defining the terms. Whose definitions would or should prevail?

Should terms be used to deliberately recognize women's greater risk of being abused by intimates? Should terms such as "wife beating" or "male violence against women" be used to drive home the point that most perpetrators of violence are male and most victims/survivors are female (see Pease 1996)? Or does such a move inadvertently stereotype women into passive victim roles and men as inevitable aggressors? Alternatively, should we be led by the terms that victims/survivors prefer (see Blagg 2000)? If we do this, how might we represent our own value-based positions, especially if we believe the terms selected disguise or distract attention away from forms of abuse/violence that we believe are important?

Not seeing a single way forward, I have experimented with terminology used to describe love and abuse. I have tried to remain interested in the debates about terminology and sensitive to the contexts in which the words are used. I have found it helpful to express interest in learning more about how particular terms have been adopted or discarded. I have been particularly interested in reflecting on the language used when love and abuse co-exist.

Summary

In this chapter I have explained why Anglo-American-dominated social work has been reticent in discussing questions relating to love, sex, and desire. I have argued that this reticence has meant that very little knowledge has been produced about the politics of love. The politics of love are important because they are central to many women's experiences of intimate abuse. Not being attuned to the politics of love runs the risk of social workers and other health and welfare professionals reaching for stereotypes and drawing on "common sense," neither of which may be fair or even useful to many of the people we serve. As I have suggested, un-inspected ideas about love and abuse are problematic because they are likely to promote dominant love styles (such as traditional heterosexual romance) over alternative styles, including those that prioritize the values of democracy, respect, desire, and freedom. In the final section of the chapter, I identified some of the debates about terminology used to represent abuse in love relationships. I have also pointed to the central point of this book, which is that even though love and abuse *should* not co-exist, they often do.

> *The decision to get married offers many attractions. Not only is there the promise of security, and the opportunity to replace the uncertain emotional unrest of passionate love with the stability of companionate affection, but there are also important developmental opportunities which apply specifically to married or cohabiting couples.*
>
> (Petersen 1984, p. 348)

2

DOMINANT STORIES ABOUT LOVE
History (Never) Repeats

IN THE PREVIOUS CHAPTER I DEFINED LOVE broadly and gave a rationale for social workers and other health and welfare professionals to study love. I argued that if love continues to be neglected, workers are liable to import into their practice ideas that they think "everybody" shares, ideas that are "common sense." This is a problem because "common sense" ideas are often simplistic formulations that, more often than not, resemble dominant love stories that favour some groups over others.

In this chapter, I survey a wide range of dominant stories about love, noting the claims that they make. Guided by the question about how love is represented in Anglo-American-dominated cultures, I begin by reviewing academic discourses about love, starting with those offered by philosophers and psychologists. These accounts are useful, particularly for the ways they reveal some of the emotional and embodied dimensions of love. I then turn to the disciplines of history and sociology to consider some of the ways that love has been codified and regulated. Finally, my attention is cast on the cultural conventions for loving during postmodernity.

Philosophical and Psychological Love Stories

Philosophers and psychologists have contributed to the growing body of literature now produced about love (Livermore 1993). From these scholars, love is constructed as an emotional state, a drive, a need, a disposition, an expectation, a role, an attitude, an embodied experience, a condition, a virus, a decision, a habit, a myth, and a fantasy. As a result, different interpretations are made about how love affects individuals. Embedded in them are claims that are worth inspecting because they influence the conclusions drawn about love. For instance, when love is viewed through the lens of behaviourism, love is likely to be viewed as a product of classical conditioning. Dichotomized from hate, love is portrayed by behaviourists as a conduit (or channel) to positive reinforcement. It is also likely to be seen to increase feelings of pleasure while avoiding "negative stimuli" (Snyder 1992). With a relatively simple plot, this discourse presents love as an escape from pain and suffering.

Dramatically different claims about love emerge from those social theorists who use ideas from existentialism, psychoanalysis, phenomenology, and social constructionism. From these theorists love is presented as a paradoxical phenomenon that produces agony as well as ecstasy. Rather than offering an escape from negative stimuli, love is said to be riddled with contradictions and productive of many mixed emotions (Snyder 1992). This is particularly evident when individuals fall in love.

Falling in Love

With other existentially inclined philosophers, Barthes (1978) assumed that falling in love was a cataclysmic event that involved lovers becoming "thunderstruck," hypnotized by the tingling, emotionally intense sensations of love. Moments of magic, anticipation, exuberance, compassion, tenderness, union, and festivity were said to follow with life feeling very meaningful, yet lurking among these sensations were those far less pleasurable. According to this way of thinking, lovers express anxiety, jealousy, drama, and catastrophe due to the fear that their love will not be reciprocated.

Williams (1997) narrated a similar story about falling in love. For him, the lovestruck were likely to experience fleeting happiness but also be flooded with doubts. Similar to Barthes (1978), he claimed that in-love individuals were prone to doubt because time spent together did not assuage all fears of the love relationship ending, with time spent apart just making matters worse (Williams 1997). Lovers worried that their fantasized reunions would not eventuate, fretting that they would then be abandoned. This is why the parting of lovers has been described as "little deaths" (Cixous 1984) and are said to take their toll:

> You have left me so many times in the past, the present, the future that the event has to pierce through thick layers of time to reach me.

And yet it is already there. Once again death, your death, reaches me even before I can discern it. Enters me furtively and predictably. Was I not still convalescing from your last departure? (Irigaray 1992, p. 49)

Sexual love is an embodied affair. Lips, tongues, eyes, ears, hands, backs, faces, hearts, genitals, hair, and every other plane, recess, and orifice of the body are important as they provide the sites for all manner of connections (Lupton 1998). According to Lupton (1998), when an individual experiences a heightened sense of embodiment, rapid pulse rates, tensed muscles, surges of adrenalin, altered breathing patterns, the churning stomach of nervousness, and the prickling sense of anticipation are common. With people who are in love, the senses are awakened and touch speaks a language of its own (Barthes 1978; Cixous 1984; Irigaray 1992). In the lovestruck, human contact precipitates waves of excitation, enchantment, empathy, idealization, acute longing, disappointment, and despair.

Even when lovers are relating well to each other, their existential anxiety is not necessarily resolved because of the tensions stimulated between merging and individuating (Barthes 1978; Benjamin 1988; Cixous 1984; Haule 1990; Irigaray 1992). By virtue of being in love, lovers will find the borders separating themselves from others will blur, if not collapse (Barthes 1978). No longer able to view themselves as discrete, autonomous, and rational entities, they become excited by their imaginations but also destabilized from their sense of coherence and self-containment (Benjamin 1988; Cixous [1984] 1994; Haule 1990; Irigaray 1992; Lupton 1998).

Torn between merging and individuating, lovers may seem "moody" and "out of touch with reality." Barthes (1978, p. 87) went so far as to say that being thunderstruck meant "an absence and withdrawal of reality." He claimed that, "It frequently occurs to the amorous subject that he [or she] is going mad" (Barthes 1978, p. 120). Williams (1997), Dowling (1995), and Brown (1987) all agreed. Williams (1997, p. 337) described it as "the dementia of loving" and claimed that the human mind is hopelessly inadequate to fathom this distracting and electric "miracle of love" (Williams 1997, p. 33). Similarly, Dowling (1995) claimed that being in love is irrational and beyond one's control. Brown (1987) argued that when love is experienced, no justifications are required. Barthes's (1978, p. 177) added, "What is stupider than a lover?"

Does Love Impair Judgment?

In many Western societies, the proposition that love impairs judgment has so much currency that it infiltrates many of the physiological stories that are told about love. Drawing together research findings from scientists interested in the bodily effects of love, Leros (1998) maintained that when the body is aroused, it secretes pheromones that act as a catalyst for sexual attraction. When people fall in love, arousal is intensified by the natural opioids that flood the body (Fisher 1995; Leros 1998). These opioids are then said to be responsible for the natural highs that falling in love so often produces, along with associated feelings of exhilaration, euphoria, and optimism. With touch stimulating their nervous systems, lovers often find that their immune systems are boosted (Leros 1998). However, this is not the end of the story because, according to this view, love may become addictive.

In these physiologically inclined narratives, lovers have their judgment impaired by the delirium of falling in love (see Fisher 1995). Craving the rushes of adrenalin, individuals in love are often likened to drug addicts who go in search of a fix (Leros 1998). In turn, love is sometimes likened to "a virus" that "infects, takes hold, brings night sweats, is treated and subsides and at last it is gone" (Ellis 1999, p. 24).

Yet, not everyone accepts such biological accounts of love. For Lupton (1998) love is a deeply emotional experience. She was most interested in why Anglo-American cultures tend to be so distrustful of emotions, at least those that are not controlled, and bodies that are not contained. She argued that self-containment and rationality are so highly prized in Anglo cultures that great reservations are expressed about anything that generates "unruly" emotions and/or "leaky" bodies (Lupton 1998). Since lovemaking involves the exchange of bodily fluids, it is often seen to signal the "loss of control, a breakdown in the containment of the self" (Lupton 1998, p. 87).

Passionate Love and Jouissance

For many theorists who identify as postmodernist, falling in love and passionate love are social phenomena that overlap and contain desires that are limitless, insatiable, and exhausting. Using ideas from Lacan (1986), Fuery (1995, p. 26) thought about it as "desire [that] cannot be satisfied." Similarly, Cixous (1974, p. 28) pointed to the impossibility of satisfying desire when she criticized the "search for the limit." In her view, the search for limits was futile because there are no limits (Cixous 1974).

According to Cixous (1974), limitlessness is the conundrum that faces passionate lovers and lovers of passion. With their unruly emotions and leaky bodies, these lovers are often thought to yearn for limits, especially those that promise to contain excess and provide a sense of completion or closure. While limits may appear to transform chaos into order, she maintained that they are but a chimera or illusion (Cixous 1984). She added that while lovers might try to invent new ways of containing desire, they are likely to find that in the process, their desire may be restimulated.

Playing with the concepts of limits and love, Cixous (1984, p.127) inverted the axiom that it is better to be loved than to love when she argued that "to be loved that is true greatness.... Being loved, letting oneself be loved, entering the magic and dreadful circle of generosity ... that is love's real work."

Deconstructing the love-hate opposition, she wrote that "we do not only kill what we hate. We also kill what we love. We always kill a little of the beings we love ... because love is twisted ... (Cixous 1984, p. 154). For Cixous ([1974] 1994), passionate love was, therefore, always likely to be excessive, transgressive, and insatiable. It is an account that fits with Lacan's (1986) "dialectics of desire," which he referred to as "jouissance."

With its limitless potential, jouissance is an idea that also emerged in Barthes's (1978) work. "In amorous languor, something keeps going away; it is as if desire were nothing but this haemorrhage. Such is amorous fatigue: a hunger not to be satisfied, a gaping love" (Barthes 1978, p. 156). Insatiability emerged in Irigaray's (1992) accounts too, as she described love as an unquenchable thirst. Cixous ([1977] 1994, p. 76) did likewise saying, that she "was like someone dying of thirst who hasn't the strength left to drink." Mainstream psychologists refer to these aspects of passionate love when they speak of "longing" and "aching," yet they usually underplay or discredit the open-ended, transgressive, and excessive aspects of such love, preferring to focus on the psychological aspects that they have more hope of controlling.

Limerence and Fatigue

More inclined toward the modernist ideals of stability and certainty, mainstream psychologists will usually assume that lovers will become fatigued by a love that can never be satisfied (see Harris 1995). Take, for instance, Tennov (1979), who surveyed 500 North American adults who reported having fallen in love. Using the term "limerence" to describe passionate love, she said it involved 11 elements: (1) intrusive thinking about the loved one; (2) intense feelings for the loved one; (3) a high degree of empathy and sexual attraction for the beloved; (4) an acute longing for reciprocation, merger, and/or union; (5) dependency of mood on the lover's perceived actions; (6) an inability to react in this way to more than one person at a time; (7) the fear of rejection and the experience of embarrassment when in the company of the loved one; (8) occasional relief from unrequited love through imaginary forms of acceptance; (9) an aching of the heart when the level of uncertainty is high; (10) feelings that often intensify with adversity; and (11) elation when reciprocal feelings seem probable.

For Tennov (1979), this high state of arousal cannot be sustained. She estimated that limerence usually lasts between 18 months and three years. Harris (1995) agreed, estimating that after two or three years of regular contact, lovers will experience a decrease in passion. Even more skeptical of the duration of passionate love was Scott-Peck (1978), who challenged the exaltation of the in-love experience. For him, falling in love was a temporary erotic experience that results from the unhealthy collapse of ego boundaries between two individuals (Scott-Peck 1978). As couples got to know each other, they would start to rebuild their boundaries, leaving behind their identification with falling in love (also see Sprecher & Regan 1998).

For Scott-Peck (1978) and many feminists, passionate love stems from a decision rather than an experience that lies outside an individual's control. Setzman (1988), on the other hand, adopted a slightly different view. He agreed that falling in love was a decision, but went further to portray it as an outgrowth of childhood fantasy, a narcissistic attempt to recapture the first unconditional love bond that individuals have with their mothers (Setzman 1988). In time, he argued, lovers would discover that their childhood longings could never be realized (Setzman 1988). Using the words "crushes" and "puppy love," he represented passionate love as the precursor to a more mature and stable form of love, which is commonly referred to as companionate love: "Love that is freed from primitive needs and fantasies can give birth to tremendous feelings of creativity, productivity, and mature dependence or mutuality" (Setzman 1988, p. 132).

Love Styles and Attachment Theory

Many psychoanalysts still correlate adult love styles with early parental relations, and many use attachment theory to explain the process of loving (see Lasky & Silverman 1988). Bowlby (1953, 1969) first offered attachment theory as an explanation for the nature and origins of love. Drawing upon evolutionary psychology, he connected love with human survival, arguing that mother-child attachments facilitated "evolutionary adaptedness." He claimed that by the time children reached the age of seven, they have already learned that their future viability relies on the love attachments they have with their primary caretaker(s) (Bowlby cited in Chisholm 1995).

Tucker and Anders (1999) also narrated love through the lens of attachment theory. They claimed that early experiences of attachment influence the way individuals approach love in adulthood:

> *Secure individuals* feel comfortable getting close to and depending on others, *avoidant individuals* feel uncomfortable getting close to or depending on others, and *anxious/ambivalent individuals* have a strong desire to get close to others coupled with a fear of abandonment or rejection. (Tucker & Anders 1999, p. 403, emphasis added)

Using the logic of early attachment theory, Tucker and Anders (1999) created an inventory of some of the trajectories (or outcomes) that they then correlated to each attachment style, adding that "individuals with an avoidant attachment style tend[ed] to report a fear of intimacy ... as well as less dependency on their partner and less distress after the dissolution of a romantic relationship (Tucker & Anders 1999, p. 403). In contrast, "anxious individuals" were prone to experiencing love at first sight, as well as feelings of jealousy and an obsessive preoccupation with their relationships (see Feeney & Noller 1990; Tucker & Anders 1999). Finally, adults with a "secure attachment style" were said to "lack these qualities; their romantic relationships [were] characterized by interdependence, trust, and commitment" (Tucker & Anders 1999, p. 403).

Chisholm (1995) was critical of the class-based assumptions made through this typology. He noted that while attachment theorists claimed not to rank love styles, they usually presented secure attachment as normal and superior to those classified as insecure. He observed that "more children in unstressed middle-class samples are classified as secure (up to 66–75 percent) than in highly stressed poverty samples (as low as 35–50 percent)" (Chisholm 1995, p. 46). As he noted, it is plausible that children from low socio-economic backgrounds experience greater anxiety and instability in their early love relationship, yet this could be a result of their exposure to environmental stress rather than personal deficiencies. Furthermore, it is also possible that researchers are more likely to classify middle-class people as "better adjusted or adapted" because they more closely mirrored their own inclinations.

Given that attachment theorists show little interest in or sensitivity to the social injustices that constrain working-class people's lives, it is more than possible that middle-class biases infiltrate the ways love styles are devised and interpreted (Chisholm 1995). For instance, after inviting research subjects to respond to the statement "I find it relatively easy to get close to others," Tucker and Anders (1999, p. 406) classified those who disagreed as "avoidantly attached," going on to assume poor early attachments and problematic adult love relationships. In so doing, theorists such as Tucker and Anders (1999) ignore the realm of possibilities when they use their standardized research instruments. With preordained categories and definitions, they ignore the possibility that some respondents may not believe that it is important, safe, or desirable to develop intimate relationships with others, at least not at that point in their lives. For people who have suffered the effects of abuse, the desire to be close to others may not be refreshingly innocent but dangerously naive and potentially hazardous. And for women survivors of abuse, the pressures of intimate relationships may be too much to bear, particularly if it involves taking risks with people they do not know well.

Sadly, most measurement-inclined researchers, especially those using the classifications of attachment theory, do not make space available to explore the various meanings that individuals attribute to love (see Rubin 1970; Tucker & Anders 1999). Rather, their priority is to see how respondents' experiences align with their views on attachment, marital satisfaction, and the like. To reiterate, this is a problem for at least two reasons: (1) such data provide no information about whether the love styles preferred by the researchers are similar to those preferred by respondents; and (2) it gives us little or no information about whether the respondents' experiences of love resemble what they had hoped for.

The Passionate/Companionate Love Dichotomy

In contrast to theorists who are inclined toward existentialism and who mount their claims about the cataclysmic and insatiable dimensions of passionate love not on factual grounds but on philosophy, mainstream psychologists usually emphasize companionate love, which they assume to be more real and true. For instance, Dworetzky (1982, p. 603) offered the following definitions:

> *Companionate love:* A deep and abiding love that develops between two people over long periods of time. Associated with a desire to be together, share with one another, and sacrifice for one another.
>
> *Passionate love:* A strong sexual desire for another individual combined with the perception that one is in love. This perception is often the result of misattribution, in that heightened physiological arousal for any reason is attributed to love.

With its emotional intensity, heightened sexual attraction, and potential instability, passionate love is viewed as an immature mode of relating that well-adjusted adults are advised to avoid, outgrow, or transcend. It is a story that feeds off the claim that passionate love is a relatively short-lived experience that subsides or evaporates as lovers become more familiar with one another. The longer love relationships go on, the more they are presumed to either become companionate or wither away. "Wise" individuals are seen as those who do not continually follow the wiles of passion but instead, "settle" for more "sensible," "realistic," and contained love relationships (see Lewis 1963; Peterson 1984).

In contrast, compassionate love is usually thought to be (1) warm and tender rather than hot and overtly sexualized; (2) more accurate when it comes to perceiving partners' attributes and failings; (3) demonstrated through public vows of commitment; (4) exclusive, monogamous, and morally good; (5) co-operative and trusting; (6) open to the possibility of children and extended kinship arrangements; (7) arranged through joint finances and shared ownership of property; and (8) productive of more satisfaction than passionate love (Peterson 1984; Sprecher & Regan 1998; Tennov 1979).

In mainstream psychological texts companionate love is often represented as the most satisfying type of relationship. For instance, Tucker and Anders (1999) defined "satisfaction" as that which is derived from "faith," "dependability," and "commitment" rather than "excitement," "passion," and "sexual compatibility." So linked is companionate love to the institution of heterosexual marriage that Dworetzky (1982) used the terms "companionate love" and "conjugal love" interchangeably. Petersen (1984) did likewise, outlining specific "developmental opportunities," such as heterosexual couples deciding when to get married; where to buy their home; and when to have their first and last child.

Taking for granted the orthodoxies of heterosexual marital vows, material acquisition, and sexual reproduction, mainstream psychologists usually assume that companionate love is the most authentic form of love. It is distinguished from passionate love, which is represented as "infatuation" (Chisholm 1995). For example, Brown (1987, p. 35) separated "real love" from "infatuation," which he defined as "extravagant or foolish love." According to Brown (1987), infatuated individuals overvalue the target of their love; exaggerate their charms; and misjudge the depth of feeling and extent of their common interests.

As with all stories told about love, questions must be asked about who is most qualified to classify love relationships, and on what basis these classifications are being made. Is it not possible that what one person refers to as companionate love others will describe as infatuation, co-dependence, and/or abuse? And might companionate love be charged with generating its own fantasies, mostly notably those about certainty, security, and completion? Is it also possible that some individuals will find companionate love to be a lukewarm, sexually repressed, and rather unexciting version of love? With longevity used as a benchmark for genuine love, might the argument be made that some companionate lovers stay together out of a sense of duty and obligation rather than a shared appreciation of each other's needs and desires? At least for some people, might this form of love become a stultifying and suffocating life sentence? Some people certainly think so.

According to Livermore (1993, p. 36), "the world's greatest love affairs are conducted by Anxious-Ambivalents people desperately searching for a kind of security they never had." Gornick (1997, p. 30) agreed, saying that:

> Our lives might be small and frightened but, in the ideal life, it was felt the educated life, the brave life, the life out in the world love would not only be pursued, it would be achieved and once achieved, would transform existence; create a rich, deep, textured prose out of the ordinary reports of daily life.... In fact, only if we gave ourselves over to passion, without stint and without contractual assurance, would we have experience.

Also redeeming passionate love from its pejorative associations, Schulz (1987) told a more positive story about "brief interludes" and "short-term encounters." For him, passionate love relationships, however short lived, have the potential to be just as valuable, emotionally enriching, and physically satisfying as relationships that are long-term. As such, he claimed that they "should not necessarily result in their being labelled shallow, casual, light-weight or 'macho'" (Schulz 1987, p. 41).

Love as a Story

Proposing an alternative to the passionate love versus companionate love opposition, some love theorists advance the thesis that love is a story (see Plummer 1995; Sternberg 1998). Reiterating the idea that truth is multiple, unstable, and contested, Sternberg (1998, p. 17) wrote that:

Couples often argue about whose view better represents the "truth," but from the love-is-a-story standpoint, it is difficult, if not impossible, to know any truth about a relationship. This is because the information the partners have, as well as the information they give to others, is always filtered through their stories about their relationships.

Containing plots, characters, themes, and dialogues, cultural narratives about love have a bearing on the way individual lovers recount their own stories about love (Jackson 1999; Plummer 1995; Sternberg 1998). With a beginning, middle, and an end, the archetypal love story in the West is the fairytale (Westlund 1999; Wood 2001). Metaphorically, this story involves a prince and princess falling in love, overcoming obstacles, getting married, and living happily ever after (Ussher 1997; also see Chapter 4). However, this fairytale love, which Sternberg (1998) referred to as a fantasy narrative, is just one of many possible stories that are told.

Acknowledging that love stories can be grouped in a variety of ways, Sternberg (1998) detailed an assortment of heterosexual love narratives, which he then classified as "object stories," "coordination stories," "genre stories," and so on. "Asymmetrical stories" were those that involve one party (usually the man) governing the other (usually the woman). Rather than dismiss asymmetrical stories outright, he made the more controversial contention that satisfaction in relationships related more to the level of compatibility lovers had for particular genres, rather than the type of story chosen. In short, he said that although no one love story could guarantee happiness, the more discrepant the couple's stories were, the less happy they would be (Sternberg 1998).

Sternberg (1998) based his claims on the findings that he and other researchers gathered from three North American studies. In the first study, Sternberg and Lynch found that the *gardening story* is a popular narrative among the young university students they survey. In this story love was

> ... a garden that needs continually to be nurtured and otherwise cared for.... In garden stories, one of both partners strongly believe that the relationship will survive and thrive only if it is carefully watered, provided abundant sun, and never allowed to become choked with weeds or attacked by garden pests. (Sternberg 1998, p. 147)

Not surprisingly, Sternberg (1998) found gender differences in relation to preferred love narratives. Apparently young women university students were most likely to endorse process-oriented stories, such as the gardening or travel story, which views love as a journey that produces an exciting array of possible destinations. According to Sternberg (1998, p. 136), travel stories were successful so long as they "represent[ed] a process of becoming" rather than a yearning to arrive at a particular destination.

From the second study conducted with 43 heterosexual couples in North America, Sternberg (1998) found that women participants were more likely to identify with travel stories while the men were more likely to prefer art, pornography, and sacrifice stories. These love stories may be understood as follows. *Art stories* place a high premium on the physical attractiveness of lovers; *pornography stories* authorize one lover to express desire by debasing his or her partner(s). *Sacrifice stories* require one lover to repeatedly concede to the demands of his or her lover(s) (Sternberg 1998). From his analysis of this study, he said that "there was some tendency for men to be more likely to treat their partners as objects, but there was also a willingness by some men to sacrifice their relationship" (Sternberg 1998, p. 223).

In the third study, 55 (heterosexual) couples from North America were surveyed with two main types of love stories distinguished: (1) those predicated on asymmetry; and (2) those pursuant of equality. Among the asymmetrical love narratives were the *government story* where one partner becomes autocratic and governs the behaviour of the other; the *police story* where one partner monitors the other as a suspect; and the *horror story* where one partner terrorizes the other (Sternberg 1998). Of the stories that lent themselves to equality were the gardening story and the travel story (outlined above), and the knitting/sewing story. Sternberg (1998, p. 146) explained that:

> Couples with a *sewing and knitting story* do not feel bound by convention, but their behavior may be either conventional or unconventional. If it is conventional, it is because they have chosen to follow convention rather than because they have just blindly accepted it.

It is significant that in all three of the studies identified by Sternberg (1998), the female participants identified most with love stories that pursue equality whereas the male participants identified more with those that are asymmetrical. By identifying with distinctly different genres of love stories, heterosexual men and women may have been expressing conflicting demands and expectations about their love relationships. It is a pattern that contradicts the dominant view that the opposite sexes are naturally compatible, yet it remains undeveloped by Sternberg (1998), who takes for granted the primacy of heterosexuality.

Instead of contemplating the possibility that heterosexual men and women may develop conflicting expectations of their relationships of intimacy, Sternberg (1998) preferred to theorize why some subordinated lovers submit to their subjection. Without directly referencing women, he offered a cautionary tale when he said that "People getting into relationships need to be sensitive early on to the power distribution in the relationship, because once it starts to be set, it is difficult to change" (Sternberg 1998, p. 224). It is a tale elaborated by many feminists who have suggested that asymmetrical relationships are not just hard to alter but also difficult to terminate (see Chapter 4).

Historical and Sociological Love Stories

Far from being timeless, conventions of love have changed over the centuries. In the Western world, conventions for love predate Christianity to the mythology of the classical Greek period (Tarnas 1991). In the following discussion, I trace some of the historical and sociological stories about love because they illustrate how some conventions for loving have remained while others have dramatically altered.

Platonic Love

In *The Symposium* (1974, cited in Ireland 1988), Plato told a story about the development of human beings and the evolution of love. According to this myth, human beings originally appeared as male, female, or hermaphrodite with two faces and two sets of arms, legs, eyes, and genitalia. Males possessed duplicate sets of male organs; females had entirely female organs; and hermaphrodites a combination of the two. In their respective ways, these human beings were so complete that their presence was thought to have threatened the omnipotence of the gods. In response, one of these gods, Zeus, sought to weaken their power by splitting human beings into two. Now possessing only one face and one set of arms, legs, eyes, and genitalia, human beings were left to reclaim their former sense of wholeness by searching for their other half. Through men seeking out other men, women other women, and hermaphrodites members of the opposite sex, the sexual categories of homosexual, lesbian, and heterosexual were born and ranked in descending order (see Ireland 1988).

Through the search for one's other half, the idea of love's restorative powers was promoted. Plato (1974 in Ireland 1988, p. 16) wrote that:

> It is from this distant epoch, then, that we may date the innate love which human beings feel for one another, the love which restores us to our ancient state by attempting to weld two beings into one and to heal the wound which humanity has suffered.

Yet, as Plato developed his theory further, he argued for the primacy of the spiritual love (or agape) that occurred between men (Ireland 1988).

Christian Love

Centuries after Plato told his story, Classical Greece became absorbed by the Roman Empire, which rose, expanded, and then collapsed to give way to the emerging forms of Christianity (Tarnas 1991). With the advent of Christianity, love's conventions changed. Tarnas (1991) explained that the primacy of love between two males was now superseded by the view that love was a pious and familial affair, best shared with one's Creator. Inverting the idea that love is God, Christianity made the claim that God is love (Tarnas 1991). Always striving to overcome the obstacle of original sin, Christians were advised to worship God by conquering the "passions of the flesh" (French 1985; Giddens 1992; Lewis 1963; Tarnas 1991). It is a model of sexuality that Foucault (1984) referred to as abstention.

Abstention separated love from sexuality, which was imbued with guilt and shame, and promoted the concepts of virginity and celibacy (Foucault 1984; French 1985). Presenting the Virgin Mary as the archetype of earthly love, Christianity legitimated heterosexuality and scorned homosexuality, as it directed men and women to live together in "spiritual marriages" (Ireland 1988). So important was it for people to commit to a Christian marriage that the Bible claimed "It [was] better to marry than to burn" (I Corinthians 7:7, 9). However, this moral code was not applied equally to both sexes.

Along with many feminists (such as French 1985), Foucault (1984, p. 22) pointed out that during this period Christian morality was:

> ... an ethics thought, written, and taught by men, and addressed to men to free men obviously. A male ethics, consequently, in which women figured only as objects or, at most, as partners that one had best train, educate and watch over when one had them under one's power, but stay away from when they were under the power of someone else (father, husband, tutor).

Foucault (1984) also noted that in spite of the sexually austere conventions that circulated in relation to love, many transgressions still took place. Similar to Freud, Foucault (1984) explored the idea that Christianity's repression of sexuality heightened sexual desires identified as "sinful."

Courtly Love

As Western culture moved into the middle of the medieval period, new conventions for loving emerged. Tarnas (1991) explained that the development of cities and towns and the founding of universities and new industries created disruptions to the old feudal order. With a renewed interest in ancient thought and literature, he noted that:

> Troubadours and court poets celebrated a new ideal of soul-transfiguring romantic love between free individuals, in implicit rebellion against the widespread feudal convention of marriage as a social-political arrangement ratified by the Church. (Tarnas 1991, p. 173)

In a similar vein, Miller (1995) argued that romantic love originated from the aristocracy in the medieval period. He claimed the term "romantic love" first referred to idealized adulterous sexual liaisons between members of the upper class, which explains why it became known as "courtly love" (Miller 1995).

Featherstone (1998) agreed with this account, but made the often-neglected point that courtly love could also be found in India, East Asia, and Islamic societies (also see Jankowiak 1995; Lindholm 1998).

In the West, courtly love was first used to refer to the playful recreation that took place outside marriage (Lindholm 1998; Miller 1995). It was extraneous to marriage because, as Giddens (1992, pp. 38–39) argued:

> In pre-modern Europe, most marriages were contracted, not on the basis of mutual sexual attraction, but economic circumstance. Among the poor, marriage was a means of organising agrarian labour.... Only among aristocratic groups was sexual licence openly permitted among "respectable" women.... Of course this was virtually never connected with marriage.

Yet, as the troubadour poets performed their artistic works with greater regularity (Featherstone 1998), romantic love was able to find a wider audience. Luhmann (1986) said it was then that it became codified by chivalry. Once codified, romantic love shifted from its playful and external status to become known as a deep impulse and a secular ideal through which intimate alliances could be forged (Featherstone 1998; Giddens 1992; Miller 1995). It was at this point that courtly love was defined as romantic love and then constructed as "ennobling" (Spence 1996), a symbol of refinement (Jankowiak 1995), and a foundation for marriage (Foucault 1984; Giddens 1992).

The Rise of Romance

Coinciding with the rise of the novel (Giddens 1992), romantic love moved from being a "privileged body of knowledge and practice of a small group of men and women" (Featherstone 1998, p. 2) to a widespread social practice that was accessible to all members of society, irrespective of social class (Evans 1998).

Yet, Ireland (1988) argued that the rise of courtly love did not occur by way of smooth transition but was a reaction to Christianity's imposition of absolute authority and enforced religious conversions. Noting that new ideas about love took hold predominantly in areas where Christianity had most recently arrived, she claimed that courtly love was "something inherently subversive" (Ireland 1988, p. 23). Apparently, courtly love posed a threat to the authority of the Church because it elevated the status of upper-class women and undermined the primacy of the love of God. In contrast to agape (spiritual love) and even eros (passionate love), both of which were understood to be impersonal, courtly love produced the language of "amour," which referred to very specific, personalized, and individualized forms of loving (Giddens 1992; Ireland 1988).

Nevertheless, Christian love and courtly love still tended to be depicted as each other's opposites, even though they shared many similarities. For all its pomp and ceremony, courtly love was not sexually liberated, at least by current conventions. Far from being a source of raw, untrammelled, and relatively private passion, courtly love was theatrical, performance oriented, and more than a little melodramatic. Similar to Christian love, courtly love involved rituals, costumes, and public performances, and both esteemed the ethereal, the idyllic, and the saintly. Both centred their activities on worshipping a deity. And both aspire to great heights that some claim are unreachable.

The pantomime of courtly love is no more clearly expressed than through the story of the knight demonstrating his valour to the lady or princess with whom he is in love (Featherstone 1998; Ireland 1988). In this legend, fearless knights and beautiful ladies take centre stage, but are allocated two quite different roles. The lady observes the knight in shining armour who completes a daring array of challenges so that her father might be persuaded to give him his daughter's hand in marriage (see Spence 1996).

To this day, many children's fairytales endorse the plot of male suitors proving their love for a particular young woman by overcoming a series of obstacles. As early as 1976, Bettelheim explained that in children's fairytales (such as *Snow White* and *Cinderella*):

> The rescuers fall in love with these heroines because of their beauty, which symbolizes perfection. Being in love, the rescuers have to become active and prove that they are worthy of the women they love—something quite different from the heroine's passive acceptance of being loved. (1976, p. 277)

Despite sometimes being subjected to ridicule, the fairytale script of the white knight in shining armour "sweeping a lady off her feet" continues to be reproduced in the Anglo-American lexicon of popular romance.

Modern Love

During the Enlightenment, the discourses of individuality and scientific rationality ascended and affected the way love was culturally represented. With its emphasis on personal distinctiveness and self-determination, individuality offered romantic love a new platform from which it could be asserted (Giddens 1992; Luhmann 1986). However, this platform was by no means well developed. As Luhmann (1986, p. 108) explained, "Paths to personal individualization ... opened up, but left unchartered. Signposts, place names, warning signs and speed limits [did] not yet exist."

More clearly developed were the discourses of scientific rationality. Wilson (1998) suggested that the 18th century's romantic movement pressed hard against the emerging discourse of scientific rationality, which Giddens (1992, pp. 40–41) argued "had no place for emotion." Caught between scientific rationality and the continuing authority of Christianity, the codification of intimacy "stagnated in the eighteenth century and did not absorb important changes taking place"

(Luhmann 1986, p. 129), yet by the 19th century, Wilson (1998, p. 112) argued that "'Modern love' was romantic love."

Giddens (1992, p. 41) claimed that romantic love ascended as the dominant form of love during modernity when it moved from being "an unreal conjuring of possibilities in the realm of fiction ... [to] ... a potential avenue for controlling the future, as well as a form of psychological security (in principle) for those whose lives were touched by it." Evans (1998) agreed, adding that people during this period now started to anticipate falling in love.

For Lindholm (1998), romantic love was both a product of and reaction to industrialization and rationalization. Jackson (1999) and Langford (1999) agreed. According to Langford (1999, p. 3):

> The desire to please others and serve God gave way to individualism and self-indulgence, and the quest for spiritual salvation became a search for self-realisation through an irrational, fatalistic, exclusive and erotically charged "fusion of souls."

With this, Jackson (1999, p. 97) claimed that love began to provide "a means of communication and self-realisation in a complex, impersonal and anonymous world."

Now domesticated but still promising personal salvation, romantic love was inserted into market-oriented discourses that reinscribed the individualistic values of capitalism (Jackson 1999). It was then that romantic love was defined as the individualized and eroticized idealization of one's beloved (Lindholm 1998; Wilson 1998). Yet, because it was expressed in conjunction with stories about Christian love, the most valued love style was patriarchal heterosexuality (French 1993; Foucault 1984). "Wedded" to the concepts of exclusivity, permanence, and reproduction, romantic love gained widespread acceptance in the 20th century as the singularly most important foundation for marriage.

For some, romantic love became a popular social convention because it offered women a way to negotiate more stable relationships with men (see Gergen & Gergen 1988). Yet for others, women's rights were not protected but oppressed by heterosexual marriage (see Chapter 4). With members of other Western social movements, feminists also enunciated some of the disadvantages and imminent risks involved with the privatization of sexuality and its regulation (Greer 1999; Segal 1999).

From the gay and lesbian movements and, much later, the men's movement, an assortment of perspectives on love and sexuality were then developed (Connell 1995; Jackson & Scott 1996). During the late phases of modernity, temporary alliances were negotiated with other human rights movements (such as the trade union movement and the Black rights movement) and the boundaries of convention expanded after conventions were shown to be bigoted, dogmatic, and ultimately damaging to those who did not fit comfortably within their confines

(Weeks 1998). Wishing to esteem love in multiple forms, these social movements all contributed to the development of postmodern love.

Postmodern Love

In the latter part of the 20th century, the term "postmodernity" was used to represent the many changes in Western culture. Some of these changes included the complexity of communication technologies and the increased mobility of groups and individuals. Established ideas about family and community were destabilized as fewer individuals expected successive generations of family members to work and live in the same geographical area (Simon 1996). Labour relations became increasingly more casual and risky (Probert 1995) and as individuals moved in search of work and new experiences, the authority of kinship, religion, and overarching political doctrines declined (Giddens 1992; Melucci 1996; Weeks 1998). With growing numbers of people unemployed, Lee (1998, p. 33) claimed that the lower classes "required absorbing diversions. What is more amusing, distracting, even obsessive, than love?"

Faced with a proliferation of choices, people were now thought to have individuated in ways that defied linear trajectories of self-realization (Simon 1996). Increasingly, people were said to have engaged more consciously with the production of the self (Weeks 1998). The activity of shopping took on a new set of meanings as citizens were redefined as consumers. Bombarded with messages about how they might best consume love, individualism was raised to new heights.

Today individuals are expected to gratify their needs and desires immediately, whereas deferred gratification—the linchpin of lasting, committed marriage—is no longer viewed so favourably (hooks 2000). For some people, these trends are alarming and dangerous. Warnings of excess ensued and in some circles, moral conservatism has been reasserted as a new force with which to be reckoned (Jackson & Scott 1996; Plummer 2003; Weeks 1998).

In the 21st century, at least in the West, work has become increasingly specialized and more people have enrolled in university courses. With the expansion of academic audiences, more love narratives have been produced in the academy. Conflicting accounts have been given by a diverse array of theorists, including those who base their work on ideas from neo-conservatism and postmodernism. In turn, as the symbolic nature of human life is emphasized, love and sexuality have become more elaborately contested (Plummer 1995, 2003).

As only one of many possible discourses about sexuality, romantic love was now read by many as a paradoxical discourse, a form of narrative, and a cliché that was as much exalted as it was ridiculed (Illouz 1998; Simon 1996). No longer the sole prerogative of heterosexuality and untied from the institution of marriage, multiple accounts of love have been insinuated into everyday life (Melucci 1996). According to some social theorists, especially Giddens (1992), sexuality was now deemed to be "plastic."

Giddens (1992, p. 52) first recognized the diverse sexual proclivities of individuals before claiming the prominence of the ideal of the "pure relationship." Unmoored from biology and kinship relationships, the "pure relationship" was not about sexual purity or material security, but mutual emotional satisfaction. According to Giddens (1992, p. 52), the "pure relationship" could enjoy romance without hoping for "eternal love."

With this mix of aspirations more individuals, especially young women, experiment with love and sexuality to pursue what Giddens (1992) referred to as "confluent love." In this type of love, it is the special relationship that is sought rather than the special person. Illouz (1998, pp. 175–176) agreed, saying that:

> Postmodern romance saw the collapse of overarching, life-long romantic narratives, which it compressed into the briefer and repeatable form of the affair ..., [which] is a cultural form that attempts to immobilize and repeat, compulsively, the primordial experience of "novelty." Moreover, the affair is undergirded by a consumerist approach to the choice of a mate.

Viewed in this light, postmodern love has been represented as fragmented and hybridized. Stemming from no single source, love is stylized into many forms, and produces a wide variety of effects (Lee 1998; Simon 1996). In turn, lovers are depicted as active, fickle, sophisticated, and strategic (see Illouz 1998). Dispersed across the mainstream and into the margins of deviance, they are seen to interact with love discourses in contradictory ways and able to convert disparaging labels into emblems of pride (hence the use of the term "queer").

In many postmodern love discourses, individuals who enact tradition are viewed ironically, whereas those who pursue narratives of liberation and revolution may be disparaged as conformists. In the plurality of postmodern loves, both the subversive and the orthodox are accommodated. Instead of privileging the interpretations of "experts," more attempts are made to decipher the meanings "ordinary" people attribute to love by the stories that they tell about it (see Lee 1998; Plummer 1995, 2003; Sternberg 1998). Writing from the discipline of social work, Schulz (1987, p. 40) declared that "intimacy is what the client says it is."

The Irony of Romance

Often encouraging actors to momentarily suspend their disbelief, proponents of postmodern love advised individuals to be playfully experimental rather than bound by convention (see Illouz 1998; Melucci 1996). Different forms of love "play" were mobilized through the new communication technologies such as the Internet, facsimile machines, telephones, and mobile phones (Simon 1996). "Virtual" love was deemed indistinguishable from the "real," which was just one more form of simulacra (imitation). The increased consumption of ecstasy, otherwise known as the "love drug," was used to suggest that many people seek immediate experiences of euphoria (Donovan 2000). The same could be said about Viagra.

In recent decades many people have learned that love matches were not only to be found face to face. Personal columns and chat rooms have started to be legitimated as valid sites where individuals could meet potential lovers. With new sites of love matches made available through electronic forms of technology, the marketing of the self has become a common social practice, particularly through the promotion of personal traits and accumulated material resources (Jagger 1998). In some instances, love appeared to be an investment through which shareholders might "merge" so that "dividends" could be produced. In other instances, pragmatism was an important reason for rejecting an otherwise suitable love match (see Illouz 1998).

Depicted as shopping around for prospective sexual partners, many people have started to relinquish the idea that love unions will last forever. Less permanent forms of commitment have been expressed and, for many, marriage is an option that may be repeated over a lifetime (Mackay 1999). Serial love relationships may be pursued because they offer the chance to minimize the experience of isolation and experiment with identities related to being in a couple (Simon 1996; Wood 2001). In this context, coupledom in all its guises often appears as a refuge from a rapidly changing, risk-saturated, and chaotic world (Langford 1999; Lindholm 1995; Simon 1996). It is one of the many discourses regularly discussed in the mass media, with popular culture playing an ever-increasing role in the production of love discourses in everyday life (see Chapter 3).

Summary

This chapter was designed to respond to the question about how love is represented in Anglo-American dominated societies. In so doing it contains analyses of many of the competing discourses told about love. By exploring many of the claims that are made through these stories, I have suggested that love has many realities and truths; that even when love is a constant preoccupation, it is never fully captured by one human being, academic discipline, or site of production. This is because love defies scientific measurement and meddles with time. It is a story or a series of stories, but it is conducted in material, spiritual, and emotional worlds.

I have also portrayed love as paradoxical in so far as it can help establish social conventions as well as disrupt them. Organic and synthetic, love is seen to be something that comes naturally but must also be learned. As I suggest in the next chapter, popular culture is one very common way through which people learn how they should love.

Love gives you wings, romance helps you fly.
(Parv 1997, p. 41)

3
POPULAR STORIES ABOUT LOVE
Love, Love Me Do

EARLIER I SUGGESTED THAT SOCIAL WORKers and associated health and welfare professionals have not tended to study love. I considered why this was the case, noting that in the absence of studying love, social workers were liable to import into their practice popular ideas about love (see Chapter 1). Neither innocent nor universal, popular ideas about love (especially those misleadingly described as "common sense") need inspection because they privilege particular love styles, usually those that reinforce the idea of heterosexual male dominance (also see Chapters 4 and 5).

A consistent message of this book is that social workers will be in a better position to understand intimate abuse if they study love and its connections to abuse. That is why Chapter 2 was dedicated to studying love from a range of disciplines, including history and psychology. It is also why this chapter on popular love stories has been included. In the following discussion I traverse a wide range of popular texts as I further consider how love is represented in Anglo-American-dominated societies.

The Production of Love in Popular Culture

Similar to words such as "love" and "abuse," "popular culture" does not possess one single meaning. Although it has been used to refer to novels, movies, magazines, mass concerts, sporting events, billboards, and graffiti, it has also been represented as the culture of "ordinary" people and, more politically, a "terrain of struggle" (Cranny-Francis 1994).

"High" and "Low" Culture

Until the late phases of modernity, texts and performances produced for the masses have tended to be seen as shallow, artificial, and crass. Having "everyday accessibility" (de Certeau 1984), popular culture has a history of being seen as an inferior form of entertainment, mostly enjoyed by the working classes. In contrast, "high culture" has ordinarily been thought to produce texts that are less accessible to individuals who are not well read. Believed to contain depth, truth, and refinement, high culture has traditionally been associated with audiences that are formally educated, affluent, and socially esteemed.

During postmodernity, however, some social theorists have contested such assumptions and have been more interested in learning about how discourses (from either domain) achieve dominance. Understanding how different groups and individuals relate to discourses of all kinds is part of their curiosity, as well as how counter-discourses are articulated. Rather than wondering whether particular programs or texts are indicative of a "dumbing down of society," they have set about deconstructing how high and low cultural discourses generate excitement.

Being Engrossed in Love Stories

From both high and low culture, much excitement has been generated about love. In opera, ballet, theatre, and classical music, love is a dominant theme, particularly fairytale love. Take, for instance, some of the most enduring texts of high culture, such as *Madame Butterfly*, *Swan Lake*, *The Nutcracker*, *Miss Saigon*, *Carmen*, *La Bohème*, *La Traviata*, *Aida*, *Les Misérables*, *Pygmalion*, and *Doctor Zhivago*. Performed across media and genres, love stories can excite audiences and generate huge profits.

Love can be used to produce so much profit that promoters of the film *Titanic* (1998) were able to secure its success only when they belatedly marketed the film as a love affair rather than a shipping film (Kramer 1998). And this is not an exceptional case. Bear in mind that over *300 million* romance novels are sold annually around the world (Parv 1997). Add in the personal columns, Valentine's Day cards, and Internet sites dedicated to matching or advising lovers. Think about the array of love songs across music genres as well as the endless stream of romance movies, such as *Notting Hill*, *Bridget Jones' Diary*, and *Ever After*. Put this with the other love-related products, such as t-shirts, handbags, and other paraphernalia bearing messages about love and possible love unions, and the merchandising of love produces billions of dollars each year.

In spite of their flaws, popular love stories strike a chord with many people's experiences and fantasies. One of the ways they do this is by speaking to the desire to feel alive in what might be a humdrum life or, worse still, a life filled with violence and abuse. The film *The Mirror Has Two Faces* (1996) captured this nicely:

> We all want to fall in love. Why? Because that experience makes us feel completely alive. Where every sense is heightened, every emotion is magnified, our everyday reality is shattered and we are flying into the heavens. It may only last a moment, an hour, or an afternoon. But that doesn't diminish its value. Because we are left with memories that we treasure for the rest of our lives.

Memorable moments are not, however, the only reason why popular love stories are so hungrily consumed. Another reason is because they are easy to access and digest. Most plots are fairly simple, adhering to well-worn formulas. When viewed uncritically, these stories can be exciting and comforting at the same time. Sometimes this is achieved when love is represented as a balm or escape. Not requiring people to move outside their suburbs or relinquish their current commitments, love is often depicted as an innocent pursuit, a motivational force that helps people to hope that a better life might be just around the corner.

"True" Love Stories

Having faith in the magic of romantic love, Parv (1997) considered how "true love" might be found and maintained. Keeping "true love" alive is necessary because it is popularly portrayed to be love that never ends. The plot of people searching for their one true love patterns many novels, especially those promoted by romance publishers such as Mills & Boon and Harlequin. In these romance novels, there is the assumption that for every woman in the world, there is a Mr. Right whom she is destined to meet if only she tries hard enough to find (and please) him.

In many television programs the heterosexual discourse of true love is reiterated. For instance, in the repeatedly screened sitcoms such as "Bewitched" and "I Dream of Jeannie," lovers are so destined to be together that they traverse the otherwise impossible obstacles of coming from different spiritual planes. Yet, in some of the more recent television shows, the search for the one true love narrative has been modified to show "true" love as something that involves partners laughing, touching, and talking a lot with each other. Take, for instance, sitcoms such as "Roseanne" (1988–1997), "Mad about You" (1992–1999), and "Everybody Loves Raymond" (1996–2005). In "Roseanne," some attempt was made to explore working-class life in America. In "Mad about You," the newly fashioned ideal couple (that is, urban, middle-class, and heterosexual) was represented seeking the help of therapists (rather than parents or priests) to work on their issues. In "Everybody Loves Raymond," there was a return to more traditional gender roles, and involvement of extended family as middle-class suburban life is portrayed. Consistent in all three shows is the idea that humour is the best way to diffuse tension, especially that which arises between the "opposite" sexes.

Many other television programs in the 1990s and early 2000s have reflected cultural trends, including the trend that Giddens (1992, p. 61) described as the "separating and divorcing society." Take, for instance, the long-running successful series "Friends," "Seinfeld," and "Ally McBeal" in which love is portrayed as crucially important but nevertheless time-limited. For shows such as these, serial monogamy is the name of the game. Love is worth the effort not because it lasts but because it offers individuals the chance to be transported to places unknown. In "Mad about You," this message is so embedded that each episode opened with the theme song inviting viewers to "Step into the final frontier."

Love as an adventure appears in many other texts too. Catering to mass audiences around the world, North American author John Gray (1993, p. 282) wrote, "You are a pioneer. You are travelling in new territory. Expect to be lost sometimes. Expect your partner to be lost. Use this guide as a map to lead you through uncharted lands again and again." Presumably this map is necessary given men and women are so opposite that they "come from different planets." Taking for granted the idea that love is an essential feature of human life and assuming that love relationships will be heterosexual and monogamous, he used *Men Are from Mars, Women Are from Venus* texts to portray love as a crowning achievement (Gray 1993, 1996).

It is not just books, songs, and televisions shows that represent love as an achievement and, at the same time, a natural event. Many news reports do too, even between unlikely characters. Take, for instance, a recent news report about Pauline Hanson falling in love. The 52-year-old woman, who used to run a fast-food store and went on to head the ultra-right-wing party in Australia called One Nation, declared that she and her country music-singing boyfriend were each other's "perfect partner" after only three weeks (*Herald Sun* newspaper, accessed and written on February 14, 2007, http://www.news.com.au/herald-sun/story/0,21985,21228641-29277,00.html).

According to P. Gray (1993, p. 48), "people will buy and do almost anything that promises them a chance at the bliss of romance." This constant hum creates a cultural "injunction to love" (P. Gray 1993, p. 48). Crossing the borders of time, class, and culture, these stories often contain the subtext that love makes people human. Irrespective of birthplace or lineage, humans are represented as *born to love*. Indeed, the flowering of love is thought to be possible even in the most unusual or hostile of contexts. Yet, on closer inspection it becomes apparent that many believe that love must be carefully nurtured rather than blithely assumed (see Dowrick 1997). Thus, the faith in love's perfection and capacity to reproduce has exploded into many stories about how love might be realized.

Contradictory Advice for Loving

In popular culture, much advice is dispensed about love through the various "agony" columns, talk-back radio shows, and the countless self-help texts produced each year. It is also available on a growing number of Web sites, such as www.lovingyou.com, www.theartofloving.com, or www.whatittakes.com (all accessed 2007). However, much of the advice given is contradictory. On the one hand, love is constructed as natural and spontaneous, as suggested by stories about falling in love and love at first sight. Yet, on the other hand, love is said to involve effort and work (Bellafante 1998).

Blogs from Internet chat rooms illustrate the mixed messages that love "just happens" or is due to "hard work." Consider the responses made to the question "How do I find love?" According to one chat room member, "Roubini," "There is no recipe! It comes without notice!" According to "Angel," love comes "When you stop looking for it." "Dorene" thought love occurred "When the time is right." "Kipper" agreed, saying that "You can't find it like treasure or a scavenger hunt. Love hits you like a ton of bricks...." However, "Best Bet 77" thought more active pursuit of love was the way forward. She or he claimed that love was found through "exposure" gained through going on many dates and having lots of brief sexual encounters. "Fahim" took a similar perspective. She or he advised others to "Advertise in a newspaper or on the Internet with your bio-data" (Blogs on Yahoo!7 Answers, http://au.answers.yahoo.com/, accessed February 16, 2007).

Because women are the largest consumers of love narratives (hooks 2000; Wood 2001), it follows that women are the most likely to come into contact with these conflicting instructions about how they should love. In some texts, readers are urged to extricate themselves from traditional gender roles so that they can push against the boundaries of convention (also see Chapters 4 and 5). In other texts, women are told either directly or indirectly that feminism is to blame for divorce and/or the escalating numbers of women dissatisfied with their love lives.

Take the early classic, *Women Who Love Too Much*, written by Robin Norwood (1976). Hybridizing liberal feminist ideas with those about love as an addiction, she tried to steer readers toward more "healthy" and "happy" relationships. Inverting the adage that "love hurts," she claimed that "When being in love means being in pain, we are loving too much" (Norwood 1976, p. 1). With this as her point of departure, she then outlined a program for women who, she claimed, were "recovering from the disease of loving too much" (Norwood 1976, p. 1). More than a few popular self-help books have followed this vein.

Appealing to a younger generation of women, Heimel (1993) used a blend of liberal feminist and psychoanalytic ideas to instruct readers of the popular women's magazine, *Cosmopolitan*. Rather than assuming that love is a disease or an addiction, she encouraged women to understand their families' patterns, as well as their self-destructive tendencies so that they can strategically choose a mate (Heimel 1993). It was a template that would be used by many other women's magazines in years to come, interspersed with concerns raised about women who were not making enough effort to secure a love relationship.

In the late nineties, Dowrick (1997) articulated fears that would surface over and again over the next decade when she talked about the growing reservations women were expressing about forming love relationships. Entitling her book, *Forgiveness and Other Acts of Love*, she urged women to find "the courage to love." With Jungian psychology, Christianity, and liberal feminism influencing her work, she worked with the cliché that individuals must first love themselves if they were to be capable of really loving anyone else. Expected to walk a fine line between loving themselves and being selfish, readers were then cautioned against martyrdom while encouraged to display the virtues of fidelity, forgiveness, and restraint.

Adopting a distinctly anti-feminist tone, Fein and Schneider's (1995) *The Rules* advised readers to abide by traditional methods of solving love's problems. Taking heterosexuality for granted, they urge women to play hard to get with men who might not otherwise pop the question. It was so popular that it became a series of six books, including one called *The Rules for Online Dating, Capturing the Heart of Mr. Right in Cyberspace* (Fein & Schneider 2002). Influenced by this text and others like it, Doyle (2000) described her conversion to traditional femininity in her book, *The Surrendered Wife*. Appealing to traditional family values, she eschewed any new sexual conventions that might otherwise be represented in television shows such as "Sex in the City" and "Queer as Folk."

Speaking more playfully, appealing to common sense, and blending conventional thinking with post-feminist ideas, Behrendt and Tuccillo (2004) used their book, *He's Just Not That into You* to argue that all heterosexual women were effectively "dating the same guy," who needs to chase women. For this pair of authors and many others now being published in the genre of "chick-lit," it's obvious that a man is not that interested if he does not ask you out, call you, date you, and have sex with you and only you. Nor is a man "into you" if he sees you only when he's drunk, doesn't want to marry you, breaks up with you, has disappeared, is already married or otherwise unavailable, a selfish jerk, a bully, or a freak (Behrendt & Tuccillo 2004).

Love "in Reality"

Reaching vast audiences, "reality" television shows also instruct women about how to maximize their chances of finding love. Across Britain, the United States, Canada, and Australia, shows such as "Big Brother," "Survivor," "Idol" (Canadian, American, or Australian 2000–2006), "The Biggest Loser" (2004–2006) "Changing Wives" (2004), and "Australian Princess" (2005 and 2006) continue to produce advice about how women should look, act, and think. Having watched these shows for some years now, I have noticed the following seven imperatives conveyed: (1) life and love are mostly about individuals competing with one another; (2) on-air personal disclosures are good even if they evoke public criticism; (3) participating in the show is a life-changing journey; (4) contestants must try their hardest to emulate dominant ideas about beauty; (5) it is smart to use one's sexuality for material rewards; (6) money and recognition—not familial obligations or intimacy—are the biggest motivators of people; and (7) overt references to politics or religion of any hue is not conducive to happiness or the creation of a good society.

Taking these ideas to new and, some might say, ludicrous heights is the show "Shopping for Love." It quite literally implies that one might shop for love the way one shops for shoes. Prioritizing relationship compatibility on the basis of shared preferences for particular brands of clothing, footwear, and accessories, I detected no trace of irony from either the hosts or contestants. While purporting to be a "reality show," the only people I saw participating were young, heterosexual, slim, and able-bodied, White, and Western, with English as their first language.

Nevertheless, I have also noticed evidence where other television shows have satirized and at times ridiculed the promotion of such ideals or norms. Some really good examples include the times when the public—the majority of whom are girls and women—vote for contestants who fail to live up to the espoused norms. Periodically, this occurs when viewers defy prevailing norms by supporting individual contestants who are otherwise described as fat, ugly, unrefined, and/or untalented.

Parodying Romantic Love

> *Old-timer wants to find girl before*
> *becoming completely bald and impotent.*
> (MrFluffy, 2005, dating Web site:
> http://www.rsvp.com.au)

In contrast to the beautifully groomed characters on the reality shows, comedies that deliberately blur the line between "reality" and soap opera are often critical of competitive individualism and fairytales of happy-ever-after. Good examples of this include Australia's "Kath and Kim," England's "Absolutely Fabulous," "The Vicar of Dibley," "Men Behaving Badly," and Canada's "Trailer Park Boys." Each television show engages viewers in stories that show the light-hearted or funny side of dominant cultural norms.

Often, badly dressed, uncouth working- and lower middle-class characters are used to mock—affectionately and not so affectionately—the messages culturally promulgated about life, love, work, and sex. Take, for instance, "Kath and Kim," the satire that has enthralled viewers in Australia, Britain, New Zealand, the United States, and Canada alike. Illustrating how Australian culture can play out in working-class Anglo Australians' aspirations and love relationships, this comedy series does not just mock fashion trends and beauty standards, it also mocks well-established gender conventions about how men and women should relate to one another:

> *Kel Knight:* Let me prove it to you that I'm a real man, right here, right now, on the shag! (see http://www.kathandkim.com/forum/index.php)

In a completely different setting than Kath and Kim's fictitious working-class suburb of Fountain Gate, the characters of "Absolutely Fabulous" (1992–2003) also subvert the idea that people should be sober, thrifty, hard-working, law-abiding, sexually modest Christians, committed to creating a predictable and safe family life. Ironically, "The Vicar of Dibley" does likewise. Created at the time when great debates raged in the Anglican Church (and others) about whether women should be allowed to be ordained as vicars, this comedy series deviated from many other television shows by dealing, quite overtly, with a wide range of political and social issues. Consider, for instance, the episodes "We All Hate Granny," in which a couple have trouble trying to get rid of their children's grandmother (see http://dawnfrench.tripod.com/murderguide1.html). Another good example is the 2006 Christmas special of "The Vicar of Dibley," which ends with Dawn French (who plays the vicar) getting married to an accountant in her pajamas at a wedding that was based on the theme of *Doctor Who*. More than 12 million people in Britain alone are estimated to have watched this episode (see http://www.tvheaven.ca/dibley.htm).

Equally irreverent, the Canadian series in the early 2000s called "Trailer Park Boys" is "about love, friends, and family or perhaps it's about everything that can go wrong with love, friends and family" (see http://www.tv.com/trailer-park-boys/show/10334/summary.html). Literally set in a trailer park, dope-smoking and unemployed characters such as Julian, cat-loving eccentrics such as Bubbles, and hard-drinking Ricky are just some of the real-life, working-class Canadians who challenge the refined and dignified ways in which love relationships are meant to be developed, maintained, or dissolved. In one of their Christmas specials, Julian bails Ricky out of jail on Christmas Eve. However, rather than appreciate this gesture, Ricky is furious because "he always has a good time in jail at Xmas, whereas he doesn't know what to do on the outside" ("Trailer Park Boys" official Web site, accessed January 15, 2007).

While not renowned for its use of irony, American television may have less of a presence where subversive content is concerned, but there are still some memorable examples. Take, for instance, the airbrushed but quite ridiculous portraits of sexual relationships conveyed through shows such as "Desperate Housewives," "Buffy the Vampire Slayer," and "Charmed."

Love Hurts

Yet, not all love stories are playful. Some genres of popular love stories are far from fun or sweet. Consider the stories that emanate from alternative production houses as well as the odd Hollywood film that might be classified as "gritty realism," such as *Bubble* (2006). It sits beside the now classic films *Extremities*, *Fatal Attraction*, *and Thelma and Louise*, all of which have deconstructed the happy-ever-after ideal. Consider, too, songs by Nick Cave (1996), who declared that "People Ain't No Good," or Leonard Cohen (1992), who sang "Dance Me to the End of Love." Ultimately these love stories share the view that love is no panacea to life's problems. More interested in the underbelly of love, they promote the possibility that love hurts.

Usually the characters involved in gritty, realist love stories are not young, beautiful, and wealthy but people who live on the margins, and who conduct their love relationships in laundromats, taverns, diners, and trailer parks— again, see *Bubble* (2006). Raymond Carver's compilation of short stories (1988) *Where I'm Calling from* (1988), and film *Short Cuts* (1993) are also good examples. Most of the characters are chain-smoking heavy drinkers who are either unemployed or work at minimum-wage jobs. They are emotionally battered, prematurely aged, and not in good physical shape. Not afraid to speak their minds, they talk about the possibility of reviling the ones they once loved. For instance, in his story *What We Talk about When We Talk about Love*, Carver (1988, p. 138) wrote that Terri "said the man she lived with before she lived with Mel loved her so much he tried to kill her." Whereas Mel says that "There was a time when I thought I loved my first wife more than life itself. But now I hate her guts. How do you explain that? What happened to that love?" (Carver 1988, p. 143).

Attracting more mainstream attention, Hollywood films such as *American Beauty* (1999) and *Lolita* (1997) took a different turn by exploring some of the dirty secrets of bourgeois family life. In *American Beauty*, Kevin Spacey played the middle-aged, supposedly downtrodden husband trapped within the confines of middle-American suburbia that is, until he becomes sexually obsessed with his daughter's 14-year-old friend. In a similar vein, Jeremy Irons played the part of an aging academic who claimed to have fallen in love with 14-year-old Lolita, a child whom he was supposed to father. Using the compulsive-obsessive love defence to justify the sexual abuse he perpetrated against her, he was supposedly devastated when Lolita revealed to him that she would rather return to the arms of an unrepentant child porn merchant than her lecherous "daddy."

Expressing even more hostility to sentimental accounts of love is Ravenhill's (1996) play, *Shopping and F***ing*. With four of the characters scarred by child abuse and now slaves to illicit drugs, all declarations of love are mocked as hollow and pathetic. Contesting the idea that love is a "civilizing influence," Ravenhill

(1996, p. 85) used the repugnant character of Brian to argue that money is the only true source of meaning:

> *Brian:* It's not perfect, I don't deny it. We haven't reached perfection. But it's the closest thing we've come to meaning. Civilization is *money*.

Summary

Social workers and other health and welfare professionals are advised to take an interest in popular culture because popular culture plays an important role in shaping our understanding of love. Across its mediums (radio, television, print, theatre, and so on), popular culture does this not just because of the extent of its reach into our daily lives, but also because love is a central theme of so many of its programs and products. Yet the task does not end there. Studying love in popular culture is complicated by the many mixed messages it produces. From this array of messages, we are faced with the task of interpreting their meanings.

Love is a slippery subject to study because even when it is a constant preoccupation, it is never fully captured by one human being, academic discipline, or site of production. This is because love defies scientific measurement and meddles with time. It is a story or a series of stories, but it is conducted in material, spiritual, and emotional worlds. These worlds are imbued with desires, dreams, and hopes, which are undergirded and overlain by personal experiences of many kinds. That is why some people reject the notion of falling in love while experiencing it as a form of escape, if not one of life's great adventures.

What should not be forgotten is that people perform love relationships. Love relationships do not just happen to us. Using our bodies and minds (and, some might add, souls) people are sorted through the classifications of gender, sex, class, race, age, and ability. As I elaborate in the next chapter, while love is often equated with liberty and freedom, it is also subject to much regulation and can involve many costs, particularly for people not ranked highly in the social order.

*It is, after all, disturbing to think that perhaps
we might not be living happily ever after.*
(Delmar 1972, p. 1)

4
FIRST AND SECOND WAVE FEMINIST STORIES ABOUT LOVE AND ABUSE
All's (Not) Fair in Love and War

IN THE LAST CHAPTER I EXPLAINED WHY social workers should take love seriously. In chapters 2 and 3 I traced some of the stories told about love in the academy and popular culture. I noted that competing ideas have been expressed about love and that conflicting advice has been dispensed, mostly to women, about how to maximize their chances of being loved. In so doing, I considered the idea that while romantic love genres continue to promote the happily-ever-after ideal, other stories have been told about love's potential to cause great harm.

This chapter is dedicated to examining how Western first and second wave feminists analyzed love, power, and women's relationships of sexual intimacy. This historical material is important because it provides insights into the sociopolitical contexts of love lives staged in Anglo-American-dominated societies, especially those in Canada, the United States, Britain, Australia, and New Zealand. It also provides insights into how women have fought collectively to change social policies and practices associated with loving and caring for others. As will become evident, as feminists struggled into the second wave to have abuse recognized as a pressing social problem, more damning views circulated about women loving men. Before this could take place, however, women had to fight for basic citizenship rights.

The First Wave of Western Feminism

From the late 18th to the early 20th centuries, the first wave of feminists contested assumptions about women's inferiority and struggled to have women recognized as citizens in their own right. Some of the strategies they employed include exposing the ways women were rendered invisible through accounts of history; pathologized as the "weaker sex"; precluded from voting and restricted from participating in public life; obstructed in their attempts to be formally educated; prevented from owning property; expected to approximate passive behavioural codes ascribed to the feminine; coerced into financially and emotionally dependent relationships with men; castigated for prioritizing their own sexual desires; prohibited from taking steps to control their fertility; and stigmatized if they transgressed convention.

Chivalry, the "Fair Sex," and Forbidden Love

Across the waves, feminists have narrated different stories about love. In the first wave, however, much attention was given to chivalrous love and its capacity to authorize male tyranny. Wollstonecraft ([1792] 1975) was one very early feminist who provided a good example of this. Arguing against all "respectable" notions of womanhood circulating in pre-industrial England, Wollstonecraft ([1792] 1975) first had to oppose the puritanical and patriarchal doctrines dominating British culture. Only then could she mount her argument about the exaggerated emphasis placed on women's sexual reputation, and the ensuing expectations that they behave in socially and sexually modest ways.

Referring to love as "the common passion," Wollstonecraft ([1792] 1975, p. 115) challenged the idea that women were the "fair sex," and criticized philosophers, such as Rousseau, for arguing that girls should be educated in the ways that "render them pleasing [to men]." Nevertheless, she was deeply optimistic that women could avoid being degraded by love relationships, using her *Vindication of the Rights of Women* to promote sexual equality in familial and sexual love relationships. Criticizing men who endorsed patriarchal love styles and the women who conformed to them, she urged women to resist being enslaved by love by (1) "developing their character"; (2) pressing for the same educational opportunities available to boys; and (3) forming love relationships that were built on friendship, compassion, and respect.

Almost 50 years later, Charlotte Brontë became another notable first wave feminist to critically analyze the (hetero)sexual conventions of England's industrial period. First publishing the novel under a male name, Brontë (1966) used the fictional portrait of *Jane Eyre* ([1848] 1966) to expose how different classes of women were governed. She did this through the story of orphaned and emotionally abused Jane, who entered an upper-class household at 18 to work as a governess. It was there that she fell in love with Rochester, the man of the house. Before their love could be realized, she had to endure all manner of obstacles, including the knowledge that his first wife had been imprisoned in the attic.

Given that marriage was ordinarily used by the upper class to consolidate status and resources, not diminish it, the storyline of the prince-like Rochester falling in love with the Cinderella-like Jane *and* wanting to marry her was deeply transgressive. Yet, through the fictional characters and the themes of longing and confusion, Brontë (1966) did not use direct argument but gentle persuasion to encourage readers to consider new ways of loving and new ways of understanding abuse.

Working from a similar perspective to Brontë and Wollstonecraft, Emma Goldman also promoted the idea that love possessed much greater possibilities than the conventions that governed it. Imprisoned for inciting a riot and campaigning on behalf of birth control, Goldman fought for women to be granted equal rights to men in all facets of life (Schneir 1994). Rather than rejecting love out of hand, she claimed that it had revolutionary potential if freed from the impoverishing institution of marriage:

> Love, the strongest and deepest element in all life, the harbinger of hope, of joy, of ecstasy; love, the freest, the most powerful moulder of human destiny; how can such an all-compelling force be synonymous with that poor little State and Church-begotten weed, marriage? (Goldman cited in Schneir 1994, p. 323)

Goldman's redemption of love may have been connected to the love she experienced in her own life. In one of her passionate love letters to Ben Reitman, she wrote:

> You have opened up the prison gates of my womanhood. And all the passion that was unsatisfied in me for so many years, leaped into a wild reckless storm boundless as the sea.... [I]f I were asked to choose between a world of understanding and the spring that fills my body with fire, I should have to choose the spring. It is life, sunshine, music and untold ecstasy. (Goldman 1908, cited in Schneir 1992, p. 320).

Alive with private desire, yet concerned that she would be seen as too emotional to be an activist, she added:

> If ever our correspondence should be published, the world would stand aghast that I, Emma Goldman, the strong revolutionist, the daredevil, the one who has defied laws and convention, should have been as

helpless as a shipwrecked crew on a foaming ocean. (Goldman, cited in Schneir 1992, 321)

The Suffragettes, Love, and Spinsterhood

The practice of defying laws and conventions was—and still is—common to many feminists. So, too, is the desire to be loved exclusively by one other; the hope to be able to express sexual passion; and even the romantic fantasy of being rescued. Apart from the simple pleasures that can be derived from love, love often promises a temporary escape from the hostility that is so often directed at those who transgress convention. This is one reason why love and its conventions are often deconstructed but not always reviled by those who identify as "radical." And this can be said for more than a few suffragettes who contributed a great deal to the first wave of feminism.

Decades before Brontë wrote *Jane Eyre* and Goldman used activism to protest for sexual equality, women in Britain, France, and the United States joined the suffrage movement. Although their main priority was to win the vote for women, they identified many injustices perpetrated against women, including those relating to sexual slavery (Bulbeck 1997). Consider, for instance, Elizabeth Wolstenholme-Elmy, who founded the Manchester Women's Suffrage Society in 1865. She helped to found the (British) Women's Franchise League in 1889 before creating the Women's Emancipation Union in 1891. With other suffragettes, Wolstenholme-Elmy channelled much of her energy into British law reform (Jeffreys [1985] 1997). As Jeffreys ([1985] 1997) noted, although they were unsuccessful in their bid to legally prohibit men from raping their wives, they did manage to have the Matrimonial Causes Act (1884) passed. In this Act, a husband was no longer permitted to "imprison a wife who refused conjugal rights" (Jeffreys [1985] 1997, p. 31).

Like Wollstonecraft and Brontë, Wolstenholme-Elmy did not, however, renounce all love relationships as oppressive. Inspired to conceptualize love in unconventional ways, she wrote *Phases of Love* (1897), which de-emphasized physical pleasure and promoted the "realisation of justice, equality, and sympathy between the sexes" (Jeffreys [1985] 1997, p. 31). At the time she flouted convention by living with her lover, Ben Elmy, until she became pregnant and decided to marry to avoid the harm that might befall the suffrage movement if the public learned of the scandal (Jeffreys [1985] 1997).

Similar to Wolstenholme-Elmy, Elizabeth Cady-Stanton protested against Church teachings that endorsed women being "given away," as if they were articles of merchandise. She also objected to women being made to vow obedience to their husbands, as slaves do to their masters (Nies 1977). Echoing the sentiments of other first wave feminists keen to have women's basic citizenship rights recognized, she wrote that "Womanhood is the great fact in her life; wifehood and motherhood are but incidental relations" (Elizabeth Cady-Stanton cited in DuBois 1975, p. 66).

Although first wave feminists gave a lot of attention to married women's oppression, they also considered the subordination of single women. This may have been due to the growing numbers of unmarried women, especially suffragettes, who were most likely to be publicly denigrated and discredited for being single (Summers [1975] 1994). Said to be "indelicate" because of their outspokenness and their refusal to wear the corseted dresses of their time, the suffragettes were forced to battle the stereotypes of "dirty whore" or "unloved spinster." This may also explain why Christabel Pankhurst argued so pointedly that "spinsterhood was a political decision, a deliberate choice made in response to the conditions of sexual slavery" (Jeffreys [1985] 1997, p. 89). She was reacting to the claim that single women, especially suffragettes, were either desperate to find a husband "deep down" or "too selfish" to create a family.

Contesting the assumption that all women were desperate to marry and bear children, Sarah Miles Franklin (1902) used her novel, *My Brilliant Career*, to explain why a woman might forsake love for a career. Among the themes of heartache, secrecy, guilt, and shame, she argued that women should be able to have families and careers without being seen as greedy (also see De Beauvoir [1949] 1973).

The Second Wave of Feminism

The right to have a family and a career was an ongoing struggle in the second wave of feminism (1960s to the mid-1980s). However, during this time the number of campaigns for women's rights exploded. In homes, hospitals, schools, workplaces, universities, and law courts, second wave feminists refuted assumptions made about men's superiority and women's inferiority (Hollway 1983, [1984] 1996; Oakley 1981). Rereading dominant discourses about biology, sex, and gender and cataloguing the effects of gender oppression, feminists across the political spectrum articulated large-scale plans for social change (Connell 1995; Greer 1972, 1999; Herman 1992; Segal 1999).

Ambitious plans for social change surfaced in the second wave in response to the rapid expansion of knowledge about women and injustice. In a wide range of feminist groups, membership numbers increased when women from less privileged backgrounds joined in. While the new recruits were still mostly White and suburban, the class-based issues they brought with them meant that more talk was given over to day-to-day hardships, especially those that ordinary women faced. In anarchist, liberal, and socialist feminist groups alike, more time was spent examining the implications of gender segmentation in social institutions, including the family, schools, and the labour market.

Because most feminists in the second wave prioritized building knowledge about women's oppression, love was often left to appear in the subtexts of narratives about sex and gender. From these subtexts, many divergent ideas were expressed. Often, the differences could be related to the established paradigms through which many feminists made their claims. In no order of priority, the following discussion explores some of the second wave feminist discourses (stories or theories) associated with love.

Penis Envy and the Two Lips Manifesto

For some second wave feminists, psychoanalysis offered a springboard from which new stories could be told. Providing the mainframe of psychoanalysis, Freud ([1908] 1990) argued that all human beings possess an unconscious that becomes the site of competing drives. One of the most important of these is the sex drive (Freud 1986). Born with the capacity to feel sexual desire (including pleasures derived from breast-feeding and expelling bodily fluids), individuals are believed to behave in ways that do not always make sense, often produce guilt, and are frequently self-defeating (Freud 1986).

Psychoanalysts still talk about individuals enacting scenes from the past. Representing desire as insatiable, transgressive, and inclined towards "phantasy" (Freud [1908] 1990, p. 148), they claim that individuals are compelled towards repetition because they carry into adulthood unresolved issues from childhood (Freud [1931] 1990, p. 361). With past experiences hovering overhead, "normal" individuals are understood to try to satisfy their sexual desires, while at the same time they try to win the approval of those in authority. From this contradiction many "neuroses" are generated (Freud [1915] 1990, p. 125), as well as much "hysteria" (Freud [1908] 1990, p. 146).

Most psychoanalysts still believe that a central part of being human involves satisfying and repressing sexual desire. With psyches that oscillate between libido and disgust, individuals are thought to experience much ambivalence. According to Freud ([1915] 1990, p. 125), ambivalence is a "form of sexual organization that can persist throughout life and can permanently attract a large portion of sexuality to itself." Yet, the ways in which individuals try to reconcile their ambivalence is said to depend on the "stage of psycho-sexual development" that is reached (Freud [1915] 1990, p. 125).

Freud ([1915] 1990, p. 124) claimed there are many stages of psychosexual development that "are normally passed through smoothly, without giving more than a hint of their existence." For instance, there are the oral, anal, genital, and phallic stages of development. In the *oral phase*, eating is the main site of sexual pleasure. For Freud ([1915] 1990, p. 125), the next pre-genital phase of development is the "sadistic-anal organization." This is the period when individuals express their "instinct for mastery" in relation to the anus (Freud [1915] 1990, p. 125). However, by puberty, a period traditionally assumed to involve profound biological changes between the age of 12 and 18, individuals are said to direct their sexual attention to the genitals. Once this is achieved, they are then ready to enter the phallic stage (Freud [1915] 1990).

In psychoanalytic accounts, many claims are still made about femininity and masculinity. In the *genital stage*, boys are said to discover the delights of having a penis, while girls derive pleasure from the stimulation of the clitoris. However, as girls enter the *phallic stage*, Freud ([1915] 1990, p. 138) argued that they put "aside their childish masculinity" when they begin to realize that the clitoris is a castrated version of a male penis. From this "castration complex" comes the now-famous narrative about "penis envy" (Freud [1915] 1990, p. 122). In the story of "penis envy," girls are thought not to be aware of the vagina but the penis. Freud ([1931] 1990) maintained that when girls discover that they lack a penis, they react with envy and rage. This hostility is then said to be directed toward their mothers, who are thought to share their fate. Represented as rivals for their fathers' attention, mothers apparently find that they become less important in their daughters' lives. Instead, fathers become girls' most important "love object" and the "law of the father" becomes enshrined as the most important form of authority (Brenner 1955).

With the "law of the father" as the linchpin of psychoanalysis, Freud's earlier possibilities of bisexuality gave way to the supposed primacy of heterosexuality (Freud [1931] 1990). Crucial to social legitimation, heterosexuality still requires women to abide by the conventions of femininity. Predicated on achieving heterosexual desire, part of the lexicon of femininity—or the language of what it means to be a "real woman"—includes women transferring their attention from their clitorises to their vaginas, and displaying greater receptivity to men's sexual interests (Freud [1931] 1990).

Psychoanalysis and feminism may appear to have little in common. However, since it is such a dominant story, and since it provides a rich vocabulary for understanding the psychic life of an individual, some second wave feminists believed that it had the potential to seed more progressive ideas. For instance, Juliet Mitchell (1971) used psychoanalytic ideas to explain women's resistance to changing patriarchy. She argued that by understanding how the unconscious works, particularly in relation to the rule of the father, insights might be developed about the reproduction of patriarchal culture (Mitchell 1971).

Even Michele Barrett (1980, p. 83), who identified as a socialist feminist, claimed that psychoanalysis contained many interpretative possibilities because Freud "never satisfactorily resolved ... the problem of gender." In her view, despite appearing to reinforce dominant biological stories told about women's sexuality, Freud did not find in human beings "pure masculinity or femininity ... either in a psychological or a biological sense" (Barrett 1980, p. 83).

Speaking from France, Kristeva (1984) used the logic of psychoanalysis to explore whether women who identified with their fathers did so to escape the subordinated place in the symbolic order. She claimed that this was a paradoxical move because it reinserted women into patriarchy (Kristeva 1984). Luce Irigaray (1985) is another French feminist to use the language of psychoanalysis to criticize the cultural overvaluation of the penis and subordination of female genitalia. Refuting the story of penis envy, she said that it has "left us only lacks, deficiencies, to designate ourselves. They've left us their negatives" (Irigaray 1985, p. 207).

In her *Two Lips Manifesto*, Irigaray (1985) created a radically different story about women's sexuality. Here, the female body was represented as inherently multiple, connected, and contiguous. Since both lips of the vagina are in constant contact with each other, women were understood to live in a constant state of auto-erotica, a state that is disrupted by the "violent break-in" of the penis (Irigaray 1985, p. 24). Accentuating the importance of women's sexual pleasure, Irigaray (1985, p. 203) told women to "Do what comes to mind, do what you like: without 'reasons,' without 'valid motives,' without 'justification,'" and urged women to reconsider saying "I love you" because, for her, it "lies in wait for the other" (Irigaray 1985, p. 206).

Socializing Women to Be Men's Opposites

During the 1960s and 1970s across Anglo-America, sexual libertarianism became fashionable in some circles, and new claims were made about multiple sexual liaisons. From this perspective, liaisons that were guided not by romance but sexual passion had the potential to be the precursor or beginning point to liberation. Some feminists, such as Germaine Greer, were persuaded. Yet for many others, sexual libertarianism was dismissed as "a new and loveless way of exploiting women" (Wallace 1997, p. 91). Among these debates, the campaign for sexual equality continued.

It was during the second wave that many feminists refuted the claim that men and women were biologically opposite. British feminist Ann Oakley (1972) argued that human sexuality was not biologically determined but culturally constructed. This was important given that Western societies have historically understood female sexuality to be something that involved "long arousal and slow satisfaction, inferior sex drive, susceptibility to field dependence and romantic idealism rather than lustful reality" (Oakley 1972, p. 36). In turn, traditional discourses believed that women were "naturally" inclined to respond to men's sexual urges rather than to their own (Oakley 1972).

As arguments ensued about biological differences between the sexes, Australian feminist Anne Summers ([1975] 1994) wrote *Damned Whores and God's Police*. In this text she challenged the assumptions made about marriage and motherhood, and used the discourse of gender socialization or training to explain the transmission of sexual inequality (Summers [1975] 1994). For her, gender socialization directed girls to sublimate their ambitions to narrowly circumscribed marital goals, which stood in the way of women's self-actualization (also see Hollway 1983, [1984] 1996). And in the pursuit of marriage, women were thought to be compelled to defer to men as they "slavishly adopt[ed] whatever appearance or demeanour she believe[d] [would] earn her the approval of men and, also important, other women" (Summers [1975] 1994, p. 285).

Using the works of John Stuart Mill (1970), many liberal feminists campaigned for women to have the same opportunities as men in the home, labour market, church, judicial system, and formal political arena. From their efforts, and with the support of many other types of feminists, a great variety of programs and benefits were made available to women, yet it was reform, not revolution, that was sought. Having faith in the ideals of meritocracy and pluralism, liberal feminists said little about the hegemony or domination of heterosexuality and the oppressive implications of capitalism.

Patriarchal Capitalism

In the second wave, many feminists were influenced by socialism. With faith in the public ownership of the means of production and the state in control of it, socialists aspired to radically transform the social order (Mullaly 1997). Drawing ideas from the *Communist Manifesto* (1848), socialist feminists rejected capitalism and its respect for an individual's right to accumulate profit. Yet, unlike many socialists who assumed that class was the root of all oppression, socialist feminists highlighted the system of patriarchy and were not convinced that male domination would, post-revolution, fall away on its own accord. Using ideas from Engels (1978, p. 115), they were (and still are) interested in how women could be reduced to roles of servitude by becoming slaves to "men's lust" and "instrument(s) for the production of children." With Engels (1978), they advocated for husbands and wives to share equal rights and responsibilities, which, they noted, was possible only if men shared the burden of unpaid labour and women had the opportunity to engage in paid work.

In the *Red Stocking Manifesto* (1970), "red feminists" described how women's second-class status was reproduced through relationships of intimacy. They argued that stories told about the "unique" and "private" nature of intimate relationships disguised the reproduction of male supremacy and obscured sexual inequality. In their metanarrative (or big story) about women and intimacy, they claimed that because many women lived intimately with their oppressors, they were prevented from seeing their situations in political terms.

Also assuming that women were members of an oppressed class, Michele Barrett (1980) argued that capitalist modes of production were the root cause of women's oppression. Bound by contracts and designed to maximize profit, capitalist modes of production infiltrated individuals' private lives through the convention of contracting women to men as if they were property, and exploiting their labour by denying that domestic duties qualified as real work (Barrett 1980). Catherine MacKinnon ([1982] 1996) agreed. Drawing parallels between men's violation of women's sexuality and capitalists' appropriation of workers' labour, she contended that patriarchal capitalism alienated women from their sexuality, and compelled them to internalize responsibility for stimulating men's desire, which, she said, was "a material reality of women's lives, not just a psychological, attitudinal or ideological one" (MacKinnon [1982] 1996, p. 186).

Radical feminists cited many examples of how women's lives were disfigured by male domination (see Bunch 1978; Daly 1973, 1978; Dworkin [1978] 1996; Firestone 1970; French 1978; Griffin 1981; Koedt 1970; Morgan [1970] 1971; Rich 1980; Rowbotham 1972). They also challenged many of the assumptions made about what was "natural" or "normal" for men and women. In so doing, they scrutinized all elements of society and every aspect of their lives for the social practices popularly assumed to be "standard" and "acceptable" (see Griffin 1981; Koedt 1970; Morgan [1970] 1971).

Men as "the Head of the Household"

With many socialist feminists, radical feminists highlighted the conventions that expected women to marry, relinquish their name, and assume a subsidiary identity to that of their husbands, as well as perform most of the unpaid domestic labour. Many of them cautioned women against romance and marriage through the slogan "It starts when you sink into his arms and ends with your arms in his sink" (Jackson & Scott 1996, p. 13).

Yet, in contrast to socialist feminists, radical feminists refuted the claim that patriarchy was a direct descendant of capitalism (Morgan [1970] 1971). Rowbotham (1972) cited two Russian proverbs used to encapsulate women's subordination during pre-industrial times. The first warned women that "The woman's road—threshold to stove," while the second said that "I thought I saw two people but it was only a man and his wife" (Rowbotham 1972, p. 134). These proverbs were then linked to Tsarist family law, which expected a wife to "obey her husband as the head of the family, to be loving and respectful, to be submissive in every respect and show him compliance and affection" (Rowbotham 1972, p. 138).

Through her analysis of fictional and non-fictional texts produced during the Russian Revolution, Rowbotham (1972) identified some of the competing views expressed about love and romance. In her view, many communists believed that romantic love was (and still is) a bourgeois ideal that distracts people from transforming society. The experience of falling in love—which is known to be chaotic, possessive, and jealous—was subject to close scrutiny. However, while some dismissed the in-love experience as an illusion and a form of retreat, other communists entertained the idea of love but attacked the conventions that governed it (Rowbotham 1972).

Speaking from North America, Mary Daly (1973) noted that the convention of men becoming the head of the household was not peculiarly Russian. She recognized that through modernity, Judeo-Christianity's "divine plan" started to conflate husbands with God (Daly 1973). Heralded as the natural authorities, husbands were given licence to treat their wives and children as if they were their chattels. Rather than serving as women's protection, the orthodoxies of conjugal love were said to mystify male supremacy and encourage women to have faith in the authority of their husbands (Daly 1973).

In *Gyn/Ecology*, Daly (1978) considered how words were used to create the illusion of male supremacy. She noted that by using language that was designed to colonize—including the language of love—men were able to evoke their rights through an established vocabulary, while women found that the same language obscured their interests, dismissed their experiences, and denied their claims (Daly 1978). One of the ways this was achieved was through the language of spinsterhood. Marilyn French (1978) agreed, noting that unlike the male stereotype of "the bachelor," "the lonely spinster" still fills many women with fear and dread (French 1978). So as to avoid being discredited as unlovable, many women were said to seek refuge in romantic love (French 1978).

Women's Rivalry

For many women, the prospect of being seen as unlovable *is* unbearable. Culturally expected to love, women are still given many inducements to enter into sexually intimate relationships. Yet, as Charlotte Bunch (1978) pointed out, women are given inducements to love men, not other women. According to her, heterosexuality separates women from each other and encourages them to compete against one another for men's affections (Bunch 1978). Those who "win" this competition are rewarded with the status that is conferred to women who are legally bonded to men. Believing that heterosexual courtship and marriage are pivotal sites of gender inequality, she argued that women will be liberated only when they prioritize the relationships they have with other women.

Bunch (1978) used a logic similar to that of Shulamith Firestone (1970), who had already written her text, *The Dialectic of Sex: The Case for Feminist Revolution*. In this text, women were understood to seek male recognition since there was and is so little recognition given to them in other areas of their lives. Transcending their inferior status through the unions they developed with men, women were thought to pursue monogamous heterosexual coupledom because "it becomes easier to try for the recognition of one man than many" (Firestone 1970, p. 132).

Firestone (1970) argued that while women were at risk of developing identities based on men's approval, men failed to appreciate how it might feel to be so reliant on the status of another (also see Greer 1972). Instead of understanding the implications of women deriving vicarious pleasure from the love relationship they had with men, women were liable to be pathologized as "clingy" or "needy" (Firestone 1970; Greer 1999). In conventional love stories, this dynamic tends to be seen as a "misunderstanding" that occurs between the sexes, part of the overall "mystery of love" (Firestone 1970). For this reason and others, Firestone (1970) declared that love relationships were the pivot of women's oppression.

Compulsory Heterosexuality

Also concerned with the dominant myths about sexuality, Anne Koedt (1970) produced "The Myth of the Vaginal Orgasm." In it she argued that the vagina was not a highly sensitive area; that claims made regarding vaginal orgasms were fake; and that men used the myth of the vaginal orgasm to justify the centrality of penile penetration. She said that women who confessed to not being able to achieve vaginal orgasm were likely to be described as "frigid" even though they may derive pleasure from having their clitoris stimulated (Koedt 1970). From this she argued that:

> The recognition of clitoral orgasm as fact would threaten the heterosexual institution. For it would indicate that sexual pleasure was obtainable from either men or women, thus making heterosexuality not an absolute but an option. (Koedt 1970, p. 166)

In agreement, Adrienne Rich (1980) considered how "male power" insinuated itself into women's lives through enforced heterosexuality. For her, the "power of men" was used to (1) deny women their own sexuality; (2) force male sexuality upon them; (3) exploit their labour and control their production; (4) control or rob them of their children; (5) confine them physically and prevent their movement; (6) use them as objects in male transactions; (7) cramp their creativeness; and (8) withhold from them large areas of society's knowledge and cultural attainment (Rich 1980, p. 132).

Rich (1980) linked women's conformity to hetero-patriarchy to the idealization of heterosexual romance in art, literature, media, advertising, and other dominant forms of cultural expression. She noted that in contrast to heterosexual romance, lesbian love narratives were located "on a scale ranging from deviant to abhorrent or simply rendered invisible" (Rich 1980, p. 130). Understood to be a bitter reaction to men rather than a legitimate form of sexual expression, lesbianism was (and, in many instances, still is) simultaneously erased and pathologized by a system that Rich (1980) referred to as "compulsory heterosexuality."

"The Male Protection Racquet"

Many other feminists used the compulsory-heterosexuality thesis for a wide range of purposes (Valverde 1985). For instance, Cheryl Clarke ([1981] 1996) used it to explain why women of colour may use their sexuality to appease men. She claimed that the romantic narrative of men "taking care" of women is ironic and duplicitous as it mystified the work that women did to "take care of their men" and legitimated the control men exercised over the women they claim to love (Clarke [1981] 1996).

Susan Griffin (1981) argued that underlying all forms of chivalry was the threat of sexual violence. Her now-famous argument may be summarized as follows. In hetero-patriarchy, rape served as a warning to all women and paid a dividend to all men (Griffin 1981). This ever-present threat of rape was used to justify why only women were expected to trade their liberty for protection (Griffin 1981). They do this by calling upon the protection of their male partner, who was or is thought to shield them from the "uncontrollable sexual urges" of other men (Griffin 1981). It is a "protection racquet" not only because it naturalized men's sexual aggression but also because it concealed the violence that men inflicted upon the women they were supposed to be protecting.

Andrea Dworkin (1981) narrated a similar story to Griffin (1981). Exposing the widespread violence perpetrated against women, often by their male intimates, she concluded that:

> Men control the sexual and reproductive uses of women's bodies. The institutions of control include law, marriage, prostitution, pornography, health care, the economy, organized religion, and systematized physical aggression against women (for instance, in rape and battery).... The metaphysics of male sexual domination is that women are whores. (Dworkin 1981, p. 203)

Dworkin ([1978] 1996, 1981, 1997) was particularly critical of the way heterosexual romance narratives encouraged women to demonstrate their love for men by their willingness to be hurt by them. Pointing to the sanctions used against women who attempted to leave violent spouses, she refuted the idea that women were masochists, arguing instead than men were sadists (Dworkin 1981).

Speaking as a Black feminist, bell hooks ([1986] 1991) reiterated some of the problems with patriarchy and encouraged women to collaborate with one another. For her,

> Male supremacist ideology encourages women to believe we are valueless and obtain value only by relating to or bonding with men. We are taught that our relationships with one another diminish rather than enrich our experience. We are taught that women are "natural" enemies, that solidarity will never exist between us because we cannot, should not, and do not bond with one another. We have learned these lessons well. We must unlearn them if we are to build a sustained feminist movement. We must learn to live and work in solidarity. We must learn the true meaning and value of sisterhood. (hooks [1986] 1991, p. 29)

Promoting the importance of women's solidarity, many consciousness-raising groups took place during the 1970s and 1980s. Emphasizing women's commonalities rather than their differences, many of these groups spent time scrutinizing acts of male domination (Baines 1997). By splitting love from abuse and rendering them incompatible, many members contested the dominant discourses that implicated or blamed women for male aggression (Dworkin [1978] 1996; Morgan [1970] 1971).

Campaigns to Publicly Recognize Abuse against Women

Concerns about male violence were so pressing in the second wave of Anglo-American feminism that many public campaigns were specifically orchestrated to combat it (Connell 1995; Herman 1992; Segal 1999). Discourses of "female provocation" and "the uncontrollable male sex drive" were condemned as patriarchal and charged with revictimizing women (Ehrenreich & English 1978; Griffin 1981). Much energy was expended theorizing the etiology of wife battering, sexual assault, and child sexual abuse (Herman 1992), yet by no means were these times easy.

Similar to today, debates about abuse raged and sparked great emotion, particularly anger. Anger can be frightening, especially if one has been trained to be conciliatory rather than confrontational. To muster the energy and conviction needed to stand up to the anger so often induced in opponents, women used consciousness-raising groups to "speak bitterness." Speaking bitterness helped to harness the women's anger and motivate them into social action. For White, middle-class women, this was very important since they were the primary members of most consciousness-raising groups, as well as the prime targets for the idea that a woman should behave "like a lady," which effectively meant being passive, dependent, and "nice" (Baines 1997).

To externalize responsibility for male aggression, second wave feminists had to be anything but passive, dependent, and nice if they were to de-pathologize and de-individualize women's experiences of abuse (see Bunch 1978; Herman 1992). De-individualizing and de-pathologizing women's experience of abuse required the public airing of "private matters." Sometimes taken for granted today, the public airing of "private matters" was pivotal to the development of policies, programs, and services subsequently designed to combat the spectrum of male violence against women. Across the divides, many feminists knew this. They knew that public perceptions of violence, torture, and trauma had to expand if they were going to include assaults that occurred in family homes (see Herman 1992).

The Development of Women's Services

In Australia, the United Kingdom, and across North America, women identifying as feminist were central to the development of women's services, especially those related to fertility control, domestic violence, sexual assault, and women's homelessness. Sometimes with state funding, women mostly delivered these services to other women affected by or at risk of abuse (Herman 1992; Scutt 1990; Weeks 1995, 2000). Through their counselling, advocacy, and crisis interventions, more women were exposed to feminist ideas, which expanded debates about male violence even further. There were frequent arguments among feminists and non-feminists alike about the real causes of these social problems.

Located on the "frontline" of the "war against women," a sizable proportion of the women who delivered services to abused women identified with radical feminism (Chester 1979). Through their work and their theoretical orientation, radical feminists were aware of the most harmful aspects of intimate relationships and, in many cases, were the most outspoken about the injustices they saw before them (Bunch 1978). Most were—and some still are—deeply suspicious of heterosexual love's colonizing, proprietary, and exploitative tendencies.

Inside women's refuges, sexual assault centres, and women's policy advisory units, radical, socialist, anarchic, and liberal feminists policitized the personal. In their respective ways, they criticized institutions that were ordinarily considered sacrosanct (Chester 1979; Friedan 1963; Oakley 1981). Segal (1999, p. 147) wrote that "By asking new questions about men's power over women and children, within and beyond the family, [second wave] feminists gave rise to stories of sexual abuse and ways to challenge and survive it." Some of these stories were expressed in new social policies that reached into schools, churches, and family homes.

Some stories are legendary today, especially the radical feminist call that all women renounce the institutions of marriage, motherhood, and penetrative sex as patriarchal (Griffin 1981; Mackinnon [1982] 1996; Rich 1980; Rowbotham 1972). For some, liberation was possible only when women stop "sleeping with the enemy" and committed themselves to political lesbianism (Bunch 1978; Griffin 1981; Rich 1980). For others, however, liberation could be found only through transgressing all conventions, including those promoted by feminists.

Heterosexuality and Sado-masochism

As a self-professed "lesbian sadist," Pat Califia ([1981] 1996) offered her radical feminist thesis about sado-masochism. In this thesis, Califia ([1981] 1996) claimed that sado-masochistic relationships were usually egalitarian; that partners opted for the role of "bottom" (slave, masochist), or "top" (master, sadist) as they pleased. A form of sexual ritual or pantomime, sado-masochistic relationships parodied power differentials; they did not take them seriously. Free to experiment, lovers could access forbidden pleasures (Califia [1981] 1996). These relationships were safe and healthy because they were consensual. Knowing it was a game, either party was free to say "no" or "I've had enough." In contrast, chivalry was perverse and destructive because it compelled men to assume that they were dominant and women subordinate (Califia [1981] 1996). Locked into these roles, both sexes were prohibited from playing with power and expressing sexual fantasies in potentially unusual but consensually pleasurable ways.

Critical of the women's movement's tendency to adopt self-righteous and moralistic stances on sex, Califia ([1981] 1996) urged feminists not to act as the "Brain Police." Instead, she called for feminists to radically revise their assumptions about sex and become more open to transgressive sexual practices that were ordinarily thought of as sinful (Califia [1981] 1996). Yet, her contention that sado-masochism had the potential to liberate women from the shackles of conventional femininity generated strong reactions from other feminists (Califia

[1981] 1996). For instance, Sheila Jeffreys ([1985] 1997, p. 238) claimed that sado-masochism was "a contradiction to the most cherished precepts of feminism." In her view, feminists should not eroticize sexual practices that involved domination and submission in any form (Jeffreys [1985] 1997).

Arguing a slightly different point of view, Ellen Willis (1992) viewed sado-masochism—however it is expressed—as a sad reflection of a social order that naturalized injustice and inequality. Yet, unlike some of her radical feminist compatriots, she did not assume that women who profess to enjoy penile penetration have "false consciousness" (Willis 1992). Instead, she hoped the women's movement would become less puritanical about sex and more interested in women's sexual desires (Willis 1992). Amber Hollibaugh ([1989] 1996, p. 229) did likewise, asserting that "we can never afford to build a movement in which a woman can 'lose her reputation.'"

Summary

This chapter has shown some of the ways in which first and second wave Western feminists have handled the politics of love. In the first wave, chivalry was deconstructed for the ways in which it romanticized gender inequality by casting women as feeble, and denying them the right to education and personal autonomy. The label "spinster" was criticized for preying on women's fear of isolation and coercing them into asymmetrical gender relations. Most vocal were the suffragettes who waged campaigns over girls' right to be educated and women's right to vote. As they did so, they were often cast as "lonely spinsters" and unfeminine spinsters at that.

In the second wave, there was an explosion of feminist activity and a mushrooming of perspectives about women, sex, and love. Feminist analyses across the political spectrum were published more widely and on a wide range of topics identified as relevant to women's lives. Political campaigns were staged with vigour and great regularity. Theories related to patriarchy and patriarchal capitalism gained momentum, tying many women's oppressive experiences together. Many women's services were developed. Providing refuge for women abused by violent husbands was made a priority, as was publicizing the ways in which husbands were violating their wives. In so doing, second wave feminists exposed the underbelly of heterosexual romance, and showed how it was being used to eroticize women's oppression. Yet, as I will suggest in the next chapter, they did so in ways that some third wave feminists would come to contest, if not detest.

> *Falling in love can cause in us seismic shocks
> that will, if we let them, help to re-evaluate what things
> matter, what things we take for granted.*
> (Winterson 1996, pp. 113–114)

5
THIRD WAVE FEMINIST STORIES ABOUT LOVE AND ABUSE
Pleasures and Paradoxes

IN CHAPTER 4 I EXPLORED SOME OF THE main stories of love and abuse in the first and second waves of feminism. In this chapter I consider more recent feminist stories about love and abuse. Ultimately, I argue that many third wave feminists analyze love and abuse quite differently than most second wave feminists. Less polemical in tone, their writings reflect broader changes in social theorizing as well as more possibilities about what love relationships might mean and how they might unfold.

The chapter is divided into two parts. In the first section I explore some of the socio-cultural changes that have taken place within feminist circles over the last couple of decades. I note that alongside shifts in feminist paradigms, more emphasis is placed on individual agency (personal power). With this, more attention is given to the ways in which language is said to create meanings. These ideas lead into the second section of the chapter where I examine how love is re-evaluated by feminists, many of whom believe that love, including heterosexual love relationships, have more potential for women's pleasure and well-being than previously thought.

Love and Abuse in the Third Wave of Western Feminism

Loosely dated from the mid to late 1980s to the present time, the third wave of Anglo-American feminism occurred during a period of massive economic and socio-political change that yielded mixed results for different subgroups of women (Probert 1995). With the ascendancy of economic conservatism, some women have enjoyed greater prosperity in their material living conditions, while many more have experienced a dramatic decline in their access to resources and opportunities to participate in community life (Bell & Klein 1996; Ebert 1996; Weeks 2000; Young 1997), yet, at the same time, there has been an expansion in knowledge about the politics of everyday life. Many progressive cultural changes have ensued for women and other "minority groups" (Connell 1995; Plummer 1995).

Against this backdrop, third wave feminists have become more diverse, dispersed, and fragmented. Challenging all received ideas, including those provided by feminists during the second wave, feminists in the third wave articulated divergent views about the nature and extent of gender in/equality; credibility of modernist epistemologies; the stability of categories such as "women," "lesbian," "heterosexual," and "working class"; the utility of trying to decipher the causes of women's oppression; the possibility of leading a congruent life; and the interpretations that may be made about women's sexually intimate relationships.

Feminist Backlash or Balderdash?

Among third wave feminists there have been many disputes about the nature and extent of gender inequality. For instance, while Summers ([1975] 1994) claimed that younger women had more access to formal rights and opportunities than their mothers, grandmothers, and great-grandmothers, Pringle (1995, pp. 199–200) argued that "patriarchal relations have been substantially dismantled." Mann (1994) announced the arrival of post-patriarchy, yet Young (1997, p. 3) maintained that "the basic social conditions to which feminists called attention twenty years ago, for the most part, have not improved, and in some areas of the world they have deteriorated."

Younger North American feminist Naomi Wolf (1990) cut across these analyses to narrate *The Beauty Myth*, in which she asserted that women have paid a high price for their inclusion into public life. With Susan Faludi (1992), who wrote *Backlash*, Wolf (1990) talked about the new masculinist regimes that compelled new generations of women to accept the rigid prescriptions of feminine beauty, particularly those disseminated through the mass media (Bell & Klein 1996; Faludi 1992; Wolf 1990). Both claimed that the closer women moved to positions of power historically reserved for men, the more they have been expected to downplay their intellect; diet to an emaciated masculine ideal of what women's bodies should look like; and comply to stringent beauty practices in order to "get their man." Portraying women as having to walk a tightrope between being labelled "sexually frigid" or "promiscuous," they argued that women were also expected to manage the competing demands of the paid workplace and family life, and resist complaining about sexual harassment or any other form of sexual violence (Faludi 1992; Wolf 1990). As Gerhard (2005, p. 40) wrote, their books were "intended to rouse a distracted feminist nation back to action," and in some large-scale studies, a good number of their claims were supported.

In *The Hite Report on Love, Passion, and Emotional Violence*, Shere Hite (1991) also processed responses made by 15,000 anonymous American women to show that women's "progress" toward sexual equality was not as extensive as many claimed. She revealed that 59 percent of the heterosexual women surveyed believed their status remained closely connected to the status they derived from loving men. Eighty-four percent said that while they prioritized their love relationships, they felt that men did not. Ninety-three percent said that they initiated much more "emotional outreach." Eighty-three percent believed that most men did not understand the basic issues involved in making intimate relationships work. Seventy-eight percent said they were treated as equals to male intimates only sporadically, and that they often had to fight for their rights to be respected. Nevertheless, 41 percent of married women said they got married to avoid the exhaustion, depression, and lack of respect they experienced when they were single. Seventy-two percent of married women said that the best features of marriage were "belonging somewhere," companionship, and security. Notably, 69 percent of the married women and 47 percent of the single women said they did not trust being in love. This may be why 92 percent of the single women said they spent a lot of time trying to figure out the casual relationships they were having (Hite 1991).

From these findings, Hite (1991) argued that love was a prescribed lifestyle for women. She was most concerned that the lifestyle prescribed did not encourage women to love themselves but to find a man who would do it for them. Wrestling with questions about whether heterosexual love emancipated or enslaved women, Hite (1991) believed the problem was not love per se, but the patriarchal conventions used to govern love relationships.

"Victim Feminism"

A few years after Hite's (1991) work was disseminated to Anglo-American audiences, some older liberal feminists criticized younger women for complaining too much, and not demonstrating enough gratitude to second wave feminists for achieving an expansion in opportunities now available to women. For instance, in her "Letter to the Next Generation," Summers ([1975] 1994, p. 193) chastised younger women for wanting to "have it all"; not identifying with the women's movement; and portraying older feminists as "a bunch of sad and lonely people who lived only for their jobs and politics." Beatrice Faust (1994) alleged that the backlash thesis is "balderdash." Literally calling her text *Backlash? Balderdash!*

Faust criticized feminists such as Wolf (1990) and Faludi (1992) for propagating "wimp feminism" and "victim feminism."

Amid the controversy being waged about "victim feminism," Wolf released her next book *Fire with Fire* (1993). Softening her earlier ideas, she claimed that the masculine empire had now declined but has been replaced with a fear of feminine power. As she reconceptualized feminine conventions, she claimed that through "the traditional wedding ceremony ... women who are not beauty queens can revel in their queenliness" (Wolf 1993, p. 282). By 1997, she used her book *Promiscuities* to reiterate the difficulties young women face as they negotiate the dichotomous labels of "cold bitch" and "slut." At times returning to her earlier, more polemical style, she outlined the practice of young women "waiting to be claimed" (Wolf 1997, p. 97), yet she also talked about how "special girls can feel when boys pay real attention to you" (Wolf 1997, p. 35).

Wolf's (1990, 1993, 1997) tendency to prevaricate about the causes of women's oppression and the conclusions that may be drawn about heterosexual women's love relationships can be traced to the rise of postmodern and post-structural feminisms. Constituting an important part of the third wave of Western feminism, postmodernist and post-structural feminists deconstruct the modernist epistemologies or ways of knowing that are used to narrate stories about women, sex, and love.

Shifts in Feminist Paradigms

Some feminists in the third wave used the ideas and pursued the same goals as those in the second wave. However, others, particularly those bearing the prefix of postmodern or post-structural, started to deconstruct modernist epistemologies. In crude terms, this meant that they started to debunk some of the prevailing ideas that older feminists had handed down to them. Mostly the feminists inclined to use the prefix *post-* charged all meta-narratives (or big stories) with essentializing women and homogenizing their experiences (that is, suggesting that they have the same essence and share the same kind of experiences) (see Mann 1994; Pringle 1995; Weedon 1987). This latter group of feminists criticized second wave feminists for their tendency to represent the interests of a predominantly White, heterosexual, middle-class, able-bodied constituency (Ang 1995; Baines 1997; Young 1997). Drawing on ideas from post-colonialism and gay and lesbian texts, many claimed that second wave feminist discourses oppressed those women whose interests and experiences did not coincide.

Many postmodern feminists argued that meta-narratives generated overarching and totalizing claims about women's lives, locking them into an unending set of "false dichotomies" (Butler 1990; Grosz 1987, 1991, 1994; Mann 1994; Weedon 1987; Weir 1996). False dichotomies or the split between men/women, Blacks/Whites, feminine/masculine, rationality/emotionality, object(ive)/subject(ive), sane/insane, good/bad, inside/outside, powerful/powerless, and so on were subjected to much scrutiny and criticisms were mounted about their tendency to shut down discussion (Grosz 1994; Mann 1994; Weir 1996).

Rejecting the mind/body split, many postmodern and post-structural feminists still believe that consciousness is not located in an individual's head but infuses the entire body (see Grosz 1987, 1991, 1994). Viewed through this lens, bodies were now examined in relation to the regimes that regulate, discipline, and celebrate them (Butler 1990, 1997). As these discussions ensued, increasingly abstracted language was used to theorize women's bodies, desires, and relationships (see Grosz 1994).

New Ideas about Language and Power

With their second wave sisters, postmodern and post-structural feminists conceptualized language as a site of political struggle (Gillis & Munford 2004; Grosz 1987, 1994; Weedon 1987; Wood 2001). Rather than functioning either as a pre-given, fixed, and neutral medium through which individuality might be expressed, language was thought to construct the social world. The idea of "a real meaning" was called into question as language was said to contain many interpretative possibilities. Yet, it was in the third wave that less attention was paid to authorial intention (or what the speaker meant). More attention has been given to the way readers interpret texts (Cranny-Francis 1994). Yeatman (1994) referred to this as the "desacralization of meanings," the process where gaps, pauses, hesitations, and absences are not considered peripheral to the text.

Rejecting linear causality (a + b = c), many postmodern and post-structural feminists claimed that it was not possible to understand the origins of human suffering (Butler 1990; Weedon 1987). Some accentuated the instability and potential unreliability of knowledge, calling upon the work of Nietzche (1977, p. 7), who argued that "facts are precisely what there is not, only interpretations." Hoping to validate knowledge that was marginalized and parochial, most argued that the production of knowledge could not be disaggregated from the operations of power (Butler 1990, 1997; Grosz 1994; Yeatman 1994).

Many post-structural feminists contested the claims that structural/material feminists made about power. Rejecting the idea that people were powerful or powerless, they examined practices of domination and control, taking a keen interest in the micro-politics of life (see Mann 1994). Most shied away from the belief that women's collective liberation was possible. Most focused on individual subordinates railing against their oppressors, but not necessarily mobilizing, protesting, and campaigning like their second wave sisters (Weeks 1995).

In contrast to material feminists (who were most dominant in the second wave), post-structural feminists understood power to be fluid, ubiquitous, and dispersed (Grosz 1991; Hollway 1983; Weedon 1987). Contextualized but not determined by social structures, power was now thought to be expressed both positively and negatively. Power now had the potential to be good and bad. Irrespective of social status, all individuals were thought to exercise power, and in ways that were not always predictable (Butler 1997). Honing in on resistance at the micro-level, many challenged the possessive vocabulary used to describe the operations of power. Using relational and social constructivist notions of power, they contested, for example, the claim that women "give up" or "hand over" their power to men (Butler 1997; Mann 1994). Similarly, they refuted the assumption that lesbian relationships were more likely to be equal since women hold similar amounts of power (Butler 1990, 1997).

Most postmodern feminists avoid talking about gender socialization because they believe that growing up contains more possibilities than the term implies. Similarly, they criticize the concept of patriarchy for exaggerating and/or calcifying gender differences. Patriarchy is said to overgeneralize by failing to take into account changing social mores.

According to Mann (1994), contemporary expressions of race, class, gender, and sexuality have unmoored (or lifted up) traditional analyses of structural domination. No longer so clear-cut, gender politics based on oppositional categories and polarized analyses were thought to do little but artificially divide men and women's interests (Caine & Pringle 1995; Mann 1994).

In a time described by Bail as "D.I.Y. Feminism," there is no single feminist enemy. Men, the state, and global corporations may be variously embraced, scorned, or ignored (see Bail 1996). Alliances formed are no longer predictable. Disorganized and argumentative, D.I.Y. feminists of the 1990s and 2000s were said to pursue individual achievements rather than collective action (see Bail 1996). They hang together rather than mobilize. If they do mobilize to protest, they may do so in cyberspace. According to Caine and Pringle (1995, p. xi), "The fundamental question is whether it is still meaningful to target institutions and practices as major sites of oppression."

With this noticeable paradigm shift, third wave feminists actively debated whether any kind of women's experience or collective identity could be used as an organizing principle for political action. Butler (1990) caused a stir when she asked whether the category of "women" was still viable, given the multiple subject positions women might occupy. Eager to avoid locking women into a fixed identity, postmodern feminist still speak of women's multiplicity, agency, and subjectivity. Some refer to Cixous's (1977, p. 32) idea that the "'I' becomes multiple," while others claim that viewing women's actions in postmodern or post-structural terms "liberated a multitude of political subjectivities" and "made visible a wide variety of possible interventions" (Gibson-Graham 1995, p. 183).

Re-evaluating Love and Its Contradictions

Many third wave feminists have worked from the premise that post-structural feminism offers ways to understand women's lives in more lateral and expansive ways. In turn, many of them have re-examined ideas about gender politics and sexual intimacy. Arguably, this has been possible because of the increased public awareness of intimate abuse, and the greater forms of public assistance made available to women who are abused by intimates (Scutt 1990; Weeks 1995, 2000). With these supports in place, it seems that the conditions have been ripe for feminists to be more curious about love and more able to consider how love and abuse might cross paths.

Re-examining Love Narratives

No longer presuming that any particular form of intimacy is innocent or sinister, many third wave feminists have evaluated love in light of the narratives that are told about them (Jackson 1999; Rowland 1996; Wurtzel 1998; Young 1997). For instance, Goodison (1983) claimed that second wave feminists usually gave falling in love bad press because they believed it made women helpless, passive, uncomprehending, and dependent. Romance, in her view, did not have to be like this. It did not have to objectify women's bodies and privatize their lives. The fact that it could be used to do this justified why more attention needed to be given to exploring why love stories appeal to such a diverse range of women:

> Perhaps somewhere between the traditional view of accepting it as an inevitable part of human nature, and the tendency to dismiss it as a capitalist con, there is a third path: one which involves looking at the experience in detail and grappling with its process. (Goodison 1983, p. 48)

Similarly, Angela Hamblin (1983, p. 119) objected to heterosexual women being portrayed as "collaborat[ing] with the enemy." She claimed that such a view stifled attempts to create new forms of feminist heterosexuality (Hamblin 1983). According to her, feminist attempts to transform heterosexual relationships had "not as yet been validated by the women's liberation movement as a whole" (Hamblin 1983, p. 105).

Subscribing to the psychoanalytic story about falling in love and psychic mis-recognition, Wendy Hollway (1983) argued that men tried to avoid feelings of dependency by displacing these feelings onto women. According to her, some men were so reliant on seeing women as dependent that if the women close to them took on paid work (or started to earn more money than they did), their sexual desire for them was likely to diminish. Some men were said to become so threatened by their spouses' attempts to become independent that they portrayed "their" women as "ball crushers" and retreated from sexual activity on the basis that they no longer felt aroused by them (Hollway 1983). In this instance, the problem was not that men were too sexually demanding but that they were not sexually responsive to women who were striving toward equality.

Hollway (1983) was interested to learn more about how desire might be a site of power and resistance, arguing for feminists to theorize men's sexuality as well as women's. As she said, it is important that feminists are not "trapped in a discourse which sees power as being solely the property of men—a possession which we can never acquire by virtue of our sex" (Hollway 1983, p. 140). She was (and is) not alone in this quest, given the number of feminists who have shifted their focus from the dominant feminist concerns of the second wave to the micro-political struggles between male and female intimates.

Connecting women's willingness to perform traditional gender roles with low self-esteem, second-wave feminist Gloria Steinem (1992, p. 258) claimed that the promise of romance inspired many women (especially young women) to "seek refuge and approval in exaggerated versions of their gender roles." For her, girls were likely to have low self-esteem because of the social denigration they received for being female, as well as the negative treatment they received when single. She concluded by saying that it is "No wonder many women need romance more than men do" (Steinem 1992, p. 255).

Striking a different pose, Australian writer Susan Johnson (1992) claimed that many women were aware of the contradictions and paradoxes of their lives, with many of them becoming confused and embarrassed if they harboured the mythical ideas about "true love and rescue." Aware of the more recent cultural expectation that women pursue careers and strive toward more emancipatory goals than romantic love, she talked about the number of younger women who have become too embarrassed to reveal the attraction that they have to love:

> The longing for connection is still vibrantly alive, the pain of love's failures just as acute. To admit needing love in a modern world is to acknowledge the dark and inadmissible, and everyone knows that the submerged will eventually rise up. (Johnson 1992, p. xi)

Popular radio broadcaster Helen Razer (1996) picked up the idea that younger women could be both attracted to, and cynical about, the orthodoxies of romantic love. She claimed that women are often "a little too eager to meld" because intimate bonds are a route to "easy equality" (Razer 1996, pp. 100–101), yet she did not assume that it is only heterosexual women who do so. In her view, lesbians were just as likely to use love as an escape from a masculinist world, adding that since "phallocracy [is] crushing us in the public sphere and all, we can at least expect a little veneration and foot rubbing at home" (Razer 1996, p. 100).

With many other feminist commentators in the third wave, Razer (1996) used humour and irony to entertain her predominantly female audience. Self-parodying attempts to emulate the ideals of feminine beauty, she discussed some of the penalties levelled at women who refused to conform, yet she did so in recognition of some of the paradoxes that women can face when they try to rebel (Razer 1996).

Catherine Lumby's (1997) *Bad Girls* also revolved around the themes of contradiction and complexity. Criticizing earlier feminist stances taken in relation to pornography, prostitution, and heterosexual intercourse, she promoted more active depictions of women's sexuality, reclaiming the label of "bad girl" (Lumby 1997). Similar to Razer (1996), she described how women interacted with dominant discourses in multiple conflicting ways; they were not just dominated by them.

Reclaiming Women's Sexual Pleasure

Lumby (1997, p. 77) argued that young women could view heterosexual love with "renewed optimism" now that women's citizenship rights had been more fully recognized (also see Peplau & Garnets 2000). Pointing to the ways in which the conventions for marriage, motherhood, and sexuality have been extended, and the laws passed that have granted women better access to fertility control, divorce, and equal property settlements, she believed women were in a much better position to explore their sexual pleasure (Lumby 1997; also see Peplau & Garnets 2000).

English novelist Jeannette Winterson (1989, 1992, 1997) shared this interest in women's sexual pleasure, first writing that:

> Holy water and crosses and mountain air and the protection of saints and a diet of watercress are all thought to save us as a species from rotting. But what can save us as a species from love? (Winterson 1989, p. 73)

In *Written on the Body*, Winterson (1992, p. 9) continued to examine women's relationships to sexual pleasure. As she indicated, although love is popularly associated with heterosexuality, not everyone plays by the rules:

> Love demands expression. It will not stay still, stay silent, be good, be modest, no. It will break out in tongues of praise, the high note that smashes the glass and spills the liquid. It is no conservationist love. It is a big game hunter and you are the game. A curse on this game. How can you stick at a game when the rules keep changing?

In *Gut Symmetries*, Winterson's (1997) interest in women's sexual desires resurfaced. Blurring the boundaries between domination/submission, reality/fantasy, men/women, and heterosexuality/homosexuality, she subverted the convention of women competing against one another for a man to tell a story that ends with "the wife" and "the mistress" developing a sexual relationship of their own (Winterson 1997).

Winterson (1989, 1992, 1996, 1997) was by no means the only third wave feminist to urge the women's movement to rewrite new stories about their sex lives. Stevi Jackson (1996, 1999) echoed this sentiment when she urged feminists to problematize heterosexuality without reducing all heterosexual pleasure to eroticized domination. "We do need to think further about the possibility of engaging with the positive aspects of pleasure while remaining critical of current sexual desires and processes" (Jackson 1996, p. 24). Keen to recognize heterosexual feminists' ongoing protests against sexism, she argued that "It cannot be assumed all women who take pleasure in heterosexual sex are simply wallowing in a masochistic eroticisation of our subordination" (Jackson 1996, p. 177), yet resistance to hetero-normativity was not always easy. As she said, some groups of women, especially those with strong emotional support, easy access to education, and good access to material resources, usually found it easier to dictate the terms and conditions of love relationships than socially disadvantaged women (Jackson 1996).

From different social locations, women were now understood to participate in the project of identity construction, but not always in liberating ways (see Peplau & Garnets 2000). Jackson (1996, p. 31) wrote that

> ... women's identities may be shaped by heterosexual imperatives by the need to attract and please a man. The desire to be sexually attractive appears to be profoundly important to women's sense of self-worth and closely bound up with the gendered disciplinary practices through which docile, feminine bodies are produced.

Robyn Rowland (1996) was another radical feminist who called for a "new politics of heterosexual intimacy." Her analysis was as follows: "Though patriarchal institutions and ideologies are implicit in our intimate relationships, at [the individual] level there is sometimes more room for negotiation" (Rowland 1996, p. 81). Using Jeffrey's (1990) notion of "eroticised equality," Rowland (1996, p. 82) encouraged women to

> ... struggle to keep identity and life roles separate within heterosexual relationships ... [by] conceptualising the self as single, but in partnership ... [and by refusing to] engage in domestic, sexual and emotional servicing.

Other strategies Rowland (1996) promoted include women developing networks of intimacy with other women; recognizing and respecting each other's need for independence in working lives; and refusing to play the romantic role of the woman who is self-sacrificing and self-abnegating. It was the kind of images that many women gravitated toward as they gathered each week to view new stories about women's sex lives.

In 1998 "Sex and the City" (SATC) was launched on HBO television network and was extraordinarily popular among younger women, feminists included, through to 2004. According to Gerhard (2005, p. 37) who analyzed the show in great detail, "Sex and the City" "shadowboxes with history, or specifically, with second wave feminism." Scathing of "bad fashion" and women who "let themselves go," the series is haunted by "the ghost of 70's feminism ... through a repressed, nightmarish vision of autonomous womanhood, the lesbian/feminist, a man-hating, definitely humourless, and certainly fashioned challenged caricature" (Gerhard 2005, p. 39).

Destabilizing the assumed homogeneity (or sameness) of the identity of the heterosexual woman, "Sex and the City" explored the challenges women face in their attempts to be independent and sexually liberated, but also socially connected. Almost until the end it maintained that women's friendships were paramount to health, trumping all other relationships, including those with potential spouses and family members (Gerhard 2005). Yet, as discussed earlier, it did, however, only explore the antics of young, good-looking, White, able-bodied, middle-class, well-educated, urban, and heterosexual women; that is, women with prized identities in all but one realm of life. Yet, given the wide demographic of women who followed the series, it was an issue that did not seem to perturb too many viewers. For Gerhard (2005, pp. 39–40), this was because SATC posed "'new answers to old problems,' allowing viewers to 'step down from high feminist alert' ... to [see] likeable feminine characters 'making it' in modern (a.k.a. equal) work settings. In short, viewers seemed to like the idea that if they so chose, [they] can work, talk, and have sex 'like men' while still maintaining all the privileges associated with being an attractive woman" (Gerhard 2005, p. 37).

A Rejoinder to Stay "Real"

However, not all feminists were convinced by this change in style. Indeed, many raised criticisms about how feminism came to be about privilege and style, with many pointing the finger at postmodernism for this turn. For instance, Kristin Waters (1996, p. 281) claimed that the

> ... post-modern emphasis on style is another way of putting the old-fashioned "feminine" back into feminism—by shifting attention away from substance that has concrete and material ramifications, toward a style which is elusive and obscure, ungrounded and apolitical.

Along with Waters (1996) and Coney (1996), Sue Wilkinson and Celia Kitzinger (1996, p. 376) rejected the postmodern feminist refutation of "the real." They have been especially hostile to the ways in which structural feminist analyses have been discredited as "totalising grand narratives." Angry at the way radical and socialist feminist analyses have been dismissed as "totalizing grand narratives" (or oversimplified, grandiose stories), they also challenged queer theory's argument about gender-as-simulated-performances, condemning the way individual pleasure was being prioritized over collective resistance. For them, the

> ... key queer strategy, the gender fuck, is about parody, pastiche and exaggeration. It replaces resistance to dominant cultural meanings of "sex" with carnivalesque reversals and transgressions of traditional gender roles and sexualities, which revel in their own artificiality. (Wilkinson & Kitzinger 1996, p. 377)

In a similar manner, Joan Hoff (1996, p. 394) pointed to the "paralyzing consequences" of post-structural feminism. With Mary Daly (1996), who was also alarmed by the assertion that patriarchy no longer exists, Hoff (1996) warned of the hazards of losing a framework to understand women's continuing material and sexual disadvantage. Teresa Ebert (1996, p. 9) shared this concern arguing that post-structural feminism "mystified the social contradictions and material conditions of women's exploitation in patriarchal capitalism."

Ebert (1996) referred to postmodern feminism as "ludic feminism" because she was critical of the way they overemphasized desire, difference, and discourse. On each count, she offered a competing view. First, she argued that desire was more than a "free-floating autonomous performance" (Ebert 1996, p. 49). Second, she contended that material conditions amounted to more than a language practice (Ebert 1996). Third, she claimed that differences were not only produced through language, nor were they always worth celebrating. And fourth, she refuted the assumption that the powerful were—or are—indistinguishable from the powerless (Ebert 1996).

Growing Global Inequalities in Work and Love

Ebert (1996) substantiated her argument that under global capitalism, the material conditions of most women's lives have worsened. She claimed that without question, "access to economic (educational) resources has not changed: it remains monopolized by the dominant class" (Ebert 1996, p. 11). Thus, by emphasizing desire and subordinating concerns about equality, justice, and need, she maintained that postmodern feminists provided "an alibi for inscribing and universalizing the interests of the dominant class in contemporary knowledge" (Ebert 1996, p. 57). Viewed from this perspective, postmodern feminism was and is a thinly veiled form of neo-conservatism that decontextualized women's lives and exaggerates their freedom.

By the start of the millennium many other sobering accounts of women's lives have been provided by feminists who shared Ebert's (1996) concern about sexual and material inequality. For Peggy Orenstein (2000, p. 2), women were struggling to negotiate "the clash of expectations" precipitated by "life in a half changed world." More cynical was Laura Kipnis (2003), who argued that "Love is both intoxicating and delusional, but in the end, toxic: an extended exercise in self-deception" (also see Jackson 1999). Yet for Susan Maushart (2001), the problem was not love per se, but gender inequality in love relationships. In her view,

> Our new egalitarian convictions have made it even harder to penetrate beyond the veil, as it were. Both males and females in our society publicly profess their dedication to the ideal of what social researchers call "companionate marriage" a covenant between two equally loving and nurturant partners, in which the divisions of labour and leisure are negotiated rationally, equitably and, above all, without reference to gender.... But when a woman marries, what she sees is not what she gets. (Maushart 2001, pp. 3–4)

Echoing a similar sentiment, Lynne Segal (1999) called for women to identify as feminists and for feminists to remain connected to overtly "political" analyses. She asked, "Why feminism? Because it's most radical goal, both personal and collective, has yet to be realized: a world which is a better place not just for some women, but for all women and men" (Segal 1999, p. 232). It was an argument supported by Kearney (2001, p. 280), who fixed her feminist gaze not on the pleasures of shopping or casual sex, but on the abuse of women in intimate relationships:

> Many abused women have chosen to conceal their abuse from health care providers, not only because of fear of retaliation from their abusers but also because of perceived time pressure and provider lack of interest or sympathy.

Not concerned with academic debates about matters such as the "queer fuck," health practitioners such as Kearney (2001, p. 280) called for the extension of provisions for women who were not coasting through life, women whose

> ... depression and substance use [was a] correlate of intimate partner violence ... that may increase women's immobilization, which in turn may lead to lack of self-care agency....

Especially for people working on the front line of health and welfare services for women in very oppressive conditions, paradoxes and pleasures seemed not as important as the need for safety, decent wages, and housing.

Summary

Those in the second wave were so committed to the ideals of equality and justice that they became known as "equality feminists" (Segal 1999). However, by the third wave, new theories were produced about power, and new ideas were used to interpret women's relationships to love. From feminists who identified as postmodern or post-structural, there were calls for a more nuanced (subtle, layered) understanding of women's desire and a more complex analysis of their relationships of intimacy. However, in response to these demands, fears have been expressed about the potential of "ludic feminism" to induce nihilism (apathy, breakdown) in the women's movement. Fears have also been expressed that with such a concentration on desire and little commitment to collective efforts, the abuse of women in and outside intimate relationships might once again go unchecked.

> We begin the day narrating to ourselves and
> probably to others our expectations, plans, desires,
> fantasies and intentions.... We meet our colleagues, family,
> friends, intimates, acquaintances, strangers and exchange
> stories overtly and covertly. We may try to tell all, in true
> confession, or tell half-truths or lies, or refuse to do more
> than tell the story of the weather, the car or the food....
> Even when we try to escape narrative, as when we listen
> to music or do mathematics, we tend to lapse.
> (Hardy 1975 cited in Plummer 1995, pp. 5–6)

6

USING A NARRATIVE FEMINIST PERSPECTIVE
Analyzing Women's Stories of Love and Abuse

PART OF BEING HUMAN INVOLVES narrating stories to other people as well as ourselves. Located in imaginary worlds as well as those that are materially based, human beings use narratives to express emotions and convey beliefs about how things should be (Chanfrault-Duchet 1991; Cotterill & Letherby 1993). Through the retelling of stories, we represent our identities and our societies (Chambon 1994; Jackson 1996; Plummer 1995, 2001; Reissman 1994).

Narratives are integral to human cultures because cultures are constituted through the mosaic of stories told over time (Berger 1997). Cultures produce the conventions for living. Whether it is in the general community, workplace, or home, cultures shape the ways individuals envisage their world and speak about their places in it (Berger & Luckman 1966; Plummer 1995, 2001, 2003). However, cultures are also made by people who do not always do as they are told. Either by accident or design, individuals do not always attend to particular types of narratives or use those that are voiced in ways that are intended (Cranny-Francis 1994; Simon 1996). This means that while narratives are often used to reinforce conventions, they are also used to contest conventions produced during particular historical eras (Franzosi 1998; Jackson 1998).

This book is itself a collection of narratives. In the first chapter I narrated some of the historic influences on Anglo-American social work to consider why love and sexuality have remained outside its frame of reference. I argued that social work has been reluctant to embroil itself in debates about love and sexuality, particularly those that relate to women's sexual pleasure. I also noted that in spite of its predominantly female membership, social work publishes few texts about sexuality and of these, there is an obvious reluctance—if not refusal—to use feminist ideas to analyze love. Given these gaps, I noted that social workers may become acculturated by the popular stories in circulation, especially those relating to romantic love, and that such acculturation posed dangers for groups not well served by these stories.

In the next two chapters I illustrate how the cultural conventions for love have altered over time. By examining the love narratives that have achieved dominance at particular points in history, I have represented love as a socially constructed phenomenon rather than a biologically determined event or inevitability. In Chapters 4 and 5, I used the chronology of the waves of feminism to narrate some of the less publicized and more contentious stories told about women and love. I noted that during the third wave, when power was theorized in more lateral and relational ways, women's relationships with love and sex have attracted more attention and have been given better press. Yet, I also argued that one of the problems of this move has been to underestimate—if not ignore—the structural disadvantages that still confront particular groups of women.

The purpose of this chapter is to describe, justify, and explain the use of one type of narrative research. I begin with a discussion about the rise of narrative research because it is within these politics that narrative analysis may be located. I then consider some of the challenges associated with social workers conducting narrative interviews. In the final section, I offer practical suggestions for analyzing personal stories line by line, or segment by segment.

Approaching Narrative Methods

Narratives have become so popular in the humanities and health and welfare professions that there is now a growing network of narrative communities, a burgeoning body of literature, and a conference circuit that even the most active would have trouble keeping up with. Meeting in person, through the written word, and cyberspace, they tell stories and exchange ideas, hoping in the process that they might develop new ways of understanding their work and themselves.

Whether used in the fields of research, group work, or individual therapy, narrative methods are unashamedly non-scientific. This means that those who use narrative methods do not claim to be neutral or objective. They are not "social scientists" who "discover facts" so as to assert "the real truth of the matter," or "experts" who "know what's best," but people who are curious about the world and the people living within it. Mostly they are curious about how people make sense of their worlds, and how these meanings affect themselves and others (see Fraser 2004).

Metaphorically speaking, narrative researchers may be likened to chefs who see cooking as an art form, and who do not try to stay true to traditional recipes (also see Hollway & Jefferson 2000; Jackson 1998). Alternatively, they/we may be likened to artists who paint, sketch, and draw our impressions, or craftspeople who sculpt, create mosaics, or build their works, sometimes with the scraps that other people have left behind. The metaphors of sewing, knitting, and travelling may also be used to describe narrative research. Piecing together fragments of the fabric of conversations, researchers may be understood to sew ideas together. Similarly, we may be seen as knitters who "spin a yarn" by weaving together the threads of different stories (see Cotterill & Letherby 1993). Finally, we may be compared to travellers who embark on a journey and who try to use maps and compasses. Looking for signposts but not always finding them, we are often challenged by the forks in the road or the crossroads that may appear before us (see Olson & Shopes 1991).

The Benefits and Risks of Narrative Approaches

Yet, there are risks associated with using such metaphors, including the risk of romanticizing narrative research. Nevertheless, I believe these metaphors have utility for three main reasons. First, they shake off the illusions of scientific objectivity, and the correlating assertions of impartiality. Explicating our subjectivity, they recognize that words are never neutral or innocent (Ellerman 1998; Lawler 2002; Plummer 2001). Second, these metaphors are useful because they refer to activities that are familiar to many ordinary people (Berger Gluck 1991). Opening up space for us all, no matter how old or "educated," to participate in the analysis of narratives, these metaphors help to demystify practices that have long been associated with the White, middle-class professionalism that has been linked to orthodox masculinity. And third, the practical association of the metaphors of cooking, knitting, sewing, and travelling help many of us to envisage some of the concrete tasks involved in narrative research.

As I have argued elsewhere (Fraser 2004), narrative approaches have much to offer social work. For instance, they provide ways to make sense of language, including that which is not spoken (Berger 1997; Riessman 1990). Apart from encouraging a plurality of truths to become known, they also provide ways to understand the interactions among individuals, groups, and societies (Jackson 1998; Plummer 1995, 2001; Riessman 1993, 2002). Having the capacity to attend to context as well as idiosyncrasy (that is, people's circumstances as well as their individual peculiarities), they subdue the inclination to posture as an expert and may be used to stimulate different kinds of discussions (Drewery

& Winslade 1997; Milner 2001; Plummer 1995, 2001; White & Denborough 1998). Most importantly, they are able to authorize the stories that ordinary people tell (see Coates 1996; Gubrium & Holstein 1995; Hones 1998; McCabe & Bliss 2003).

Narrative approaches also have the capacity to recognize people's strengths and engage people in active, meaning-making dialogues. When informed by critical ideas, they may help social workers move beyond a strict problem focus to more generally explore social phenomena. Speaking about narrative therapy, in particular, Milner explained that such an approach:

> ... challenges people's beliefs that a problem speaks their identity, a "totalising" effect which conflates the person with the problem. It seeks to separate the person from the problem and develop a sense of incongruency between the two that opens up space for responsibility taking and accountability. (Milner 2001, p. 2)

Carefully used, narrative methods may be effective in cross-cultural work (McCabe & Bliss 2003) and community work (Brunt 2001). Emphasizing curiosity and reflexivity (Myerhoff & Ruby 1992; Skeggs 2002), narrative methods may aid those who seek to democratize professional relationships. By more obviously opening up points of contest and difference, they are, therefore, potentially compatible with social work values, especially those pertaining to social justice and self-determination (Hones 1998; Leonard 1997; Milner 2001).

As with all new trends, however, questions must also be asked about the risks associated with social workers using a narrative approach:

> How might we understand the meanings of the infatuation with constructivist/narrative pursuits in this time and space? Why have we become so entranced with a search for meaning, for language, with its elegant and seductive philosophies? Is it because our social surround is falling apart? (Laird 1994, p. 185)

These questions are hard to ignore given the rise of the narrative movement that occurred during a sustained period of economic conservatism, at least in most of Anglo-American societies. Pointing out that governments have "destroyed the social programs we cared about and re-channelled resources to the already rich," Laird (1994, p. 185) wonders whether "there is something 'escapist' about the story metaphor?"

Having wrestled with this question during the last 10 years, I recognize that narrative approaches are escapist if they ignore "the politics of narratives and the extent to which they support or contest social structures and practices" (Jackson 1998, p. 62). They are also escapist if they assume that social hierarchy is inevitable or immutable or, conversely, that the practices of domination and social exclusion are mere fictions that are amenable to simplistic notions of reframing and positive self-talk. Understanding this helps researchers to avoid becoming either a "witless relativist" (that is, someone who erases the impact of social structures and cultural-political contexts), or a social determinant (that is, someone who focuses so much on social structures and cultural contexts that individual agency is denied) (see Gubrium & Holstein 1995).

Narrative research should not only reflect people's "reality" but also challenge taken-for-granted beliefs, assertions, and assumptions, including those made by revered social theorists (Jackson 1998). As Drewery and Winslade (1997, p. 42) argued, "although we do not have complete control over the possibilities of our lives, we can only ever speak ourselves into existence within the terms or stories available to us." This means that narrative researchers need to retain an awareness of social conditions of people's lives when reflecting on the stories participants and researchers tell (Lawler 2002; Riessman 1993, 1994, 2002, 2003).

Doing Narrative Feminist Research

Narrative feminist research has many possible faces. For instance, it might involve promoting women's stories so that women's interests might be better served. Or it might use a gendered lens to inspect stories that men have told about women. Or it might be used for any number of endeavours that are explicitly interested in gender, stories, and women's rights (also see Jackson 1998).

Narrative feminist research is undertaken by people still willing to identify with feminism despite any pejorative connotations. Although women who call themselves feminist may, quite legitimately, be seen to be promoters of self-interest, they/we are also people who wrestle with questions about power, rights, and justice. Often, this makes life uncomfortable for others *but also ourselves*. Not always right and more than occasionally argumentative, feminists may vary in their views, yet what we share is the impetus to think beyond gender conventions so that new societies and practices might be envisaged (also see Jackson 1998). For many of us, feminism(s) invite(s) us to step outside the ever-mutating system(s) of gender inequality, to bear witness to the privileges accorded relatively few women—namely, women who are young, White, Western, middle or upper class, professionally trained, heterosexual, able-bodied, and/or conventionally beautiful—while the vast majority of women remain marginalized (also see Coates 1996; Ehrenreich & Hochschild 2003; Jackson 1998; Segal 1999; Young 1997). And rather than pretending that research is a disembodied neutral affair, we use it to further these aims.

Surveying Women's Stories

I designed this research to "survey through stories" (Cotterill & Letherby 1993). I undertook narrative feminist interviews because although I know that quantitative and qualitative research each has a part to play in the production of knowledge, I wanted to ensure that a wide range of women's love stories were incorporated into the discussion. As Reinharz (1992) maintained, feminist research interviews have the potential to validate ordinary women's knowledge. They do this by helping us to enter into dialogues that unearth hidden or subordinated ideas (Borland 1991) as well as those that are more obvious or conventional. Because I wanted the chance to get up close to the women presenting these views, I conducted face-to-face narrative interviews with 10 women in Australia in 2000 and 74 women in Canada during 2004.

Loosely using a topic-based interview schedule, I asked the women to tell me what love meant to them; what they experienced through loving others; what they were hoping for; and whether they were satisfied. Focusing most on sexualized love relationships, I was particularly interested to hear if they were interested in democratic love relationships, whether they had experienced them, and how they might define them. While a range of responses ensued, what was obvious was the priority most women gave to the project of loving others.

I used ideas from scripting theory to undertake the analysis of the stories transcribed from the audio recordings made of the interviews. Initially I did this using an intense and very time-consuming form of analysis that involves trawling through meanings line by line (see Fraser 2004). However, as I became more familiar with the type of analysis I wanted to conduct, I stood back and looked for connections from a more aerial perspective (also see discussion below).

Recruiting the Australian Participants

The first 10 women I interviewed in Australia were solicited through a purposive (or "snowball") sampling technique because I deliberately wanted to reach women who had suffered some form of child abuse and/or a period of separation from their birth families while they were young. My rationale for wanting to reach this group of women was clustered around three main reasons: (1) I was skeptical of the alarmingly popular belief that such experiences in childhood will inevitably and permanently damage one's ability to love in the future; (2) I knew from my past work in the areas of child welfare and domestic violence that this criteria would more likely connect me with women who had experienced material disadvantages; and (3) I was still entertaining other people's doubts about the relevance love might have to social work. I figured that by interviewing abuse victims, any concerns that I had moved too far away from the "real" business of social work would be quelled.

Recruiting the Canadian Participants

The much larger second group of Canadian women were more loosely recruited. They just had to be interested in the topic of love, over 18 years of age, not in the midst of a personal crisis, and willing to talk with me about their love lives. I did this because I wanted to extend the discussions to women who had experienced relatively uneventful childhoods so as to ascertain whether there was any clear difference between women who had been abused as children and those who had not. I also wanted to talk with more lesbians, bisexual women, and women who were not keen to form monogamous relationships. As I realized how much energy was being generated through the research, I extended the sample because I saw how I could help to move these discussions into the community. Repeatedly women told me of the conversations they had with friends, family members, workmates, and even people on the bus with whom they had struck up conversations before and after they were interviewed. Over and again women urged me to interview their mother, sister, friend, or colleague. Some even wondered if I might talk with their husbands.

Recruiting participants was much easier after the *Winnipeg Free Press* ran a story about an Australian woman wanting to talk to Canadian women about love (February 2004). The local television channel CKY then picked it up and led with a story about "Dr. Love." After this I was inundated with offers far and wide, with one woman emailing me from China asking whether she could do a phone interview. Sticking to my decision to do face-to-face interviews, I ended up interviewing 74 women, mostly in Winnipeg but also in Ottawa and Toronto. I stopped in September 2004 after I had been able to speak with women who were not just White, straight, and articulate. I also stopped before my interviewing energy ran out and the excitement for the project subsided.

Using a Conversational Interviewing Style

The interviews spanned an average of two hours per person. While most of the women identified as heterosexual, about a dozen identified as lesbian or bisexual. Ranging in age between 18 and 80, most of the women are of European descent, but of this group, quite a few are French, Ukrainian, Jewish, or Mennonite. A few others are Native Canadian, Métis, or from the Philippines.

As I have already suggested, my interviewing style was relatively informal and open-ended. I wore jeans, which happens to be my usual attire, and tried to present myself as chatty, down to earth, and willing to talk about my own life in ways that conveyed my own sense of uncertainty. I made it clear to each participant that while people sometimes fear that they will not make sense or sound very intelligent (especially on the audio-tape), it was my job to make sense of what they were saying, not theirs.

Because I did not want to sanitize the research or create a clinical atmosphere, I used many other forms of affirmation to maximize the possibility that participants would feel at ease and derive some benefit from their participation (also see Hones 1998). While some of the women were initially reserved and perhaps a little guarded, I worked to put them at ease, keep them engaged, and make sure that I understood what they were saying (also see Coates 1996). I can honestly say that all the women in Australia and Canada amazed me by their candour and generosity. Although I was not able to pay anyone for their time, I tried to make them comfortable, often providing food or a drink. Moreover,

I wanted to compensate the women for giving up their time and energy by making the research process one that they would find worthwhile. As I said to each woman in the preamble to them signing the consent form, I hoped they would leave the interview feeling as if they had gotten something out of it—a new insight or a sense that they knew a lot about love, perhaps more than they had initially thought. Judging by the tone of the responses made by many of the women at the end of the interview and the emails I received afterwards, this aim was achieved.

Conducting Narrative Analysis

During the interviews and then after I had conducted them, I listened to the women's stories. Sometimes I played the tapes while I was painting, letting the conversations wash over me in ways that were not simply rational and intellectual. Listening for what was said and not said, I paid attention to the content of their stories and also the emotions conveyed with their narrations (also see Borland 1991; Olson & Shopes 1991). I used a journal to note key points, including any points of confusion or disagreement between the participant and me. I considered how each interview started, unfolded, and ended because I knew that such an exercise can provide clues about the genres of stories narrated (also see Cohler 1994; Plummer 2001).

After the interviews were transcribed, I worked on piecing together meanings that I intended to use in the writing-up phase (also see Riessman 1993). Part of this involved me noting the type(s) and direction(s) of the stories, as well as any contradictions. Disaggregating long chunks of talk into specific stories, or segments of narratives, I scanned for plots, characterization, motives, and themes (also see Chanfrault-Duchet 1991). Sometimes it was relatively easy to see where a story began because narrators used literal conventions such as, "It all started with...." At other times, the first line was not evident until the whole story had been told.

Accepting that there may be disputes about the exact point of where the story began or ended, I also examined any commentaries or explanations that were given. Appreciating that judgments made about stories are bounded by cultural conventions of speaking (also see Coates 2003; Riessman 1993), I bracketed my own comments so that readers are able to see my interjections. I also named some of the stories I was planning on using in the final analysis so that I could more easily recall some of their features. For example, I called Christina's story "Paying the Debt":

> And I realized years ago that I always had this feeling because I'd received so much charity in my life that I had to give back to society. Because that's what you were brought up with the notion that you'd received so much, that it's time for you to give it back.

Connecting the Personal with the Political

To avoid fixating on one element of a story, I scanned for different domains of experience (also see McCabe & Bliss 2003). Guided by my theoretical framework, I looked for any intrapsychic, interpersonal, and cultural scripts in operation (see Gagnon & Simon 1974; Simon 1996). This helped me to make explicit how the personal is political. Interested in the socio-political role of storytelling, I noticed references to popular discourses (also see Brown 1990; Cranny-Francis 1994; Riessman 1993). For example, I took note when participants spoke of falling in love (see Ellwood 1996; Westlund 1999) or coming out (see Plummer 1995). I also noted how particular tales were told because as Riessman (1993, p. 70) explains, "how someone tells her tale—shapes how we can legitimately interpret it."

I tried to keep my eye on how humour, metaphors, language choice, and narrative style were used, bearing in mind that they are usually mediated by time, place, gender, culture, class, and a host of other variables that researchers may not share with their informants (also see Olson & Shopes 1991). Sometimes I noticed this only after I had undertaken multiple readings. I also examined the transcripts for commonalities and differences between and among participants. For instance, I noticed that many of the women survivors of abuse used a form of mocking laughter to convey their disgust toward those who had abused them, yet when it came to questions of shame, blame, and ongoing impact, there were notable differences (see Fraser 2002).

I acknowledge that since narrators were not given a chance to comment on the conclusions I have drawn from their stories, they may not approve of the political implications that I have drawn (also see Borland 1991). Rather than hoping to produce "the right" knowledge or "the truth," I know that there are multiple possibilities for representing stories. I therefore proceed with my analyses of the women's stories knowing that "A narrative is never concluded, it is always subject to reconstruction and reinterpretation" (Hyden 1994, p. 109).

Summary

In the academy and elsewhere, post-positivist research has become increasingly legitimized (Leonard 1997; Reinharz 1992). With the greater acceptance of postmodern research methods, personal storytelling is now seen as a valid means of knowledge production (Cotterill & Letherby 1993; Johnson 1999; Riessman 1990, 1993; Skeggs 2002).

Narrative methods have the capacity to recognize people's strengths and engage people in active, meaning-making dialogues. Narrative methods that are informed by feminist ideas can help social workers move beyond a strict problem focus to explore the wider spheres of social phenomena as they relate to women and men. Carefully used, they may be effective methods in cross-cultural work (McCabe & Bliss 2003) and community work (Brunt 2001). Emphasizing curiosity and reflexivity (Myerhoff & Ruby 1992; Skeggs 2002), narrative feminist methods may aid those who seek to democratize professional relationships. By more obviously opening up points of contest and difference, they are, therefore, potentially compatible with social work values, especially those pertaining to social justice and self-determination (Leonard 1997; Milner 2001).

> Christina: *We all have different concepts of what love is, especially when you're growing up without that kind of love. You have different ideas of what it is supposed to be....*

7
LOVE AND ABUSE IN CHILDHOOD
It's Not All Sugar and Spice

"LOVE" IS A CODE WORD THAT PEOPLE USE to describe a wide range of experiences, including some that hurt. In earlier chapters I explored this proposition as I examined some of the prominent and official stories told about love and abuse. In the last chapter I explored the idea of narrative and considered the ways in which I have used a narrative feminist perspective to analyze the women's stories of love and abuse. This chapter then turns the spotlight onto ordinary women's stories.

I begin by considering how one's family background, and early experiences of love and/or abuse, can linger over time. Through the stories women have told me, I examine the relationships they have with mothers, fathers, and siblings. Because I am interested in learning more about the connections between love and abuse, I hone in on the stories that women told me about relationships where love and abuse are evident. I pay particular attention to the narratives that adult victims/survivors of child abuse told me, especially those who spent time away from their birth families, who were in kinship or substitute care, and/or group homes and other institutions. Toward the end the discussion turns to how the hopes for love might be kept alive in even the most hostile of contexts.

Love, Abuse, and Family Background

Few people would dispute that birth families influence an individual's experience of childhood. Birth families have much currency in a person's life not just because they provide the first context for love but also because families are conduits (or channels) for meanings ascribed to race, ethnicity, class, and gender. Birth families influence individuals' access to resources and participation in community life. They convey expectations and assumptions about the wider world. They are the first site of identity, even for those removed from mothers at birth. Birth families—and the stories that are told about birth families—set the stage for any number of psychodramas in later life.

In contemporary Western societies birth families cannot help but influence individuals' early constructions of love because they are assumed to provide individuals with their first love experience. As I have suggested in chapters 1 to 3, mainstream discourses about family life often take for granted love's existence. In these discourses, questions are raised not about whether love will eventuate but how it is best expressed. Although the conventions for familial love change over time and are modified by social contexts, they are often used to classify whether a family is normal, healthy, and functioning. For families who are classified as dysfunctional, deviant, and unhealthy, the implications can be profound (Doyle 1990; Mullaly 2007; Ryan 1976).

Family Background, Social Status, and Abuse

Although different discourses or stories about the family provide a range of explanations about how family life can affect an individual, none dismiss out of hand the significance of the birth family. Take for instance, Stephanie, a 23-year-old middle-class Canadian, who echoed the customary idea that loving families produce children who are more likely to "know how to love":

> I've experienced love in my family. My family was very loving. We didn't have a lot of money, but I never felt like I grew up badly. Like, I always felt cared for. So, I've never been without love, which I think would put my [current] relationship into a totally different kind of zone.

"What kind of zone?" I asked. From other stories she told me, I gathered that had she not experienced such love, she would have been more inclined to look for love in all the wrong places. Quite simply, it would have made Stephanie more vulnerable to young men's false promises, and more likely to settle for a relationship that would not be conducive to her feeling respected or happy:

> My parents were loving and I saw what a loving relationship was and is. I've seen many of them. My grandparents on both sides—they are very loving couples. And they respected each other. I think respect is

really important—and trust. And, uh, because of that, I wasn't going to settle....

Similar to many other women with whom I spoke, Stephanie hated the idea of settling for substandard love. She also knew that family background and social status are so important because we rely on them so heavily, at least when we are young. If we cannot rely on them, we risk being exposed to outside scrutiny, and all the attendant difficulties that can stem from being viewed as a child who has been abused or neglected. It is not radical to suggest that the most intense scrutiny is usually felt by families identified as working class or, more vulnerable still, underclass. Nor is it radical to suggest that resource-poor families are more likely to struggle with issues such as insecure housing, inadequate income, inferior educational opportunities, and fewer labour market opportunities, which, in turn, can directly impede their ability to create safe and happy home environments (see Mullaly 2007).

In short, this means that our families will yield some influence over how we are likely to evolve (also see Jenkins 1990). The question is, how much? Many of the women I interviewed wondered this with me. Many women made explicit comments about how their family backgrounds had marked their social status in ways that were not always advantageous to them. For those who were removed from their birth families and placed in some kind of state care arrangement, the impact on social status was most profound. This was especially true for the women who spent significant periods of time in orphanages or other state institutions (including group homes).

Abuse: "What Does It Say about Me?'

Although not *all* children who enter state/substitute/alternative care do so because of abuse, most do. For many, abuse creates effects that can take a long time to manage. When perpetrated by a trusted family member in the family home, abuse can be especially hard. This is not just because the discovery of abuse often requires victims (not perpetrators) to leave their homes. It can also be hard to handle because families are still popularly assumed to be happy, safe, and loving. In these idealized places, parents are scripted to love, cherish, and protect them, no matter what material, social, or psychological obstacles stand in their way. Children, on the other hand, are scripted to display their "innocence" while they "love, honour, and obey" their parents. For children whose childhoods are anything but "innocent," unquestioning obedience may still be expected.

It can be a slow and difficult process admitting to oneself, let alone others, that a "loved one" has abused you. Most victims/survivors know that abuse disclosures may cast shame and dishonour across the whole family. Negative judgments made about one's family can reflect badly on a child and may corrode his or her feelings of self-worth (Friday 1996; Kaplan 1995). Denial and repression of abuse may ensue. As Doyle (1990, p. 3) explained, "Children bathe in their parents' reflected glory so they [often] have a vested interest in interpreting their parents' cruel behaviour as a display of strength." And in a society that celebrates "winners" and castigates "losers," the shame associated with coming from an abusive or dysfunctional family, added to the stigma of being a ward of the state, may be very difficult to manage (see Doyle 1990).

Children who do not experience parental love and care, or who experience it as abusive, usually know that their lives deviate from the idealized images of family life. Often, they have to negotiate some difficult questions such as: Why was I abused? Why me? Why have I been removed from the family home? What does this say about my family and me?

As many survivors of abuse and substitute care are aware, just identifying as someone who had a trouble background can be hazardous, let alone disclosing details of abuse (Fraser 1998, 1999, 2000; Herman 1992; Hudson 1984; Kaplan 1995). Apart from exposing them to the curiosity of others, such disclosures may spark debates about culpability and may restimulate feelings of shame, guilt, sadness, and anger (Saraga 1993). Through this exchange, many survivors are also aware that abuse may be used to stigmatize victims as well as perpetrators. Frequently survivors ask, "What did I do to deserve it?" In response, those who bear no such scars may respond with embarrassment and/or pity, which can then entrench feelings of low self-esteem and social status in victims/survivors.

Abuse disclosures can also be difficult because assumptions are often made about the victims'/survivors' future prospects for love. Mainstream psychoanalysts and many developmental psychologists often regard adult love styles as correlated with or even determined by childhood trauma. A straight line is often drawn between difficulties experienced in childhood to those experienced in adolescence and adulthood. Often, abused young people are professionally classified as "anxiously" or "avoidantly attached" (Chisholm 1995). For different reasons, some feminists have unintentionally consolidated the idea that early experiences of abuse do not augur well for future love relationships (see Burke Draucker 1999; Dworkin 1997). Stories told about abuse scarring and damaging victims are common and have some utility. They are useful in so far as they underline the seriousness of abuse while promoting victims' rights. However, their Achilles heel is their tendency to permanently affix victims to abuse, and by extension, to their perpetrators. The challenge is to point to the possibility of harm without suffocating future hopes for change.

Although I appreciate that such accounts are often well meaning and sometimes strategic, I am not inclined to draw a straight line between difficulties in childhood with those that are experienced in later life. Instead, I take my lead from many people I have counselled or interviewed who reiterate that the impact of abuse is more complex and convoluted than the aforementioned discourses imply. Working from the assumption that abuse is something that survivors usually wrestle with rather than passively endure, I am open to the possibility that women or men will not necessarily hate the loved ones who have abused them.

Yet, at the same time, I acknowledge that personal experiences of deprivation, abuse, and displacement from birth families *may* affect the kind of love stories pursued in later life (also see Benjamin 1988; Kaplan 1979, 1995).

"Mommy Dearest": Maternal Love and Abuse

Audrey was a good example of someone who believed that her childhood experiences constricted her ability to love. Born in England to White, working-class parents, she endured multiple placements in a range of settings (foster care, children's homes, and youth shelters). When she was about 10 she migrated to Australia, was disowned by her parents, and ended up living in a youth detention centre despite committing no crime. Audrey's overall narrative serves as a sobering reminder of how low status, abuse, and deprivation can affect an individual. As she spoke about the concept of love, one of the most pressing issues she raised was her relationship with her mother. In a story she told not long after the interview began, I recognized the appearance of two very popular discourses about love and motherhood. They included the story of mothers bonding with their children, and the story about mothers being "good":

> *Audrey:* Um, I just found this out recently. When I was born, I never got to bond with my mother. I got dragged off because she was crazy.
> *Heather:* She had a psychiatric—
> *Audrey (interrupting):* Twelve hours after I was born, she went to hospital and I didn't really know her. And err, she—both my parents—I would class as "Double D's."
> *Heather:* Double D's?
> *Audrey:* Dumb as dog shit. [laughs cynically]

Audrey's story underlined her mother's failure to bond with her at birth. Audrey knew from her nursing studies, and her general life, that mothers were meant to form deep attachments with their child(ren) (see Benjamin 1988; Kaplan 1995). With it ingrained in popular thinking, Audrey also knew that mothers were supposed to fall in love with their babies and know instinctively how to care for them. By suggesting that her mother was "crazy" and that she was "dragged off" of her, she was, therefore, able to establish the possibility that her mother did not voluntarily reject her.

Viewing the situation through her own eyes, not her mother's, Audrey subverted the professional jargon I tried to use to restate the fact of her removal and denounce her parents as "dumb as dog shit." Having established that it was not her fault for the failed maternal bond, she was also able to undermine the possibility that she was a "chip off the old block." Representing herself as *not* like her mother was especially important given the harrowing stories she would go on to tell about her mother abusing her. Take, for instance, the story "Locked in the Bedroom":

Audrey: She was not a very good mother. She used to leave us in a room for days on end and I used to pick the lock to get sugar and bread. I've got clear memories of being three years old and walking into the kitchen. If we got caught leaving the bedroom—
Heather (interrupting): She would *lock* you in the room?
Audrey: Yeah. I've got clear memories of shit on the wall because my brother would start. He'd get bored so he'd play with his own feces and paint pictures. No one in the neighbourhood could go into the house because they couldn't stand the smell. We used to eat sugar and bread. I'd tip a whole lot of sugar on the bread and run in and give it to my brother and sister because I was the only one quick enough to do it. We were taken away and given to three families.

With the extent of the deprivation quickly established, Audrey's use of the words "I've got clear memories" pre-empted the possibility of her not being believed. Imprisoned in a room, her role was to pick the lock so that she could steal food for their survival. In the meantime, her younger brother amused himself by painting the walls with his excrement. These images are extremely evocative, especially when it is revealed that there was little chance of them being rescued. No one visited. Indeed, no one approached the house because of the smell. Without us knowing what her sister was doing, the story suddenly ended. With no indication of who intervened and how it occurred, the children are separated from each other and "given" to three different families, almost as if they were puppies.

Roughly the same age but from the other side of the world, Jesobel (an Aboriginal-Canadian woman in her mid-forties) could relate to Audrey's experience of maternal deprivation, and to the way she eventually gave up hoping for her mother's love. Yet, for Jesobel, the detachment occurred much later in life and generated more subtle results for her and her sister:

I think after watching her [her mother] disrespect our childhoods, disrespecting us as adults, we became very detached from her. I remember a really fleeting moment—it was from my grandmother—I said to my sister, "I may love her, but I don't like her." And she said, "I feel the same way." And it was just the sense of liberation because I had said something that I had thought for years. And I know it affected my relationships. Even today, Jeff [current partner] said something that I found a little surprising. I went to go see the film *The Passion of the Christ*, and I cried buckets.... The next day he was telling people [about it].... He said that I was normally very detached and very cold emotionally. And that just surprised me. I asked him about it, and he said, "Oh yeah, but I can see past all of that."

The effects of abuse on Jesobel and Audrey were not that unusual. The devastating—but not necessarily permanent—repercussions of maternal ill health, incompetence, and cruelty can be seen from many of the women who were abused by their mothers.

The Primacy of the Mother and the Erasure of the Father

While there have been recent cultural changes that have seen fathers take a more serious role as primary caretakers, maternal love, for the most part, continues to be the first line of defence for children. When mothers are unable or unwilling to enact scripts of maternal love, the implications for children can be profound. When they are abusive, children's lives may be jeopardized (see Fraser 2000).

I reiterate these points not because they are novel but because they were threaded through many women's stories. For instance, Cecilia, Karen, and Linda explained that after their mother had a stroke and was permanently hospitalized, they were sent to an orphanage. This happened even though their father was said to have been a loving and caring man. Indeed, that was the problem: He was a man, and men are—or at least were—not meant to be the primary caregivers of children, especially daughters.

Christina and her four brothers were sent to an orphanage when their single mother did not have enough resources to care for them. Again, no mention was made of the possibility of their father stepping in. The same can be said about Samantha's father. After her mother failed to return from a holiday abroad, there was no attempt to ascertain whether he might be able to look after her. Instead, she was placed in the care of neighbours who, in subsequent years, became her foster parents. Granted, part of the problem related to the lack of contact she had with her dad. As Samantha said,

> My mum and dad were divorced when I was a baby. I hardly ever saw my dad. I think I saw my dad maybe three or four times in my life up until I found him myself.

From other stories she told about her father, I knew that Samantha managed to track him down when she was 15 years old. This means that on average, she saw him once every three to four years.

In contrast to Samantha, Dallas, Emily, and Vera had more extensive contact with their fathers. Even so, this contact was eclipsed by the expectations they had about their mothers. For instance, when I interviewed Vera, I asked her to comment on the relationship she had with her parents when she returned to their care at the age of six. It is interesting that she interpreted my question as one that related only to her mother:

Heather: When you think of being away from your mother and father for that period of time, do you think that affected your relationship when you returned to them?
Vera: I think so. I don't think Mum had that bonding with me. I think, had she had me around her all the time.... She had a hard time having me. She had to go to hospital for … nearly six months before I was born.... So, she'd had a hard time having me and I don't think it was probably easy for her to … be … away from me.... I'm not saying it was easy for her. Her first marriage had failed and she wanted her second one to succeed, so I can understand that now as an adult why … it happened.

Relying heavily on the concept of the maternal bond, Vera tried to explain why she was not able to live with her parents in her early years, mostly from her mother's perspective, yet she faltered as she tried to prevent her mother from being seen as irresponsible or callous. Her line of defence assumed that her mother would have jeopardized her second marriage if Vera had lived with them in the early years. This is interesting because it subverts the possibility that a difficult pregnancy might be a precursor to a stronger mother-child bond. It also suggests that marital relationships may be undermined—not enhanced—by children. And it erases the possibility of her father taking primary responsibility for her care.

Parental expectations were thematically expressed in many other participants' stories. With Audrey, Dallas narrated stories that portrayed her mother as dangerous:

> When Mum was in one of her rampages, Dad would say, "Quick, girls, get behind me!" And he would take the knives, or the pots of hot stew, or the pots of hot soup, or the bottle, or whatever else she could lay her hands on to throw.... But if she decided to lay into us, there was nothing Dad could do about it. The police were there so many times, wanting to lock her up and charge her. But Dad would say, "No!" because that meant that we would have been taken off him. Back then a *man* didn't get to keep the kids because he had to work. There wasn't social security and all of that then.

Through the expression "one of her rampages," Dallas signalled that her mother was frequently enraged by her and her sister, and how her father tried but failed to protect them. Awkwardly she admitted that there were times when there was "nothing that he could do" to prevent their mother from "lay[ing] into" them. Then, in defence of him, she pointed to the conundrum her father faced: Allow the abuse to continue or betray his wife by instituting police charges against her and risk losing custody of his children.

Dallas's defence of her father was striking given she told me a story about being so desperate to escape her family's home that she spent long periods living with the family of a school friend:

> *Dallas:* They had a family that you only ever see on "My Three Sons" type of thing. That made me hate my family even more. I hated going home because I never knew what I was going home to. Um, so then, that became acceptable to me because there was there wasn't any physical hurt there. *Never* any physical hurt.
> *Heather:* So the price to pay for being part of that apparently happy family was to be involved as…?
> *Dallas:* As a prostitute. A prostitute. A prostitute—pornography stuff.
> *Heather:* And that was better than going home?
> *Dallas:* Yep, yep, far better than going home.

Through 12-year-old Dallas's eyes, her school friend's family seemed to be leading the perfect life. It was such a contrast to her own home life that she started to hate her family even more. It may be because "hate" is a word ordinarily forbidden to be used against family members that she softened her discussion by explaining why she "hated going home," yet the story of the "perfect" family is torn apart when Dallas revealed being sexually exploited. From previous stories I knew that her friend's father groomed her and other children to pose for pornographic photographs. I also knew that the violence her mother perpetrated was so frequent and extreme that she was willing to "pay the price," as I worded it, for the place she occupied in her friend's family. Reiterating the word "prostitution" three times, she suggested that no matter what I might have been thinking, she still believed it was preferable to returning home.

Counterintuitive Patterns

From the first study I conducted with women who had been abused and spent time away from their birth families, I could include many other stories about maternal abuse. I have to admit that I was unprepared for the number and intensity of stories about maternal neglect and cruelty. I would have assumed that at least one or two mothers might be described at some point as triumphing over hardship and rescuing their children from future perils. This did not occur. Instead, some of the most poignant love stories told about childhood relate to their fathers. These stories caught my attention because I would have assumed that many more of the women's fathers would be described as absent, emotionally unavailable, and/or abusive.

Having spent so many years working as a social worker in a range of women's services, I was unsettled by the interview material and aware of my feminist inclination to justify—perhaps defensively—why many of the women's mothers are not described as loving. For it can be said that motherhood is so idealized in

Western society that most women would be hard pressed to achieve the status of the "good mother." Without easy access to fertility control and with so much responsibility allocated to mothers, it is not surprising that some women fail to meet these idealized expectations (Maushart 2001; Oakley 1981). In contrast, far fewer demands are usually made of fathers, at least in Anglo-American societies. In these cultures, it is easier for a man to perform the script of the "good father" than it is for a woman to perform the script of the "good mother." Finally, let us not forget that men are the main perpetrators of familial abuse, but that even when they do so, they are more likely to be forgiven (Greer 1999).

That said, I know that cultural explanations cannot account for abuse entirely. As a narrative feminist researcher, I am committed to understanding social phenomena across the domains of experience (intrapersonal, interpersonal, cultural, and structural), not just fixating on one domain. I also know that my purpose is not to defend women per se, nor deny that they are capable of committing abuse. I also have no interest in devaluing the positive influences that fathers may have on their daughters' lives. Instead, I have seen my task as exploring some of the complexities of women's experiences, including those that are out of step with wider social patterns.

Father-Daughter Relationships: Daddy as the "First Prince"?

Many of the women I interviewed in Australia and Canada spoke highly of their fathers. I was particularly interested in the references women made to the ways in which father-daughter relationships influenced their early constructions of love. I noticed the script for "being Daddy's princess" (Ussher 1997) even though I have never experienced it.

I thought it was worth exploring the idea of "being Daddy's princess" because it is one of the archetypal types of father-daughter relationships that often gets occluded when discussions of child abuse ensue. It is important that this type of relationship does not get blocked from view because many heterosexual women use it or part of it as a template for their future adult love relationships. Take, for instance, Ada, a Native Canadian, who is now in her mid-forties and who told me that "I had always been my dad's little girl, even before that when my parents were still together."

From other stories I knew that Ada's mother struggled with alcohol addiction and left the care of her children mostly to their father. Ada was especially appreciative of the little gifts he would bring home for her after being away as a travelling salesman.

With respect to the notion of the little princess, Ada's portrayal of her father did not, however, go as far as Vera's:

> *Vera:* My father never ever chastised me or, um, he always defended me in every way. With everything that went wrong in my life, he'd have an answer for it. He'd always have an excuse for why it happened.

Heather: So you felt he was a protector?
Vera: Definitely! My champion!

Vera remembered her father as someone who jumped to her defence when she was in trouble. Although I was interested to know whether he defended her mostly in front of her mother, I hesitated because I knew that she was uncomfortable with questions that inferred any shortcomings of her mother. Instead of asking this question, I opted for the safer question about whether she could relate to the concept of the father as protector. Categorically, she agreed, declaring him to be her "champion."

Since the word "champion" reminded me of the word "hero," I initiated the next story when I asked the following:

Heather: Were you his "princess"?
Vera: I would say so. I would say so.
Heather: Did he ever say so?
Vera: He, he, never—he didn't. He tried not to treat me as a favourite, I think, but I don't think he could help it. He didn't say anything to make the rest of the family feel bad, but he definitely used to treat me as his favourite, I think, because we did a lot of things together. We used to make pickled onions together and we used to go to the pictures together because he liked that. And he used to take me to the pictures on his own and buy me a box of chocolates.

Vera stumbled to respond to me because, without initially realizing it, I had again put her in a bind. While on the one hand she liked the idea that she was his "princess," on the other, she feared this would show him as a father who "played favourites." To get around this, she explained why he "couldn't help" making her his princess. She did this mostly by attributing it to the amount of time they spent together and the common interests they developed. However, as she provided examples of the activities they used to do together, I was struck by the way she ended the sentence with the phrase "because he liked that." I was struck because it inverts the script of parents sacrificing their own interests to amuse their children, and because it may be seen as a precursor to her later life when she sublimated her own interests for those of her husband's (also see de Beauvoir 1963).

Even though it might appear to be a tenuous connection for me to have made, I wondered whether Vera's father helped her to rehearse some of the conventions of heterosexual love relationships. In the last line of her story, my suspicions were confirmed. It is the line when Vera recalled with pride and affection how her father took her to the movies "on his own" and bought her a box of chocolates. Arguably, these three images: going to the movies, being unchaperoned, and buying the (little) "lady" a box of chocolates are traditional symbols of a date. And while such actions may be read as an innocent way for loving fathers to behave toward their "darling" daughters, the romantic (and thus sexual) undertones means that the script operates on the edge of danger. As adults who are charged with the care of minors, it is fathers who must ensure that these relationships are not sexually exploitative.

The Story of the Good Father

In mainstream accounts (but not those psychoanalytically inclined), "good" fathers are those who find the idea of developing sexual relations with the daughters unimaginable and/or repugnant (Hall & Kondora 1997). However, with the rise of the second wave of feminism, concerns raised about the eroticization of father-daughter relationships have made their way into the mainstream. For instance, in popular culture, it is no longer considered acceptable to expect a daughter to fulfill the role of a deceased or absent mother. Yet, in many family homes, it is still acceptable for fathers to refer to their daughters as "princesses," "fairies," or "angels." I was interested in knowing whether the women I interviewed saw this as a problem. I was intrigued to learn that most of the women I asked did not. Indeed, they were more likely to remember feeling reassured and loved by their fathers, *as long as this was not the only form of affirmation their fathers gave to them.*

Cecilia was a case in point. She was referring to her father when she said the following:

> He called me "fairy" when I was little; his fairy. [pause] Before I went into the orphanage, my self-esteem was pretty, pretty good. And I would say that 90 percent of that was due to the fact of my father being, being such a: "You're a good little girl. You're a lovely little girl. You're a good student. You're a good scholar."

Even as an adult, Cecilia derived pleasure from remembering herself as "his fairy," and hearing him refer to her as "good" and "lovely," yet after the interview, as I looked much closer at her words, I have to admit that I remained suspicious. From my vantage point, pet names such as "fairy" are so gender specific that they cannot be presumed to be innocent. I say this because the term "fairy" may be a derivative of "fairy princess," which can sugar-coat patriarchal power relations (or the rule of the father), and reify (or fix) rigid class hierarchies. I also know that since few mothers are likely to use this reference with their daughters and even fewer with their sons that traditionally feminine traits were being affirmed—namely, those associated with being small, lightweight, naive, and pleasing. To some extent, there is evidence of this when Cecilia used the words "good," "little," and "girl" in quick succession. However, what I also noticed was how other terms were woven into the story, words that validated behaviours not traditionally associated with femininity. They are the affirmations she was given for being "a good student" and "scholar," affirmations that she has still held onto as an adult in her late forties.

For many of the women in this study, the love and support they received from their fathers has reverberated into their adult lives, including periods when they were not in regular contact (also see de Beauvoir 1963; Jenkins 1990). Interestingly, such support does not require a blood relationship. Take, for instance, Jesobel, the Aboriginal-Canadian woman I mentioned earlier. Now in her mid-forties and working as a journalist in Toronto, she still remembered with great fondness the care her stepfather provided to her and her sisters:

> *Jesobel:* My younger sisters have the same dad, but I don't. Our stepfather raised us. My biological father, he had—and this is an estimate—we believe he had nine children with different women.... My dad or my stepdad—well, I called him Dad since he raised me—he was a gentle, sweet man, but throughout the years, through the abuse that my mother handed down to him, it made him very distant and very angry.... He changed when I think I was about six. I noticed he changed. He wasn't Daddy anymore. He was different. Of course I'm too young to put a finger on it then, but then I think I know what it was because it just escalated as the years went by.
> *Heather:* The physical abuse?
> *Jesobel:* Yeah, physical abuse. And verbal abuse because she was very nasty. He committed suicide when I was 24. It's so strange because he shot himself just two days after my sister's birthday....

It is significant that Jesobel recalls her stepfather's love when he provided her with a diminishing level of care after she turned six. It is also striking that to this day, she attributed her stepfather's suicide not to any personal inadequacy but to the legacy of her mother's brutality.

Kate was another woman whose sense of self has been positively shaped by the relationship she had with her father. Even though he died some years ago, his love and encouragement has lived on now that she is a woman in her mid-thirties and as a sole mother to her young daughter. In her view, one of the reasons why her father's love meant so much to her was because he was her primary caregiver between the ages of 11 and 14, the period when her parents separated and her sisters lived with their mother. Out of step with the majority of children who automatically accompany their mothers, she and her father lived together and became very close.

In many respects, Kate's Anglo-Australian family was unorthodox, especially during the years that she was raised. They did not work hard to approximate gender stereotypes. Politics was a subject actively discussed among all family members and very liberal attitudes were held in relation to sex. These attitudes meant that Kate and her half-sisters were permitted an unusual degree of freedom to explore their sexuality from a relatively young age.

Many of the stories Kate told me about her father were thematic of exploration. For the most part, she was encouraged to explore life, love, and her sexuality in ways that were not circumscribed by gender conventions:

> *Heather:* So, could you tell me a little bit about the relationship that you had with your dad?
> *Kate:* That's him up there. [points to a photograph of him on the wall] He was dying with cancer when that was taken. He was only 61, but his hair went white when he was 25. He was an incredibly gentle, quiet man. He was a philosopher. He read and wrote over six or seven languages. He taught me to read when I was three. He taught me ancient Greek from six to 10 but from 10 I put a stop to that when I discovered that not everyone else had to come home to do ancient Greek homework. [both laugh] He told me I can do anything with my life and he praised me a lot for academic stuff because that was very important to him.

Similar to Cecilia's father, Kate's father esteemed her efforts to learn, yet two differences were obvious: the first related to social class and the second to conventional notions of gender. On the first point, Kate's father had both the time and the skills to teach his daughter how to read well before she was old enough to attend school. Unlike Cecilia's father, who had limited access to and experience with formal education, Kate's father was familiar with the classics. At school, this gave Kate a distinct advantage and both of us knew it. We both laughed in the acknowledgement of the privileges associated with having a father who was able to offer this tuition, but also because he was a man who could accept his daughter's right to resist it.

It was significant that Kate used the more active word "can" (rather than "could") to represent her father's encouragement. This suggests that she has felt buoyed by his faith that she "can do anything" and motivated to pursue her adult goals, even after his death. However, it was also noticeable that Kate's father praised her for activities that were *important to him*. Shortly after talking about this, Kate mentioned other limitations of his care.

In the story called "You're the Dad, You Decide," Kate's father's parenting style started to have some less desirable repercussions:

> *Kate:* He was a pretty incompetent parent in a way. I mean, things like when I fell off—I remember falling ... off a rope ladder from a tree—and he came rushing out and said, "Darling, what do you want me to do?" And I was lying there and I remember thinking, "You're the dad, you decide."

> *Heather:* Mmm … [laughing]
> *Kate:* I was sick and stunned and I'd just fallen out of a tree. He said, "Do you want me to go down the road and get Paul?" who was a doctor. And I just lay there thinking, "I don't want to make this decision."
> *Heather:* Mmm … [solemnly]
> *Kate:* And I sort of stayed with him when my parents split up because, um, I felt responsible for him.
> *Heather:* For your dad?
> *Kate:* Yeah. Actually, he did a lot of stuff that he shouldn't have, like he told me about the mortgage and stuff like that, so I'd go to school thinking, "God, the overdraft!" And we had a minor car accident and I thought, "Shit, how are we going to manage this?" He put a lot of adult responsibilities onto me, which I don't think was very fair. *But I loved him to bits. He was an amazing man.*

Because Kate had already constructed her father as a kind and loving man, she was able to criticize him for being "a pretty incompetent parent" without fearing that I would see only his flaws. She then illustrated his incompetence with three incidents: (1) the day that she fell out of the tree and he didn't know what to do; (2) his overburdening her with details of their financial stress; and (3) the management of the car accident. Having established this, she was able to identify how responsible she felt for him, even as a child, yet this was tempered with the depth of the love she felt for him and the respect she had for him being such "an amazing man."

Another woman to view her father as "an amazing man" was Marcie, a 64-year-old Canadian woman. Like Kate, her connection with her dad was very strong, developed primarily through the activities they did rather than the words that were exchanged:

> I'll tell you something. My dad and I had a connection as a child, which bothered my mother big time. They say little girls and their dads get along great, but my dad employed the idea that I was his little boy because we changed the oil in the car and he showed me how to change a tire. We would wash the car together on Saturday mornings and that sort of thing. And then when my mother became very ill, we did the housework together in a buddy system, so there was a link there that my dad treated me as an equal, which was really different.

Given Marcie's age and the era in which she was raised, it was unusual that her father treated her as an equal. It was also unusual that he treated her as "his little boy." Yet, for Marcie, this meant a great many opportunities were opened up to her in later life, especially as she went on to express her sexual desire for women during a time when lesbianism was rarely mentioned and very restricted in terms of avenues for sexual exploration.

Father-Daughter Rape

Paradoxically, it was in the Canadian study I conducted—the one where I did not call for women who had been abused during childhood to step forward—that evidence of father-daughter rape emerged most strongly. Dianne was just one of the women who disclosed this to me in the story called "He Raped Her Right Beside Me":

> *Heather:* Can you tell me when the sexual abuse started from?
> *Dianne:* With me personally? Or with my older sister?
> *Heather:* Either.
> *Dianne:* With my older sister, I was eight and I guess he basically raped her while she was laying beside me. We were out camping.
> *Heather:* So you were there when he raped her?
> *Dianne:* Right beside her, yeah. We shared a bedroom our whole life, so up until she left home when she was maybe 16.
> *Heather:* So he raped her not just the once in front of you but quite regularly?
> Dianne: Yeah.
> *Heather: Wow.* He thought he could keep you both quiet?
> *Dianne:* Yeah, with fear, yeah. Just shut us right up, or he'd beat the tar out of us. He never, ever, ever actually said, "Don't you ever say anything or you'll be really sorry." But we knew. *He was a man to be feared.*
> *Heather:* So, you knew. And you were afraid.
> *Dianne:* Well, yeah. There was the time where he was beating her in the driveway. I mean, they were both naked and he had a gun and he broke it over her back as she was trying to run away. So, I mean you see things like that and you know what your father is capable of. *There's no way in hell you're going to say anything, you know.*

Dianne and her sister were forced to endure acts of sexual depravity that many people would find hard to believe. On top of this, they were physically beaten by their father, geographically isolated, and emotionally disconnected from their mother, who Dianne said had little idea of how to get help and had submerged herself in alcohol to ease the pain of her own life. For Dianne, the impact was devastating, particularly in the early years of her life. Yet, somewhere deep within, she knew that her family relationships were not what she called loving:

> I remember being nine years old and watching my mom and dad physically fight in the driveway and thinking, you know, "This is not what love is all about. This is not what married people do." And you

know, at nine what do I know except what I see or what I've experienced? So, how I came to that conclusion at nine or 10, I don't know. I just had this idea and knew that that wasn't it. You don't treat people like that. But I still had to battle the issues and the low self-esteem that came from it.

Battling "low self-esteem" and working doggedly to leave the family home as early as she possibly could, Dianne eventually managed to meet and marry an old school friend with whom she said she had developed an extremely nurturing, respectful, and joyous relationship (see Chapter 9).

Relationships with Siblings: Protection, Camaraderie, and Rivalry

Relationships that parents have with their children can affect the way siblings relate to one another, and vice versa. Dynamics among siblings are usually complex and formative. Sibling relationships have the potential to inspire love and solidarity, yet they may also involve rivalry, torment, and abuse. The potential of sibling rivalry, especially among siblings of the same sex, has been widely discussed (see Benjamin 1988; Freud [1915] 1990). In these accounts, siblings are represented as each other's natural competitors, who rival each other for their parents' attention.

From the Australian and Canadian women, I heard about siblings acting as one another's rivals but also their comrades and protectors. Sometimes these contradictory roles were enacted simultaneously, while at other times, one or two roles may have dominated. Christina related the following in a story called "Growing up in the Orphanage with My Brothers":

> They [her brothers] were a form of protection ... because if anyone laid a hand on me, I think they would have been killed. That's how protective they were. They'd slash all the tires on their cars.

From the stories Christina had already told me, I knew that she and the other girls in the orphanage had to collaborate so as to prevent the "cottage fathers" from sexually abusing them. From this story I learned that the main advantage she had growing up with her brothers in the orphanage was the protection it afforded her. Without specifying the details, she referenced the script of big brothers looking after their "baby sisters."

In contrast to the protection Christina felt from her brothers, Dallas told stories about needing protection from her sister:

> *Dallas:* I had TB when I was four and I was in hospital for 18 months. I remember before I was in hospital that Fiona was extremely nasty to me even then, and that was before the sexual abuse, *before any sexual abuse at all*. Because when I first started to walk, my feet were turned in

and I had to have callipers. And for the first—I don't know how long it was—I had the full hip callipers. And then after a time, they got reduced. When they were reduced, the shoe part went together with a bolt. Well, Fiona delighted in tripping me up. She really delighted in tripping me up, so that was the start of my "clumsiness."

Whether she had this jealousy thing that I had to have some sort of special attention, I don't know. I can only imagine that's what it was. And then when I went to hospital, I had to have 12 months of bed rest and because she knew that the last episode at home—before I went into hospital—I was hemorrhaging, bleeding to death. Well, she thought that by making me bleed, that she'd put me back into hospital, or kill me. I could never work out why—what was behind her nastiness to me—so I was always trying to please her as well as trying to please Mum. I didn't have to work hard at pleasing Dad because I was always told, "Go on, you spoiled little bitch, run to Daddy." "Daddy's little girl." "Daddy's little princess."

Heather: Did you feel like Daddy's little princess?

Dallas: [pause] No. No. I didn't feel special at all. I never grew up feeling that Dad favoured me over Fiona because he didn't.

Making it plain that her relationship with Fiona was rivalrous and antagonistic, Dallas provided details about the treatment she received for tuberculosis. Clearly, it was a painful and distressing time that involved her learning to walk with callipers. As she said this, the image that came to my mind was of a young girl trying desperately to stand on her own two feet despite being tripped up by her sister. Twice using the word "delight," she portrayed Fiona as sadomasochistic, yet her parents were oblivious to this possibility, preferring instead to see Dallas as clumsy.

Wondering whether jealousy was the root cause of Fiona's cruel treatment, Dallas's story of sibling rivalry became more asymmetrical and sinister. Fiona appeared to be willing to do whatever it would take to return her to hospital so that she could have her parents' attention to herself, yet she was not the only person that Dallas found hard to please. Her mother was also lumped into this category. Her father, on the other hand, did not take so much work. However, even this accomplishment was problematic given it antagonized the other women in the house. Without specifying whose words she was repeating, she called upon the "Daddy's princess" script to show how it was used against her. Indicted for being a spoiled and pampered child, she recalled feeling anything but special or favoured.

Love and Abuse in Alternative Care

As Hall and Kondora (1997, p. 37) understood, "trauma experienced in childhood can reverberate with after effects in adulthood that take a significant toll on health and happiness." When trauma is a product of abuse, as it so often is, the legacy may be even more catastrophic (Glass 1993; Goddard 1996; Goddard & Carew 1993; Owen 1996). Many service users and workers know this all too well. If you have been a service user and/or worker in child welfare, or domestic violence, drug and alcohol abuse, or the justice system, you know that abuse in childhood can have a significant legacy (see Currie 1999; Glass 1993). You know it can wreak havoc with mental and emotional health, social and intellectual growth, educational progress, labour market opportunities, and other material circumstances (Doyle 1990; Goddard 1996). And it can do this for years after the abuse has stopped.

Child abuse is often so traumatic because it can involve terror and intimidation (Child Migrants' Trust 2001; Herman 1992; Owen 1996; Scutt 1990; Thorpe & Irwin 1996). Invading many individuals' material and intrapsychic worlds, abuse can leave its mark on and in the body (Currie 1999; Glass 1993; Hall & Kondora 1997). Unlike love a word typically associated with peace, harmony, and growth—abuse has the capacity to obliterate self-esteem and undermine the material conditions for living (Currie 1999; hooks 2000; Steinem 1992).

Kinship Care: The Story of Cinderella

As previously indicated, abuse may be particularly confusing when perpetrated by loved ones and results in removal from the family home. For many children, responsibility for the abuse is internalized and they assume they were removed because they were bad or inferior (Child Migrants' Trust 2001; Doyle 1990). As such, many enter alternative care arrangements wondering what they did to deserve it. Emily told stories that highlight these points. The first is about why she was separated from her parents at the age of three:

> When I was three I had a father who was 21 years older than my mother and he was Scottish. And when I was born he wanted a boy so bad, you know, like a lot of men do. Anyway, they had me. So then, when three years later my mum had my sister and she couldn't cope, my grandmother took me and my grandmother had me until I was 12.

Emily's grandmother died when she was 12 and instead of returning home, she was sent to live at her aunt's house where she was singled out as different and inferior to the other children:

> [crying] My auntie's husband couldn't see that I was decent. I was no good. He always picked at me. If I came inside, I always had to take off my shoes. His kids could run in wherever they wanted and do what they wanted, but I was always picked at. I hated it. I used to do so much for my auntie.

In between times, Emily made the occasional visit home to her birth family.

> *Emily:* Every now and then my father would pick me up. When I got older he used to take me home for the weekend. I used to have to scrub the walls. We had a wood stove like that [points to the stove in her kitchen] and there would be soot everywhere so you had to wash down the walls. They used to scrub the floors in those days and I used to do it all.
> *Heather:* Like a little servant?
> *Emily:* Yeah. They used to—my father used to entertain because he was a businessman and we used to have white starched tablecloths in those days. My mother used to dampen them down and roll them for two days. And when I used to go there, I'd have to iron them. It would take me hours and hours to iron.
> *Heather:* And your sister?
> *Emily:* She was just there. She was like the perfect angel.
> *Heather:* Sounds like the story of the princess and the ugly sister.
> *Emily: Yeah!* My father when he had people come he used to say, "Oh this one's my clever one." And I was just the one to do the garbage.

Non-kinship Care: Being an Unlovable "Charity Case"

Emily was not the only woman to be accorded inferior treatment by caregivers. Some of the women, such as Christina, Cecilia, Karen, Linda, Emily, and Samantha, mentioned how adults often justified treating them badly because they were not living with their birth parents. Excerpts from two stories that Christina told me highlight this point.

In the story called "They Would Never Do It to Their Own Children," Christina talked about the ways the orphanage staff instituted two regimes, one for their "own" children and one for the "orphans":

> *Christina:* And yet, when the public eye wasn't on you, they'd do the worst things that you can think of that they would never do to their own children. Not one day did I see their children go on their hands and knees and scrub and wash and polish and clean, and, you know, things like that. So to me, that really wasn't someone that was loving. Definitely not love.
> *Heather:* So, it was like two systems—

> *Christina (interrupting):* Yeah, a double standard—one for the public and one for us "poor, unworthy things."

Many of the women I interviewed spoke to me about how they fought against the idea that they were unlovable when they were young. Some of the women made a point of telling me how their attempts to become "a somebody" involved rejecting the claim that they were destined to be "a nobody":

> *Christina:* They would tell us to our face, you know, "You are unworthy." "You will follow in the footsteps of your parents." "You are nothing." "All this good money that the public pours into places like this is just a big waste of time."
> *Heather:* They'd say that to your face?
> *Christina:* Yeah, they'd say that. [pause] You'd grow up thinking, "Hey, if I'm going to be like this, what's the point in living?"

I found it gut-wrenching to hear how the cottage parents had no qualms telling the "orphans" that they were "unworthy"; that they were bound to replicate the lives of their parents; and that public resources allocated for their assistance were "a waste of time." Compounding the problem was and, arguably, still is the long-standing expectation that young people express gratitude toward non-familial carers and comply with their rules, regardless of the quality of care and fairness of the rules. These expectations are part of the Anglo-American tradition of distinguishing "the deserving" from "the undeserving" (see Chapter 1).

From a neo-conservative perspective, punitive treatment of "the undeserving" stands as a useful warning to those who might otherwise relinquish their familial responsibilities (Young 1997). One of the ways to reinforce these responsibilities is to make alternative supports inadequate, barren, and frightening. For children designated as orphans or state wards, this has often meant living in extremely impoverished living conditions. That said, advocates of children's rights have managed to persuade Anglo-American societies that children are implicitly deserving of compassion. Feeding the discourse of the "best interests of the child," the stories about childhood innocence, vulnerability, and need for protection have helped to improve the standards of substitute care. However, since many of the women interviewed for this study grew up during the period preceding the ascendancy of child rights, the conditions they experienced were extremely harsh, especially for those raised in orphanages or children's homes.

In the interview I had with Cecilia (who is now in her mid-forties), life in the orphanage was "an Oliver Twist kind of thing":

> Our meal of bread and butter and custard was eaten in total silence. This happened a lot according to whether the sisters stated whether

> talking was allowed or not. And I remember it being really strange. We were told that night that we weren't to speak; to sit and eat and not speak. I cried all night that first night. I had many reasons to feel miserable and hurt. I had all my clothes taken away from me and placed in a big cupboard in the workroom. I was told that it would be given back to me at holiday time. My clothes for now were two cotton day dresses, two Sunday dresses, a cardigan, underwear, and pinafore. I became known as number 90 and this was labelled on everything. So, it was that thing of you are just one of 100 children.

I can only imagine how nine-year-old Cecilia felt as she arrived at the orphanage and proceeded to enter the large dining hall where she was served a meagre meal that she and the other girls had to eat in total silence. I knew that for her it was "really strange" because it was such a contrast to the emotionally expressive atmosphere of the large Irish family that she and her sisters had left behind. So profound were these changes of circumstances that she cried all night long. Stripped of her clothing, made to wear a uniform, and allotted a particular number, she was labelled and objectified. Being just one faceless child of 100, her individual uniqueness was obliterated.

Love and the Panopticon

For Cecilia and the other women in this study who were confined to orphanage life, love had an absent presence. On the one hand it was a luxury that could not be afforded or indulged. Yet, on the other, because it was so obviously missing, it tended to exist as an ever-present longing as Cecilia described:

> This is the whole theme of the orphanage: I felt love and being loved and being cared for and having affection was *just not a part of my life*. It just wasn't there. It was, um, taken away from me like so many other things during those seven years. I just felt things were just taken away from you. There was no redress or balance. Things weren't given back. It's just like you were always in the negative, I suppose.

After I heard this story and many others from women who had grown up in orphanages, I was reminded of Jeremy Bentham's idea of the panopticon (Foucault 1984). I thought of the panopticon because the children were enclosed within a defined space and closely monitored. Expected to comply with their "masters'" commands and internalize the restrictions as normal, they were not to question why their carers rarely showed them affection. Nor were they permitted to question why, when the wardens did touch their charges, it was often brutal. What also became clear to me was that those who exhibited the required behaviours occasionally received rewards. Mostly, they went to those who accepted the institutional roles allocated to them, those who were willing to police themselves and their peers for any transgressions to the regime.

From a Marxist perspective, the stories may be seen to have a similar plot. Pressured to internalize the regulations of the ruling class, subordinated subjects were pitted against one another and encouraged to vie for their rulers' favours (Marx [1848] 1988). When this occurred, attention was deflected away from the existing injustices (Carver 1998; Marx [1848] 1988). However, as I analyzed the women's stories further, I could see how the girls staged rebellions and resisted becoming incorporated into the colonizing apparatus. From a cluster of the women's orphanage stories I could see how the girls periodically sabotaged the disciplinary regimes. In many instances, this involved the orphans deliberately defying, provoking, and riling their custodians. In popular terms, these stories were about the underdog biting back after being kicked one too many times.

Again Christina provided some of the most vivid examples of how she "bit back." Take, for instance, the story "Playing the Orphanage Staff," which ensued after she had entered the orphanage as a baby:

> I got to know them really well and I could play them like a yo-yo. After that—I tell you true—it was on everyone's mind: "Be careful of her. She can make your life miserable," you know?

Living in the orphanage from birth to adulthood gave Christina ample opportunity to observe the patterns of those in charge. This knowledge helped her to learn how to "play them." The image of the yo-yo is interesting because it suggested that Christina was the one who was pulling all the strings. As exaggerated as this might sound, it is a useful reminder of how fear can travel in both directions, between ruler and subject. She indicated this by noting how wary others became of her. Using a defiant tone, she seemed proud of the fact that she was able to make her wardens' lives "miserable."

Making others' lives miserable might sound like a spiteful way to behave, but in such impoverishing and brutal circumstances, survival sometimes requires doing more than turning the other cheek. As Christina's story suggests, resilience (or the ability to recover or spring back from hardships) often requires survivors forging a clear space between themselves and their oppressors. This is anything but easy given she was a "coloured," poor girl who was left in an orphanage by her unmarried mother. As she noted, incarcerated individuals must sometimes perform counter-attacks if they are to have the chance to develop alternative perspectives about themselves and the world.

From the interviews generally, I noticed that some of the women struggled to build and maintain positive self-concepts so as to keep alive alternative stories about love. Christina, Cecilia, Karen, and Linda were particularly vocal about this, telling me how they remember dreaming about a different and more loving life outside. As Christina described:

I'm telling myself—like my mind is talking—"Now is the right time to die." "Kill me if you think I am not worthy to live." And I felt that I heard this voice, but I'm sure it was just my imagination because ... as I said, I'd read the works of Elizabeth Barrett Browning and in there she says, "Death doesn't hold you—it's love." Right. Yeah, I thought that was so profound. Up until this day, I would read that particular thing, you know. She was so good, you know. From that—from then on—I never took it lying down when they told me, "You are worthless and that nobody will ever care for you. You are ugly, you are all kinds of things."

Summary

An assortment of stories from childhood were analyzed in this chapter related to some of the women's early experiences of love and care. While exploring the influence birth families can have over the meanings that individuals attribute to love, I referred to the "Mommy Dearest" script because it encapsulates the primacy of maternal love and also the terrors of maternal abuse. I then honed in on the script for "Being Daddy's Little Princess" because it is often used to induct women into normative heterosexual behaviours. Significantly, though, few women participants disclosed being sexually abused by their fathers. Many appreciated the support their fathers gave them, while others lamented the absence of their fathers in their lives. Another notable point was evident among siblings. While some felt the effects of sibling rivalry, many women also spoke of sibling solidarity and protection. These experiences were important to explore because they helped to mediate abuse perpetrated by adults. Overall, the pain of not feeling loved, respected, and cared for pervaded many stories. Yet, by exploring these stories I have not sought to overdetermine the effects childhood trauma may have on later life. Rather, I have tried to provide some insights about where the women might be coming from, as well as what they had to face along the way.

In the following chapter I examine aspects of the women's early adulthood experiences, focusing on stories about love, sex, and romance. In this discussion, I argue that girls are usually inducted into womanhood through sexual scripts that underline the importance of loving. Regardless of whether primary experiences of love are fraught, destructive, and/or absent, I suggest that since the project of becoming a woman may be linked to the practice of loving others, this period of the women's lives is a critical time to explore.

Samantha: *I wanted to love them, so I did.*

8
ROMANCE, LOVE, AND ABUSE IN EARLY ADULTHOOD
Cinderella's (Un)happy Ending?

FAMILIAL LOVE RELATIONSHIPS IN CHILDhood and their impact were the focus of discussion in the last chapter. In this chapter, I present and analyze some of the stories the women told me about love, sex, and romance during their early adult years. I continue being interested in the performance of sexual scripts, noting instances of conformity, collusion, and compliance, as well as acts of defiance, rebellion, and improvisation. The language the women used to represent their experiences is also a source of interest.

I start by noting that girls are often inducted into womanhood through the use of particular sexual scripts that can be so embedded in everyday talk that they are hard to notice. I focus most on women who have endured abuse during their childhood, providing snapshots of how some of them negotiated the process of becoming women. Aware of the power of their desire, and respecting their ability to make decisions, I pay attention to what they said they hoped to achieve through their love relationships, not just what they eventually experienced through their transition into womanhood.

I take note of the women's material circumstances because they help to shape how the women experienced love, sex, and romance in their early years. Because they resonate with some of the women's experiences, I also discuss some of the promises and problems associated with conventionally prescribed romantic love relations. I pay particular attention to the paradox facing most young women: how to consciously invest in love relationships, but also achieve independence. Toward the end of the chapter the discussion returns more explicitly to the impact that years of abuse and neglect have for young women survivors. A brief discussion of self-love follows as some of the women indicated that it helped them to destabilize the script of the "Poor Welfare Girl Abandoned at a Young Age." The chapter closes with ideas about "enlightened witnesses," which is a term coined by members of the Narrative (Therapy) Movement to describe how others outside birth families may help to foster unique or positive outcomes (Milner 2001; White & Denborough 1998).

Being Inducted into Womanhood through Sexual Scripts

In Western societies, adolescence is a critical period of psycho-sexual development because it is the time when people are expected to become more conscious of and curious about their sexuality. For young women, however, many concerns are still expressed about the riskiness of young women's sexual experimentation. Often these concerns manifest in the discourses (or stories) that circulate about love and romance from a diverse range of sites.

Discourses about love, sex, and romance come from family members, alternative caregivers, peers, religious authorities, the mass media, teachers, neighbours, coaches, and the state, just to mention a few. From this jumble of stories, girls are usually given and frequently look for specific instructions about how to "do" womanhood (Johnson 1993; Jong 1974, Laws & Schwartz 1977; Lees 1986, 1989; Oakley 1981; Ussher 1997; Walkerdine 1984). The kinds of instructions they receive have a bearing on the sexual scripts that they are likely to perform (Lees 1986, 1989). Navigating one's way through the mosaic of instructions is part of the process of growing up (Gilbert & Taylor 1991), yet these instructions are often inconsistent or contradictory. While they can often feel individual or interpersonal, they are part of the much wider realms we refer to as social and cultural.

"Good Girls" and "Smart Girls": Yesterday and Today

In Western societies, men still tend to be valued most for being strong, decisive, and rational, while women are esteemed most for being good, malleable, and emotional (Gilbert & Taylor 1991; Lees 1986, 1989). In conventional terms, strength is understood to be a manly virtue, something that relies on male pride and involves the flexing of muscles, the assertion of independence, and the protection of others (Connell 1995). In contrast, goodness tends to be portrayed as a feminine virtue that involves loving others and being emotionally vulnerable. Usually it has called for women to sublimate their self-interests, forgo any claims they might wish to make to independence, and be hypersensitive to others' needs (Gilbert & Taylor 1991; Gilligan 1982; Lees 1986, 1989; Summers [1975] 1994). For men, it has traditionally called upon them to demonstrate leadership, take initiative, and be in charge (Connell 1995; Goldrick-Jones 2002). They are expected to do this regardless of how they feel about it, and they are meant to do so from adolescence onward.

In contemporary Anglo-American-dominated countries today, young women and men are still encouraged, if not compelled, to abide by gender conventions. However, some changes are evident, at least for some groups of women. While some groups of women are still subjected to quite strict gender socialization practices in their families, local communities, and schools, others are allowed or even encouraged to explore work, life, and love possibilities that cut across rigid gender divisions. Amid this encouragement is the pressure to perform new sexual scripts, including those where university, career, marriage, and motherhood are all seamlessly interwoven.

Qualitatively different from older generations, many girls today watch their mothers juggling their paid work, domestic duties, and part-time studies (see Maushart 2001). Many know that intimate relationships are now expected to occur throughout the educational process, potentially over decades, not just a few years. For girls raised in families that entertain quite high educational aspirations, the challenge is to become a young woman who is sexy enough to attract potential suitors while at the same time still being good and smart enough to get a place at university. Young women raised under this kind of cultural regime know that the archetypes for "good girls" are not just related to being soft, pliable, and traditionally feminine, but also being strong enough to make it in "a man's world."

For the young women who do not have so many educational and labour market possibilities in front of them, parental hopes for the future and correlating expectations can be quite different. While usually proud of their children's achievements, particularly those related to formal education, working-class parents sometimes find themselves encouraging their daughters to either not date at all or, alternatively, not to let their studies interfere with their chances of creating a loving partnership. I know this not just from the women I interviewed but also from some of the students with whom I work. From some of the working-class women, I have learned that because they are aware that they cannot themselves easily cover the costs of education, some worry about the debts their children are accruing from university study. In these instances, some daughters are advised to balance their educational goals with those related to making money and creating a family. Part of this balance can involve expecting young women to finish whatever course they are studying before giving serious thought to the imperatives of making a home and a family.

Cultural Conventions Be Damned!

Fed a steady diet of "reality" television shows and sitcoms that depict affluent young professionals consumed with questions about their looks and relationships, young women across the board sometimes found it hard to know how to pitch themselves on the educational, labour, and sexual markets. Yet saying it can be difficult does not mean that young women are without critical faculty. As Currie (1999, p. 4) outlined in her text, *Girl Talk,* many young women, including some who appear to be devoted to it, can deconstruct the cult of femininity promulgated by the mass media.

Being able to deconstruct cultural conventions, especially those that do not fit with one's own beliefs, experiences, and hopes, means that although there are constraints, many young women will be drawn to other possibilities. It means that even though cultural conventions exist, people have and will continue to experiment with behaviours and traits that are not aligned to the templates given to them. Just as some of the young women did when they were children, people can work off the script and, in so doing, create new ones (see Chapter 7).

Working off the script does, however, entail a fair degree of improvisation. Even when people find that the scripts do not fit them well, it can sometimes be easier to follow along well-worn tracks, at least for some period of time. From the lesbian and bisexual participants in this study, I learned that the time spent trying out conventional scripts can provide a breathing space because the instructions for how to navigate through high school, friendships, dating, university, and the potential role of career woman and/or wife are clearly mapped out. Some of the women indicated to me that trying out traditional scripts, even when success seemed remote, gave them the chance to figure out how they felt about alternative ways of being, including other ways of expressing love, finding happiness, and participating in society. Even if they did not subscribe to alternative ways of being, many of the women knew that working off or away from scripts can be more difficult because it tends to be less encouraged and valued. Perhaps it is a mixed blessing that the dominant ideals expressed about love and femininity (or indeed, love and masculinity) are riddled with contradictions.

As argued in Chapters 1 to 4, love is often portrayed as a mysterious phenomenon that can never really be understood, but also as a commodity that young women are expected to demonstrate as they make their way toward womanhood (Julius-Mathews 1984; Kipnis 2003; Pilcher 1999). While they do this, young men are expected to accentuate their sexual desire by ramping up their readiness for sex as they dampen down, if not deny, any desires they may have for emotional closeness. Again, deviations *are* possible, but for the young men who do not abide by this script, there is the chance that they will be cast as overly emotional, a bit of a sissy, and/or potentially gay. In contrast, young women whom others see as not emotional enough may be questioned about their apparent coldness.

Many young women I interviewed talked about feeling frustrated with these cultural expectations. Some talked about how much they appreciated being with partners—women or men—who were emotionally expressive. Some also spoke of their frustration of being expected to moderate men's sexual urges while at the same time playing the waiting game. Carly, a 26-year-old Canadian, reiterated this when she asked rhetorically:

> Why are we still the ones who are s'posed to be responsible for making sure things don't get out of hand [sexually] when we're the ones who are meant to wait for guys to initiate, wait for them to ask us out, then wait for them to call …?

Carly was not alone. Although many younger heterosexual women in Canada and Australia realized that they had the option of messing up the rules by asking a man out or initiating a phone call, they also realized that such actions carried particular risks, especially condemnation from others who were likely to view women who display such impatience as indicative of their desperation. For most women, being seen as desperate is humiliating. Some of the women told me that to be a woman and to be desperate is to be ugly, sad, and very likely to be "left on the shelf." In men, however, the same acts are read not so much as desperate but as active, acceptable, even desirable, particularly if it is related to sexual rather than emotional need fulfilment. The biologically essentialist discourse that assumes that all men are hard-wired to want and need sex helps to entrench these expectations. Unlike the feminine, the masculine subject is rendered desperate if he is not getting any sex.

But here is the rub: On the one hand, it is popularly assumed that it is harder to be a man given all the expectations of him where initiating, inviting, and pursuing is concerned. Yet, on the other hand, many of us feminists argue that it is harder to be a woman, given that the conventions for hetero-normative romance ultimately promote the interests of men. As I have already suggested, orthodox hetero-romance does this by extolling the virtues of young women remaining chaste (or at least very careful about who they have sex with) while becoming hetero-"sexy" and investing in heterosexual relationships (also see Hey 1997; Jackson & Scott 1996; Mann 1994; Millett 1971; Pipher 1995; Ussher 1997; Wetherell 1995; Wollstonecraft [1792] 1975).

From the point of view of some of the heterosexual women with whom I spoke, the problem was not whether it is harder to be a man or a woman but that too many gender stereotypes exist in the first place. For some the conventional thinking expressed in books such as *The Rules, The Surrendered Wife* (Doyle 2000) and *He's Just Not That into You* (Behrendt & Tuccillo 2004) discount the wide variations among and between people. Oversimplifying love relationships to a series of moves that men and women are supposed to make in the game of love, these books reinforce the idea that real men and real women follow traditional pathways. According to these books, all heterosexual women long for men to take charge so that they can surrender to their will. Heterosexual men, on the other hand, are depicted as so insecure that they become emasculated and experience an inevitable diminution of their sexual desire when heterosexual women have the audacity to take the bull by the horns.

Many people, regardless of gender, are cajoled into believing these impulses are natural and true. Nevertheless, many people find these rules (or popular conventions) anything but liberating. In hetero-patriarchy, mainstream conventions for loving tend to be far from liberating because their net effect is to repress women's expression of sexual desire and shepherd them into roles that are incompatible with their individual temperaments, inclinations, and aspirations. And repressing women's sexuality is hardly conducive to the pleasure of prospective partners (heterosexual or lesbian) who want to love in expansive and imaginative ways.

Being Respected and Managing Risk

The cultures in which so many of us have been raised continue to be driven by fears regarding the dangers of women's sexuality. At the same time, concerns about women's safety are embedded in women's psyches, especially as girls grow into womanhood. Thus, it is not surprising that many of the women I interviewed talked about how much they longed to be respected (see Chapters 10–12). Even among the young women I interviewed, I heard how women still have to walk the tightrope between being "good enough" (that is, sensible and attractive) without being labelled as "frigid." What has changed over the generations is the pressure on young women now to be "bad enough" (that is, sexually desirable) without being branded a whore.

For many older women and those raised in orthodox religious households, the task of becoming a woman seemed more straightforward because the sexual constraints governing their sexuality were more clearly and narrowly defined. For older women, especially baby boomers, clear edicts were usually handed down about what girls should and should not do. While some used ideas from feminism and sexual libertarianism to play different roles, most of the ordinary women I spoke with maintained that narrow rules continue to be stipulated.

The most common rule handed down was that sex was forbidden before marriage or, at the very least, until a loving, stable, monogamous *heterosexual* relationship had taken shape. Twenty-three-year-old Stephanie, from Winnipeg, told me about the teachings her Calvinist, baby-boomer mother handed her:

> Sex was really bad and you weren't supposed to have sex until you married. You know, that sort of thing. I don't know whether it was because my parents stressed it more for me, but I know that I took it to heart

more than my brothers. My brothers have been having sex for a long time, doing their own thing, which is fine. Then my mom worried that I had taken what they'd said to heart *too much* and told me that they mean that sex is good in marriage, like, you know....

Stephanie was not the only woman to narrate stories about how she should contain her sexuality without extinguishing it. Most women I spoke with were taught to pursue the sexual scripts for having a serious relationship and getting married even if some of them decided not to do so. While not all women suggested as much, at least 40 of the 84 women I interviewed made reference to how they were taught to be very careful about how they expressed their sexuality. Of this sizable group, most were enticed by the promises of romantic love, mostly because traditional romance offered them some latitude to experience their desire and avoid being penalized for perceived acts of defiance.

Vera, a woman in her mid-sixties, is a case in point. So, too, are Cecilia and Ada, women in their forties. While Vera was vigilantly protecting her virginity, Ada said, "Sex was out of the question.... I had always thought that I would keep my virginity until I married."

Cecilia softened this position a little by using the language of romantic love to justify why she agreed to have sex before marriage. Unlike a good number of the younger women I interviewed, many of the women over 40 told me that they conformed to traditional expectations about how they should "do" womanhood, at least initially. Some said they gave a good impression that they were conforming, hiding any transgressions until they had left the family home and/or developed their own means of support. For most of the older women, this meant pursuing heterosexual, monogamous coupledom in ways that were complementary to men but not necessarily equal (see Oakley 1982). For women like Vera, Cecilia, Ada, and Emily, their early love lives also bore some resemblance to French's (1985, p. 534) claim that "Women are trained for private virtue, men for public power."

Childhood "Innocence" and Sexual Reputation
Being trained for public virtue was etched into many of Vera's stories:

> Being a Roman Catholic and going to confession on Saturday—it was just not done. You just didn't indulge in any sort of sexual activities with boys.... They were called, um, bad names.... The "village bicycle" was one of the terms. Or, um, low morals. And boys would talk about them.

For Vera, premarital sex was an indulgence. Arguably, this can also be read as a sin, a luxury, and a transgression. Transgressions are difficult because they run the risk of being "called bad names," such as "village bicycles," For a range of reasons, the metaphor of the "town bike" is an interesting concept. First, it unearths the historical assumption that heterosexual intercourse involves men actively "doing the riding" and women passively "being ridden." Second, it points to the ways in which women have been objectified as public property and discarded when their "equipment" is no longer required (see Greer 1999). Finally, it might be seen to support the feminist warning that hetero-sex can involve women "being taken for a ride" (see Bunch 1978; Morgan [1970] 1971; Rowbotham 1972).

It is significant that more than 50 years later, Vera could still recall these conversations. Apart from the social stigma associated with being seen as a "bad girl," Vera revealed how other penalties could be levelled at girls who were sexually transgressive (see Johnson 1993; Taylor et al. 1995; Ussher 1997). In a story called "Risking Her Education," I asked her whether it was ever possible for her to ignore her mother's instructions. Vera replied:

> No, because I wanted an education. I didn't want my education to be stopped. To me, my education was the most important thing in the world to me because I wanted nursing.... I could not risk being told that I would have to leave school, or that I wasn't going to be educated because that was always on their agenda.

Like a lot of other women I spoke to, Vera calculated the risks of nonconformity by weighing up what she most wanted to do. Having already decided to become a nurse, she knew that she needed to finish high school. Given that her parents were already ambivalent about her finishing school, sexual transgression seemed too risky.

According to Johnson (1993), the decades following World War Two was a time when the demands of industrializing societies competed with conflicting cultural ideas about women's role. Since it was a time when the education of girls was hotly contested, Vera's parents did not reflect idiosyncrasy but convention. As Vera said herself, "They thought that they [her brothers] would have to rear a family whereas I could get married to someone else's son, who was presumably educated. It was the tradition in those days."

From other stories Vera told, I learned how she completed high school, entered nursing, and lived in the nurses' quarters. There she met Dan, her fiancé from whom she protected her virginity until she finished her training and was permitted to marry. As I discuss in Chapters 9 and 10, it was then that she experienced some of the most profound difficulties of her life.

In contrast to Vera, Dallas, an Australian woman in her mid-forties, did not have a clear pathway to follow and her induction into womanhood was fraught with difficulties. Having already experienced sexual abuse, Dallas had to deal with violent relationships with her mother and sister (also see Chapter 7). Apart from causing great harm, this violence meant that she was not able to access the support that so often comes when female family members suggest ways to manage one's entry into womanhood. Instead of orienting her toward scripts she might find useful, her mother and sister appeared in her stories as erratic, punitive, and, at times, malicious.

According to Dallas, her mother vacillated between indifference and hyper-surveillance of her sexuality. Added to this, her sister's "bad reputation" made it difficult for her to protect her virginity. In a story called "Being Tarred with the Same Brush," she said:

> When she [Fiona] was about 13, well, let's just say that she was very well known by the Melton boys. Some of those boys must have thought, "Well, they're *sisters*," but I used to run a mile. I was terrified, absolutely terrified. At that stage, I didn't know what an erect penis was.

Dallas's story shows how young women who associated with "sluts/slags" are liable to similar classification (also see Hey 1997; Lees 1986). From a range of other younger women interviewed, I know that young women today are liable to be branded "bad" and subject to humiliation (Hey 1997; Taylor et al. 1995). Being known as a slut or a slag can be particularly hazardous. Long associated with dirt, sin, and inferiority, these terms have allowed many men to treat women with utter disregard and considerable impunity (see Moore 2000). This was why Dallas feared what the local boys might do to her. With a shadow cast over her sexual reputation because of her sister, she knew that if they harmed her, she might have little recourse, especially if it involved the police and the judicial system (also see Griffin 1981).

Although Dallas had already been sexually abused, her abuser's failure to achieve erection meant that she did not "even know what an erect penis was." By not knowing this adult "mystery," she was, however, allowed a semblance of "childhood innocence." Nevertheless, the protective features of this innocence were illusory since she was repeatedly raped by her sister's boyfriend between the ages of 13 and 15.

"Standing by Your Man"

Across countries, age groups, and religious backgrounds, the women participants exhibited some differences in the sexual scripts they deployed. Some of the young women scoffed at the idea of having to "stand by their man" whereas others actually used the phrase to identify their loyalty to love. Nevertheless, almost all were raised with the idea that loyalty was a trait they should display as young women. Being or at least pretending to be innocent was part of the role, especially for older women. In a story entitled "Script for Catholic Girls," Cecilia, a 43-year-old Australian, outlined the attitudes and behaviours that it entailed:

> Sex before marriage was *absolutely not acceptable* or pregnancy or divorce.... So, [there were] *very fixed ideas* about how I was to keep myself pure. I would only have sex with a *man*. It would only be *after* I was married, you know. Of course, you wouldn't be using contraception. And if you were going to get pregnant, you would just have to have the baby—you wouldn't go have an abortion. Um, you stay with the man forever and for life, regardless of how bad it is or how miserable you are.

For Cecilia, the expected behaviours came not just from the nuns in the orphanage but also her married, older sisters. Salecl (1998) talks about this as the discourses of sexual purity, whereas Rich (1980) referred to these expectations as compulsory heterosexuality. Even if it is not achieved, most women were forced to find a way to justify their actions if they did not save themselves for marriage, get married, and then bear their husbands' children. For women over 40 such as Cecilia, "standing by their man" forever, regardless of the misery that may have eventuated, was a common expectation that they had to navigate.

Cecilia's stories reiterate points I have made in Chapters 7 and 8 when I talk about how orphanages, group homes, and youth shelters are complicated sites from which young women are expected to perform their sexuality. Apart from their tendency to deny and/or punitively monitor residents' sexuality, youth shelters and the like are unlikely to offer positive role models for women to emulate as they negotiate their entry into womanhood. Audrey pointed to this when she told me stories about living in a youth detention centre, and then at another point in her life, in a largely unsupervised youth hostel. Christina, 43 years old, also talked about how difficult it was to become a woman without the help of close, older women. Growing up in an orphanage until she was 20, Christina searched for other ways to learn about the conventional scripts for romantic love.

Given the ease at which girls in the orphanage can be classified as "loose" and inferior, Christina's romantic aspirations may have seemed ambitious. With little support from adults in her interpersonal world, she had to draw ideas from Mills & Boon romance novels, and the fleeting observations she made of other girls in college to figure out how to become "a highly desirable girl" (Collins & Harper 1978, p. 91). Associating this sexual script with getting respect, Christina modified the traditional script for being a wife and a mother by injecting it with a greater degree of assertiveness while ensuring she was not identified as a "bad girl."

The Freedom to Be Who You Are

Younger women—such as Erin (a 27-year-old Canadian), Annie (a 30-year-old Canadian), Rachael (a 32-year-old Canadian), Fiona (a 33-year-old Canadian), Samantha (a 26-year-old Australian), and Kate (a 34-year-old Australian)—provided some contrast to their elders. This makes sense when one considers how the younger women grew up during a time when feminist ideas were more widely circulated and sexual standards governing sexuality had relaxed. Exposed to a greater diversity of discourses and a contradictory array of sexual scripts, relatively few of the younger women were persuaded to follow what Walkerdine (1984) described as the discourse of "romantic fantasy." Nevertheless, it is interesting that with the exception of Rachael, Fiona, Marnie, and Audrey, all the women used the language of falling in love to some extent. The most common pattern I noticed for younger women was straddling the scripts for having a serious monogamous, heterosexual relationship and having recreational sex, preferably with people for whom they had affection.

To put it another way, younger women such as Fiona, Rachael, Samantha, Erin, Annie, and Kate all had a greater degree of latitude than their older counterparts when it came to modifying sexual conventions. Afforded more space to engage in the postmodern project of hybridizing love narratives to suit their individual purposes (Simon 1996), their experiences of early adulthood seemed more adventurous and definitely more experimental. Take, for instance, Rachael, who proudly identified as lesbian from a young age and felt that,

> … marriage is a joke. [laughs] I think marriage is based on oppression and the ownership of women. I think that marriage is used as women's slavery. I think equal marriage is an oxymoron, especially in heterosexual relationships. That's a fallacy. It cannot exist. It cannot be possible that somebody outside of the home can have so much more privilege and access to resources in the general world and somebody can have so little and then they come into the home and shut the front door and things are automatically equal.

With her polyamorous (non-monogamous) lesbian partner, Rachael was not the slightest bit shy about stipulating how regulated she believed sexuality is, at least for the majority of the population. From her point of view, lesbianism and non-monogamous lesbianism in particular are still identified as "deviant" behaviours despite the allegedly liberal views circulating in Canada about sexuality. She said:

> We're so deviant on so many levels. You're raised and groomed since birth to get married and have kids. And then when you do grow up and get married and have kids, people call it a choice! They say, "I chose to get married." I say, "It's not a choice! You were brainwashed into it for 20 years. Congratulations, it worked. Now you chose it. Wow! I am so surprised."

The Promise of Romance and the Utility of Love

Although Rachael expressed staunch views against marriage, the promise of romance and the prospect of marriage appealed to many of the women with whom I spoke. For many, romance was tantalizing because it offered them an avenue for sexual gratification, which, in turn, led to the possibility of marriage, an institution that promises women that they will be safe, cared for, and respected.

As I have explained in Chapter 5, when family hardships are great and labour market opportunities are limited, romantic love may be particularly alluring (Hey 1997; Wearing 1996; Winterson 1996). Being "half of a whole" or at least "partners in crime" often provides young women with a literal and metaphorical home. Conventional scripts for romantic love also promise women that they will be loved for themselves (Vellerman 1999), and protected from other men's predatory sexual behaviour (Jong 1974).

The Fantasy of Romantic Salvation

In a story I have called "Lovely Con," Dallas spoke about the conventional idea of a man being her protector. She was explaining why her sister's boyfriend suddenly stopped raping:

> Then, when I met this guy, Con, I told him and he put a stop to it. And that was the first time I've ever had a male stand up for me and go to him and say, "If you ever touch her again, I'm going to fucking kill ya." And they were close mates and it stopped. Now [pause] I quite believe that I'd still be with Con if it wasn't for my mum. Mum put a stop to that relationship.... He was one of the loveliest—oh, he was lovely. His family was nice, he was nice, and he put a stop to what Rick was doing.

Unlike Dallas, who could not stop Rick from raping her, another man was able to by threatening retaliatory violence. Bearing in mind that her father was unable to protect her from maternal abuse (see Chapter 5), this was the first time that a man had been willing *and able* to protect her. Con's actions were so revered or, as Vellerman (1999) might describe, so overvalued that 30 years have not shaken her faith that she would be with him now if it were not for her mother.

Because Dallas yearned to become part of another family (see Chapter 7), Con's family was a significant draw card. As Walkerdine (1984) pointed out, conventional romance stories often promise girls from "bad" families the longed-for ideal family (also see Wearing 1996; Winterson 1996). In a story called "Fairytale Love," Dallas reiterated the appeal of Con's family:

> I just thought I was going to grow up and live happily ever after with Con and his family. That was—that would be about the only fairy tale that I could come close to even think like that…. He would have given me everything that I never, ever had.

Referring to the "have and to hold" discourse (Hollway [1984] 1996), Dallas assumed that it was possible for heterosexual couples to "live happily ever after." For her, this was the only "fairy tale" that she could imagine coming true. Given her circumstances, it was a rather bold step "to even think like that," yet it was a point that I missed because I did not listen closely enough. Instead, I mistakenly assumed that she was criticizing fairytale love as a myth. Not shy about setting me straight, she stressed that she knew that she "*would have*" lived happily ever after, and that he would have been able to "give" her that which she "never, ever had."

The Beauty System

In contrast to Dallas, Cecilia had very little contact with her mother, who remained institutionalized after having a stroke. Living in a sex-segregated orphanage until she was 17 also meant that she had little contact with boys or men until she left in 1974. At this point, she was 17 and moved into the home of Harriet, one of her older, married sisters. As a practising Catholic, Cecilia's sister endorsed the script for "good Catholic girls" while her brother-in-law encouraged her to date men. Mainly, he did so by saying that her good looks would make it easy for her to "catch a man." In a story called "Being a Nice Young Thing," she said:

> And, um, I remember when I sort of first came home, I'd be reading magazines and watching TV and I'd be hearing about boys and men and feeling really … [pause] it was almost like I'd avoid it. I remember thinking "Oh-oh!" And then a couple of times my brother-in-law, Larry, who is quite a—he's a real ocker type, you know [male chauvinist]—he would start talking about it. "Ah, you've developed right into a nice young thing with a figure there" [she laughs as she mimics Larry]…. "You're quite pretty when you're scrubbed up" and that sort of talking. He was with my sister Harriet and had a lovely married life. And I remember him starting to talk about things like he was going to keep his eye out for someone, and this or that. I remember being really frightened of this whole idea, but it was a bit like he was planting a seed, though.

Cecilia's story is just one of many that show how women are encouraged to capture male attention by subscribing to the "beauty system" (Friedan 1997; MacCannell & Flower-MacCannell 1987; Salecl 1998; Wolf 1990). Encouraged to hanker for the male gaze, they are invited to internalize strict beauty standards (Friedan 1997; Summers 1994; Ussher 1997; Wollstonecraft [1792] 1975; Wolf 1997; Zetzel Lambert 1995). The main incentive for doing so is the belief that beautiful women are able to wield power over men, which they are much less likely to be able to exercise if they do not comply with beauty regimes (Faludi 1992; Pipher 1995; Wolf 1997). And in a society that prizes women's youth and beauty, these promises are hardly hollow.

Someone to Look after You and the Baby

For Cecilia, being pretty helped her "catch" a man who would serve as her protector. Thinking back to when she was 18, she said:

> I had this real thing that I had to be looked after because I hadn't been.... And I had a thing about the person who was going to look after me had to be a big, strong—because I'm small in stature, so it was a physical thing too. Sounds like a child-like, fairytale kind of thing, but these were the things that I thought were really important. It was like a dream come true when I met my first husband.

As Emily described earlier and Dallas describes below, Cecilia constructed romantic love as the salve for her past neglect. The concept of being "looked after" by a man was so important that she stressed it four times. This is also why she was attracted to men who were physically much bigger than she was. With the notion of protection securely rooted in the story, she identified how "childish" this "fairytale" idea may sound. Nevertheless, the idea of the "tall, dark, and handsome prince" was enchanting not just because she was 17 but also because it allowed her to feel as if it was "a dream come true" (also see Pipher 1995; Radway 1991; Ussher 1997).

While Cecilia married her "dream" man and, for now, tacitly complied with conventional love scripts for women, Dallas was devastated by the relationship ending with "lovely" Con. In the stories that follow, Dallas described how she had a nervous breakdown and got mixed up with a group of older men who were on the run from the police:

> I took up with this guy who was twice my age and I started to flaunt him in front of my mum and dad. "Well, you wouldn't let me have Con. Now put a stop to this one." ... After that, I went for the type that would horrify Mum.

Nameless and faceless, "this guy" was the first of many men brought home to "horrify Mum." However, this subversion was short-lived when she accidentally became pregnant.

Dallas said that after she became pregnant, her mother stepped in and insisted that she and her boyfriend marry:

> Um, we shouldn't have got married, but we did. We had no other choice 'cos we were told to. Mum—I happened to have told her—and she said, "Well, I hope you're not going to expect me to look after you and the baby like your sister did."

Dallas capitulated to her mother's demands because the prospect of raising a child without her mother's support seemed too daunting. At just 17, she was married and ready to give birth. Before she was 20, her husband was in jail for domestic violence and she moved away with their daughter, Kelly.

Somewhere Stable to Live

Emily, 49 years old, was another woman who hoped for romantic love, but instead became trapped in a violent marriage at age 18. Although she was not directly coerced into marriage, her material and emotional circumstances steered her in this direction. Her situation was as follows: It was 1970 and with limited secondary schooling behind her, she was expected to leave her aunt and uncle's home. Since properly paid work was out of reach and the prospect of living alone was more than a little frightening, marriage seemed to be a very attractive option (also see Hey 1997; Wearing 1996). In the story called "Marrying Young for a Place to Go," Emily talked about getting married and said, "I guess the reason why I got married was because I had to get out. I had to get somewhere. I needed to be somewhere."

The plot of Emily's story is fairly simple. Getting married offered her the possibility to "get" and "be somewhere." However, as she heard herself talking, she realized how calculating it sounded and how it did not reflect the intensely passionate feelings she had for her husband at the start of their relationship:

> When he come along and give me that love, I melted. *I absolutely melted.* I thought, you know, "This is something I've never had in my whole life." ... It felt "Oh God, I'm getting all this that I've never ever had." I just didn't want to give it up, you know.

Emily then suggested that intimate relationships can help thaw the distance and detachment between people. It is a metaphor that connects with Lupton's (1998) discussion of the "leaky body," where the boundaries between the self and others dissolve (see Chapter 2). It also connects with the script for falling in love since it involves lovers lowering their defences, exposing their vulnerabilities, and feeling intense but often fleeting feelings of acceptance (Barthes 1978; Tennov 1979). Well rehearsed in everyday talk, it is not accidental that

Emily used exactly the same language as Dallas, who also wanted to be given something she had never had.

Love, romance, and practicality converged in stories told by other women, including Annie (30 years old) and Samantha (26 years old). Said Annie:

> At the time we got married, or when we were deciding to get married, the number one thing I wanted was, like, stability and security. I had a lot of wild oats to sow when I was in my younger years and when I was in college, and I dated lots and lots of guys, and I would get very attached to them. Then I'd be all broken, you know.... Like, I really wanted to be with someone. It was very important to me.

Supported by her middle-class family, Annie was not under as much pressure to settle down as Samantha, who was living in youth shelters and who explained that she "just wanted to have somewhere stable to live.... I just said to Tom, 'Do you want to move in with me?'"

Like many other young women who are trying to exit the care system, Samantha longed to stabilize her living arrangements at the tender age of 16. She tried to do this with her boyfriend, Tom, because she knew him and he seemed receptive to the idea. Also, since it was the mid-1980s and the cultural prohibition against cohabitation was no longer as strong (Jamieson 1999; Julius-Mathews 1984; Pilcher 1999), she knew that she was not likely to suffer the penalties historically levelled at women who "shacked up with men" or "lived in sin."

Sexual Excitement

While Samantha showed little interest in subscribing to the more whimsical elements of romantic love, she did enjoy the early days of her relationship with Tom. She remembered the time when they stayed in a local caravan park without the approval of the group home "parents":

> We had a *ball!* We didn't go anywhere, but you can imagine—we had a ball together. We were alone together for the first time, *aaah*.

Not weighed down with so much guilt about whether she should protect her virginity, Samantha's time with Tom was exciting. This excitement was heightened by the danger that her social worker and group home "parents" might discover them.

Like Samantha, Kate (33 years old) was able to enjoy sex and form sexual relationships in a 1980s youth shelter. In a story called "Looking after Dave," she said:

> I fascinated him and he fascinated me. You know, like, we'd make love and I'd say, "More," or "This way," or "That way," or whatever. And he'd say, "My last girlfriend never, ever said stuff like that. Now I sort of know what to do." He had my name tattooed on his knuckles, but this was a casual thing for me, you know. And sometimes he'd sneak into my room and all that sort of stuff, you know. And that's why it was really funny when the youth workers said, "Well, you can go and move in with Dave and look after him" because Dave used to get into trouble.

From Kate's report, she and Dave formed a relatively equal sexual relationship in which she felt able to express how he might best stimulate her. Swapping gender stereotypes, he demonstrated his commitment to her by having her name tattooed on his knuckles while she presumed their relationship was casual. She was, therefore, bemused by the workers' assumption that she not only move in with Dave, but also that she should "look after him" and keep him out of "trouble."

In contrast to most other women I interviewed, Kate was one of the few women to be actively encouraged to explore her sexuality (also see Chapter 7). She had the space to critique love, experiment with sexuality, and challenge gender stereotypes, including the expectation that women suppress their sexual desires:

> Well, we were punk socialists who, you know, were just little hoons really. *Love was a middle-class plot.* Well, I espoused all that stuff, of course, except underneath I thought Alan was the bees' knees and I loved him passionately. And there were times when I thought he treated me quite cruelly, as in not talking to me or not turning up when he said he would. But, you know, he kept me on a hook and I was just, like, "Wow!"

Aware of the argument that romantic love was "a middle-class plot," Kate suspended her disbelief to fall in love with Alan. Thunderstruck (see Barthes 1978), her previously cavalier attitude to love collapsed, at least temporarily, when she became captive to Alan's passionate but also "cruel" behaviour. From being "kept on a hook" Kate had a taste of how love and abuse could intersect, and in ways that were confusing, yet she would also experience great joy from love.

In the story "First Real Love," Kate described how she felt about a woman she met at university:

> Um, I remember this incredible happiness. Yeah, I had all those sensations, like the tummy tingles and what some French woman described as the "little death." As they walked past the window, you know, when they're actually going—yeah. Oh, we'd just hang out together all the time.

While she was speaking of the "incredible" feelings she had for Jenna, I thought of Lacan's (1986) concept of *jouissance* and Cixous's ([1974] 1994) argument about the limitlessness of desire (see Chapter 2). When she mentioned how she had "tummy tingles," I thought of how Lupton (1998) described the sensations of falling in love. While I was doing this, Kate referenced Irigaray's (1992) notion of lovers' separations being like "little deaths" (see Chapter 2). It is why lovers find it hard to say goodbye.

From other stories Kate told me about Jenna, I knew that it took a long time for them to acknowledge the sexual dimension of their relationship. The delay may have been because lesbian relationships were still relatively unscripted, liable to "Othering," and vulnerable to public condemnation. These three dynamics certainly faced Marcie and Amanda when they met 39 years ago:

> I am driving along and I see this gal coming home from work. She worked a night shift as a welder at a toy company, and she was dressed in work attire, but the stride on her was like John Wayne. There was a certain walk about it. I knew she was walking male. And I thought, "Holy Dina!" I took a look and went around the block for another look. She noticed that I had gone around the block twice. When I went around a third time, I rolled down the window and I said, "Hi. Do you want to go for a ride and raise some hell?" [smiling broadly] That's what I said to her, "raise a little hell." And they made a song about that later on, "raise a little hell." ... It just about didn't work, though. She got near the car and said, "Well, I don't think my old lady would appreciate that." She was telling me that she was attached, but because I was naive, she knew that I didn't understand. I said, "Well, would like me to take you over to your mom's place and ask her if it was okay?"

Abuse, Victimhood, and Resilience

In Chapters 2 and 3, I explained that in recent decades, many feminists become embroiled in disputes about the operations of power and the utility of binary oppositions such as powerful/powerless and oppressor/victim (see Butler 1997; Grosz 1994; Mann 1994; Weedon 1987). While arguing that many of these discussions have been productive for feminism, I have, however, also identified some of the dangers of using relational accounts of power. In particular, I have argued that such accounts are sometimes used to produce highly atomistic views of agency that are divorced from social constraints (Ebert 1996; Segal 1999; Young 1997).

In Chapters 5 and 6, I have argued that relational accounts of power are productive if they do not exaggerate individual agency and erase structural inequality. In so doing, I reject the inference that victimhood is self-inflicted or that it is an identity that women are liable to exploit (see Faust 1994; Garner 1995). I also approach the discourses of "co-dependence" (Cowan & Warren 1994) and "resilience" (Howe 1995; Taylor et al. 1995) with much caution because I recognize the ease with which they can be used to deflect attention away from those who perpetrate abuse as well as away from the social conditions that allow perpetrators to commit abuse with relative impunity (Langford 1999; Wood 2001).

My feminist politics are worth reiterating because I know that they are critical to the way I analyze the women's stories, especially those that relate to being a victim. I am also referring to this set of stories because in most of the women's interviews, debates and dilemmas ensued about how to attribute responsibility for the abuse that they and other women suffered. As Laws and Schwarz (1977, p. 10) wrote 31 years ago, "To find experience, and articulate sexual options outside the dominant script is more costly and involves more risk than to those who follow the script."

As I have suggested, practices that involve moving off the script require greater explanation than acts that are seen to emulate cultural norms. Explanations are often required even when digressions result not from will but circumstance. Below I will explore two examples that highlight this point. The first relates to the challenges facing girls who are sexually abused and then removed from the family home for their own protection. The second relates to the challenges facing young women who develop sexual desire not for boys but other young women.

Identities under Threat

In some detail, Samantha, Kate, Dallas, and Christina talked about the dynamics of abuse. As they did so, they reiterated debates often made about women's personal power or agency. For instance, in the story called "Wearing the Label of a Slut," Kate talked about being sexually active with both men and women while living in the youth shelter. When I asked her whether the label of "slut" was ever used to define her, she replied:

> No, but one of the boys once said, "Are you a bit like that.?" "I'm bi!" [laughs] I was pretty cocky about stuff.

Interestingly, Kate used the phallic expression of "being cocky" to deflect potential criticisms of her bisexuality. It is also interesting that while she was not identified as a "slut," she said, "there was a woman in there—like, the first time I was there—and she was perceived as a slut, and called a slut, and harassed...." When I asked what differentiated her from the other woman, she said:

> Probably her whole life. I remember she was a bit dirty, as in unwashed and she was very whiney and apologetic. She was right into the victim thing, which everyone wants you to be in, you know. I was openly hav-

ing it off with Dave and she sneakily had it off with one bloke there and suddenly she was a slut, but I wasn't. I don't know how to answer that, though, you know....

Initially Kate attributed the labelling of the other woman to the fate of her "whole life," in which she had become a "dirty ... whiney and apologetic ... victim." On second thought, however, she was not sure how the label had caught hold and why she was able to escape given she was "openly having it off with Dave." To me, it is a story that shows how uneven sexual policing can be as well as how hazardous the conditions of substitute care can be. Earlier I talked about how young women may experience threats to their identities if their living conditions are materially and emotionally impoverishing (see Chapter 7). Through the story Dallas told about how she had used a sexual relationship to horrify her mother, I have acknowledged that some forms of resistance can be self-defeating and destructive (also see Taylor et al. 1995). However, what I have yet to point out is that people who have threatened or "spoiled identities" (Breakwell 1986; Goffman 1963) often suffer re-victimization from the very people we might assume would protect them.

Dealing with Re-victimization

In a story called "Near Rape," Kate talked about the time she lived in the youth shelter and carried a knife for protection. She recalled the day she was hitchhiking and two men picked her up and had her in the car before threatening to rape and kill her. While sitting in the back of their car, she thought about using her knife. Instead of using it, she jumped out of the car when they pulled up at a traffic light. Adrenalin pumping, she made her way to a payphone and called the police in the hope that they would help her:

> I rang the police, but the police treated me really badly. They were, like, "Why did you get in the car?" I was, like, "*Because I was trying to get to town!*"—you know.

It was shocking to Kate that rather than getting details about her assailants, they incriminated her by expecting her to justify why she was hitchhiking.

According to Kate, when the police learned of her shelter address, they became even more "victim blaming" (Ryan 1976). From being a youth worker in residential care at the time of interview, Kate was aware of how easy it was for young women, especially those with low social status, to have their complaints of sexual violence trivialized and/or thrown back in their faces (see Pease 1996; Scutt 1990). Samantha reminded me of this when she told me about the time she was raped by another resident of the group home. The rape occurred very early one morning before the young assailant went to work as a baker and she was to go to school. When the house mother heard of why she was absent from school, she said, "Oh, you asked for it," according to Samantha.

Audrey suffered a similar fate when her stepmother discovered her half-brother had sexually abused her. Said Audrey, "She beat the shit out of me for it. She said I was a dirty bitch."

Traumatized by the abuse and the stepmother's reaction to it, Audrey asked, "Do you know what that kind of thing mentally does to you? When your first experience is with him? That *fucks with your head!*"

Audrey's description of her abuse fits with the accounts provided by many abuse researchers. Take, for instance, Miller (1995), Moeller and Bachman (1993), and Saakvitne et al. (1998), all of whom discuss how long-standing and profound the effects of abuse can be.

Two days after her brother's abuse was uncovered, Audrey was relocated to the care of her birth mother and stepfather. However, a few days after she arrived, her birth mother told her that they did not want her to live with them. With the help of her stepmother, her birth mother put all her belongings into garbage bags and dumped her with the bags at the local police station. Lost and alone, she then found herself at a custodial hearing where her entire family would vouch that they were not prepared to have her live with them. She said:

> I remember one time I went into court and Amanda went in there and she stood in front of the judge, who said, "Why won't you let your daughter go home?" She said, "I don't want it." And he said, "Why not?" She then said, "Because I just can't control it and Gordon will kill it if it comes home." You know, I don't know why she kept referring to me as an "it." I think the judge was disgusted at that, even though he ended up remanding me at the Callum Detention Centre.

Right into her thirties, Audrey's personal circumstances sounded soul-destroying. Stories about love, sex, and romance—even the slightest displays of affection—were notable in their absence. In the story called "Being Turned out," she talked about being prepared for the script of the drug-using street prostitute who lived in a halfway house:

> They dumped me—they dumped me in a refuge with a bunch of fuckin' druggies. I'll never forget this guy called Smithy. There was also Miranda, who was a 13-year-old prostitute who had a baby and another girl called Carol.... Smithy was a punk, a skinhead, ... a neo Nazi. He used to go out and do all sorts of shit—start fights.... He used to come home wasted on Monday morning with black eyes and bruises everywhere and all that sort of shit. Carol—she was on the game in King's Cross. [pause] Miranda was off the game, but she wanted to turn me out.... On the weekends they used to get dope ... and we used

> to stand outside and bong on [laughs] ... I stayed there about three months. I wanted to go back to school, but ... it wasn't really a safe environment for me to study, so I got a job at a nursing home.

Like so many other placements Audrey had experienced, this one was unsafe and short-term. Drug use was the main leisure activity and the possibility of study remote (also see Owen 1996). With her nurses' aide work, however, she could at least have an income and the opportunity to mix with people whose main focus was not drugs, crime, and sex work.

Battling Internalized Inferiority, Affirming Self-Love, and Resilience

In contrast to many young people who are adopted into middle-class families and sometimes granted the protection and status of their host families, Audrey lived in impoverished conditions common to many state wards, orphans, and "poor cousins," such as Cecilia, Karen, Linda, Emily, and Christina. A common thread of their stories were the institutional processes used to promote the internalization of inferiority:

> I had to learn from books how normal people behaved. When I used to go to my friends' places in college—they used to invite me for the weekend and things—I never wanted to go because I'd think "How would they behave?" Do you know what I mean? You're not taught all those things. They treat you like animals in the orphanage. Nothing nice. When I went to this one house once and I saw this lovely lace tablecloth on the table, I was stunned because I'd never seen one before—the way they laid the table. They said, "Help yourself!" We'd just have our food dumped on our enamel plates. [laughs] "That's your share and that's all your getting." You know what I mean?

Impressed by life in the outside world but without a script from which she might behave like "a young lady," Christina recounted that she

> ... started reading Mills & Boon from the time I was in grade six. I used to go and borrow them from the library.... I liked them because they took you *out of this world*. It made it possible that there were good situations. There was a way to learn about love because they wouldn't teach you about love and what it meant. You wouldn't talk about subjects like that. It was *forbidden*, you know what I mean?

As she spoke, I was reminded of Atwood's (1996) *Alias Grace*, a novel that depicts how low-class women are so often portrayed as lacking in charm, poise, and refinement, the emblems of high-class femininity.

Although some feminists have argued that the consumption of romance is indicative of "false consciousness," I am more interested in learning why women might gravitate to this material (also see Hey 1997; Radway 1991; Wetherell 1995). Christina said the romance novels helped to transport her "to another world," a common reason given by Radway's (1991) research participants. Being transported to another world helped Christina to maintain the faith that "good situations" were "possible." It also helped her to believe that love in the future might be possible.

Christina was not alone. Many women I interviewed who disclosed childhood abuse told me that love was a concept they used to project more positive future images of themselves. Take, for instance, Samantha, who said:

> Love was very important to me—it was the stability.... I've always had respect for myself. If I was in strife, I usually had enough respect for myself to try and get myself out of it even if I went the wrong way about it. I mean, you can tell I was always thinking ahead.... Through all the crises I was always trying to look after myself the best I could because I knew that there was only one me.... If I didn't look after myself or love myself, there was nothing going on at all. I would've been like all the other kids that I knew that were my friends—all my girlfriends that were having babies at 14 and 15 and getting into drugs and all that sort of stuff.

I thought of Samantha when I read Doyle's (1990) work about how young people in care are usually discouraged from modelling themselves on either their parents or peers. I thought about how hard it was for her to develop self-love and respect in her early adult years, especially since she felt the need to distance herself from her girlfriends who were getting pregnant or into drugs. Fortunately, she was able to get support from "enlightened witnesses."

Enlightened Witnesses and Unique Outcomes

Enlightened witnesses are those people who are prepared to provide empathy, support, and guidance to others so that they can pursue dreams and aspirations (White & Denborough 1998). Enlightened witnesses often help survivors of abuse to maintain the hope that more respectful and uplifting relationships may be possible in the future (Milner 2001). They often help victims/survivors to externalize the reasons for their pain and expunge any feelings of culpability or inferiority (also see Chapter 4). Sometimes this is done through actions rather than talk, actions that suggest the person has value and is worthwhile, and is not destined to be treated badly in the future.

Unique outcomes are those exceptional events, actions, thoughts, and feelings that contradict problem-saturated stories told about the self. Unique outcomes help to author more liberating and expansive stories (Milner 2001). Consider, for example, a story Christina told about a visitor to the orphanage:

> This lady was *wonderful!* She was an Austrian lady and we used to call her Mother Moss. She used to come every Saturday and take us for nature walks and show us the plants—what was good to eat and what you couldn't eat—and I thought that was *such good knowledge*. So, when you used to get punished and they wouldn't give us dinner as a form of punishment, we used to go out into the woods and gather things and come back with so much stuff. We'd have a stomach ache by the time we'd come back. [both laugh]

From other stories I knew that the children in the orphanage were instructed to address the house parents as "Mother" and "Father," especially when visitors were present. However, of their own volition, many of them called the visitor "Mother Moss." Mother Moss was a kind, patient, and sensitive character who helped them to envisage a more enriching life on the outside.

Samantha was another woman to experience the benefits of an older woman in helping her to have faith in herself and hope for the future:

> There was a social worker that wasn't appointed to me that picked me up after the court hearing thing and helped me get back on my feet a bit.... She was it and a bit! ... She's wonderful. I still talk to her now.

This unappointed social worker "picked [her] up" and helped her get "back on [her] feet." Almost a decade later, they were still in contact. This is remarkable given the workload constraints that face most who work in child welfare agencies and the professional prohibition that it is not appropriate to have contact with ex-clients.

Summary

From the women's stories about early adulthood, I have found that women conceptualize love, sex, and romance in multiple, contradictory, and shifting ways, yet they do so within gendered, classed, and generational specific constraints. As I have suggested, as girls become women, they are usually given instructions about how women should express their feminine sexuality. Most have to navigate scripts for "good" and "bad" girls, which are modified over time and are often handed down by older women relatives and authority figures. For women forced to grow up in orphanages, group homes, and youth detention centres, the process of being inducted into womanhood can be especially harsh, whatever the generation. Nevertheless, some manage to find ways to convert themselves from orphans and state wards to respectable young ladies and enchanting brides.

Across the age and geographical board, many women I interviewed found that romantic love in novels, films, and scripts offered promising visions for the future and/or an escape from day-to-day drudgery. Many women told me about exciting times they had while they were dating in their early adult years. Some honestly believed that true love could deliver them lasting happiness. As I will elaborate further in the next chapter, some women reported experiencing exactly that: lasting happiness through their love relationships. However, many more, particularly those at risk of prematurely partnering because of the socio-cultural contexts of their lives, reported experiencing disappointment, depression, and trauma after they settled down.

> Emily: *There's a lot of people out there that want to be loved. Just loved. That's all they want—to be loved—nothing else.*

9
LOVE AND ABUSE IN ADULTHOOD
When Love Is (Not) the Answer

MANY PEOPLE EQUATE LIVING WITH LOVING and yearn to be loved in uncomplicated ways. From Emily's point of view, this should not be too much to ask. Yet, in the shadows of her insistence is her lament of how hard it was to achieve this simple dream.

In this chapter, I continue to analyze stories about love and abuse in adulthood. As with the previous two chapters, I look for connections between personal experiences and wider patterns that emerge in other research, especially the kind undertaken by feminists. As I do this, I continue to explore the main plots, characters, themes, and sexual scripts. I concentrate on love stories that involve sexual intimacy so as to ascertain the potential impact sexual love relationships can have on the women's lives. I analyze the language they used to speak about love because, as I have intimated earlier, people use talk to manage their identities and account for their actions in socially plausible ways (Frith & Kitzinger 1998).

To begin, I theorize how many women in Anglo-American-dominated societies are likely to develop and maintain their sexual love relationships. Because hope plays such a significant role in the maintenance of some of the women's love relationships, I refer to Berlant and Warner's (1998) concept of "heterosexual optimism." I pay attention to the popular fairytale love scripts such as finding "The One" and "Living Happily Ever after." I also inspect the "virtues" of loyalty and perseverance as they influence a good number of the women's love performances. In the second part of the chapter, I engage with feminist arguments about emotional work and domestic labour (Baines 2004; Hochschild 1983; Jamieson 1998; Langford 1999). I do this because many of the women told stories about feeling overly responsible for their relationships remaining intact. I argue that these feelings are not surprising given the dominance of discourses about women as society's "natural" homemakers and carers. I show that when women internalize high levels of felt responsibility, it can be extremely difficult for them to resists acts of male domination, especially those enacted by lovers.

Developing Love Relationships

As I have indicated in the previous chapters, love relationships tend to cohere around specific sets of stories (see Chapters 2 to 5). In many popular love stories, the plot is drawn from fairytale love. The plot of most fairytale love stories including those that have worked their way into many contemporary movies, songs, and romance novels revolve around the script of the "princess" (or woman protagonist) enduring some form of initial hardship before meeting, testing, and "living happily ever after" with her "prince" (Sternberg 1998; Walkerdine 1984; Wood 2001). Although such a story might sound whimsical, even flaky, its lure resides in the promise that it makes (especially to women) about the possibility they will have of leading a better life. According to fairytale love, this life will not be filled just with romance but also with certainty, security, and happiness. Alas, as I am about to discuss, in "real life," ordinary women's love lives rarely unfold in a simple, stable, or permanent manner.

Avoiding "Meaningless Relationships"

Many women talked to me about not wanting to get into "dead-end" or "meaningless" relationships. Christina was a good example of this. In the language of our grandmothers, she married "above her station," which meant that she married someone from a family with much more social status than her own. Given her "humble beginnings," this was quite an accomplishment. To my knowledge she is still married to this man and has enjoyed a financially secure and emotionally stable relationship with him. Some might call it lucky, but not Christina. She was adamant that her circumstances were built, not predestined or fateful. Yet, she was still romantic in so far as she was still enchanted by popular romance novels. Many years ago this interest helped her believe that true love was possible. Nevertheless, she was aware of the obstacles to transforming herself from "the poor orphan girl" to "the respectable middle-class married woman."

In a story called "Initial Bargaining Power," Christina explained how she tried to craft a better life for herself:

> I didn't want to get into meaningless relationships because I felt I really wanted to get my degree so that I'd never be dependent on anybody or any man for my own survival. So if I have a degree and a job, I can tell people to take a hike. I'm my own boss and I can take control over my life. It's only when you are a nothing—when you've got to depend on somebody else—and then you are saying, "I'm a victim, look at me. Victimize me more." And I knew that that would give me the control over my life that I knew I wanted....

Sticking to the script of "Highly Desirable Girl" while acquiring professional credentials, Christina cast herself as assertive, independent, and judicious, someone who was not going to be overcome by emotions. Ironically, such a portrait is a far cry from the traditional "romantic woman"—that is, a woman who is passive, emotional, and submissive. Instead, she navigated her way through her love of romance by using masculine discourses about rational citizenship and individual autonomy (see Pateman 1988; Plummer 2003; Young 1990). This was a clever but unusual move given that the two sets of discourses are usually pitted against each other, and it was not easy to achieve.

It can be hard to emotionally avail oneself of love while at the same time avoid having a "meaningless relationship." It can be hard to figure out in advance whether a relationship would end up being the real thing or a short-lived infatuation. Clues often exist, but for many of the women I spoke to, reading the signs sometimes felt like a crap shoot. For women who were unlikely to endure penalties for having a brief encounter, this was not such a problem. However, for a woman such as Christina, a brief encounter would jeopardize her sexual reputation. In turn, if her sexual reputation was sullied, she lowered her prospects for a good marriage.

While it may now seem absurd, heterosexual women who married and had children have long been expected to become men's dependants (Oakley 1981). Christina knew this, but still vowed never to become financially beholden to any man. She knew that breadwinners have long been positioned to lead, if not control their homemaking dependants (see Julius-Matthews 1984; Millett 1971; Oakley 1981). Yet she was determined to be responsible for her own survival so much so that she repeated the word "control" and placed it in opposition with being "a victim," which she equated with being out of control. She ended by saying that "I was determined I wasn't going to let someone get me into bed and spoil my life, you know."

Prizing Heterosexual Romance

Like many people I with whom I have spoken, Christina assumed that meaningful relationships were heterosexual, romantic, monogamous, and committed. Unless otherwise specified, heterosexuality is still typically represented as the norm (Westlund 1999). That is why Christina presumed that I would read the "someone" in the story above as male.

Yet heterosexuality is not a "single ideology nor a unified set of shared beliefs" (Berlant & Warner 1998, p. 548) but consolidated through a wide variety of practices that naturalize male-female sexual relations. Part of this consolidation is achieved through people subscribing to mainstream discourses about heterosexual romance (Rich 1980; Summers [1975] 1994; Ussher 1997). And as I have indicated in Chapter 2, heterosexual romance has been promoted from the medieval period right through to postmodernity (Evans 1998; Luhmann 1986). However, during modernity, dominant love discourses reinforced the idea that romance on its own was not enough. It was not sufficient because the popular script for "Having a Meaningful Relationship" required monogamy and commitment. And, as Overall (1998) pointed out, although the term "monogamy" was used historically to refer to a man being married to just one woman, it is now used to describe couples who profess sexual exclusivity to each other.

Even today, sexual fidelity (at least in the form of serial monogamy) is still represented as one of the hallmarks of "true" or "real" love. The majority of the women I interviewed thought this, believing that when a person was truly in love, she or he would not want to make love to anyone else. Some maintained, however, that fidelity was harder for men to achieve because they possessed a more active sexuality (see Fisher 1995). Others protested that this assumption was sexist, with some declaring they were as sexually motivated, if not more, than their male counterparts.

Crossing ages, religions, and classes, the women questioned many beliefs about heterosexual romance. Some women agreed with Gergen and Gergen (1988), who claimed that women were most advantaged by the long-term commitment of marriage, and that marriage offers women a way to control their male intimates (see Gergen & Gergen 1988). Others made the counter-argument that men benefited most from marriage because exclusivity and marriage were instituted to help men feel more confident that their offspring were theirs. Still others dismissed marriage outright or celebrated it as a way for equal partners to come together (see Chapters 10 and 11). For all their differences, all accepted that heterosexual romance was the most socially and culturally prized form of intimacy, even if they were not the least bit interested in it.

Believing in Love and Convincing Others

From Christina's point of view, my deconstruction of marriage was not the least bit interesting. Politely waiting for me to finish, she joined many other women who argued that heterosexual romance offered women many benefits. Most of the benefits cited related to women having the chance to escape from the "dating game" (Denzin 1991); find a place in which they might belong; and a route through which they could be "respectable" (Julius-Matthews 1984; Oakley 1981; Summers [1975] 1994).

Yet for women like Christina, who were in low socio-economic circumstances, these achievements were not automatic. Spousal selection was important, as Christina explained:

> I felt he believed in me and what I wanted to do. That was important to me; that a person was in love with my mind rather than my looks. [laughs] Not that I'm saying that I'm not good looking, but, you know.... And that was really good for me because he's really tall and I'm really short and anyone who looked at us thought ... well, his family thought he could have made a better choice, you know, but now they realize that I am [the] best choice for him and they don't stop telling me that....

Providing a living example of how women can be advised to date and mate, Christina knew at a relatively young age that she should be strategic about her choice of mate. She looked for a man who would love her not only for her looks but also for her mind and the things she wanted to do. Without mentioning it directly, she knew that women's physical attractiveness is a highly valued aspect of heterosexual relationships (Ussher 1997; Wolf 1990). She also looked for someone who supported what she wanted to do because she knew how easily women's goals can be eclipsed by their husbands (Greer 1999; Kingston 2004; Kollantai 1972; Oakley 1981; Summers [1975] 1994). Taking care to seek out a partner with whom she could connect, she modified traditional sexual scripts that underestimate heterosexual women's interest in developing intellectual intimacy with their partners (Jamieson 1998).

Christina also showed how we can entertain contradictory ideas about love, and how we can move back and forth between conventional and alternative discourses. For instance, while she blurred the boundary between the mind and the body, she used the conventional tall/short opposition to reinforce the idea that opposites are attracted to one another. Wanting to be loved for her mind did not mean that she wasn't "good-looking." What she did have to struggle with was how to reverse her middle-class in-laws' concern that she was not a suitable choice of bride. As she expressed in the next story, her orphanage background needed to be managed. Mostly it involved her going beyond what would normally be expected of a bride by inspiring her husband to do more through her own example:

> Like, when I met my husband and I fell in love, his family were not that happy really, when you come to think of it. My mother-in-law told me

that "You seemed to have doped my son. He's head over heels in love with you." And I said, "What do you mean? I'm just as equal as he is." And he follows in my footsteps. I've done my master's years ago and he's just finishing his. I'm doing something else. I've inspired him a lot. He's done so much more with his life than he would have ever done if he'd never met me. He would never have done so much.

Taken in their entirety, Christina's stories indicate how she has successfully traversed some of the challenges of contemporary married life. To some extent, Christina was optimistic that her hopes and dreams would turn out well given the obstacles in her way.

Heterosexual Optimism

With many possible manifestations, heterosexual optimism (Berlant & Warner 1998) is the hope that everything will fall into place if there is enough love in the relationship. Sometimes it is expressed when people say, "See? It can work!" In this study I talked to women who had adopted this view, irrespective of whether the odds of it eventuating were weighted in their favour. Take, for instance, Dallas, who talked about her relationship with her second husband:

> I didn't know that Gill would turn out to be a complete and utter arsehole like he did. [pause] Maybe it was only at the start, when he was drinking, that he'd lay into me. But then when he was on a binge, I knew what that meant. But then when he wasn't on a binge, he was a completely different person. And that's how it went for the next six years.... I think I was *totally smitten*. [pause] I had what lots of other girls wanted. Yeah ... it's not that I consciously wanted the other girls to be jealous that didn't even enter my head. Um, I suppose it was that I had somebody tall, dark, and handsome. [both laugh]

Dallas's optimism was striking given the high rates of unhappy heterosexual unions (Melucci 1996; Oakley 1981; Scutt 1990; Westlund 1999) and the fact that her first marriage ended because of violence. Her optimism is also evident by the surprise she expressed at the way her second husband turned out. After struggling to remember when his abuse began, she reached for the popular discourse that holds alcohol responsible for violence. By depicting him as a "completely different person" when he was drunk, she was able to de-personalize the assaults he inflicted on her. This also helped her to deflect the possibility that he was like the many other men who treat "their women" in a similar fashion (Astbury 1996; Scutt 1990; Westlund 1999). It was a move that helped her to retain the hope that marriage as an institution could benefit women.

I was interested in learning more about how Dallas sustained her sense of optimism through the six years of abuse, so I asked her whether sexual desire played a role. She said it did, that she was "totally smitten" by Gill. Far from being an idiosyncratic expression, "being smitten" is part of the popular vernacular of falling in love. With its heightened sexual excitation and promise that dreams *can* come true, being smitten appeals to many people, including some feminists (Gornick 1997; Jackson 1999; Walkerdine 1984). Part of the appeal is the permission it gives to otherwise sensible people to engage in acts that others perceive as madness (see Chapter 2). For Dallas this was the case. Also, with "girls falling at his feet," her proximity to his popularity elevated her social status (also see Benjamin 1988; Oakley 1981; Summers [1975] 1994). Having admitted this, Dallas wanted me to know that she had not consciously intended to whip up other women's jealousy. In so doing, she prompted me to think about the largely second wave feminist concern expressed about the potential for men to induce rivalry among heterosexual women.

Often constructed as each other's competitors, women are stereotypically portrayed as fighting over men. With such rivalry jeopardizing, if not eliminating, the possibility of women joining together to share friendship and join with one another in the fight against male dominance, heterosexual relationships have long been seen to possess the potential to isolate women further and make them more susceptible to men's violent regulation of their territory. This is certainly what many radical feminists have maintained over the years (see, for instance, Bell & Klein 1996; Bunch 1978; Dworkin 1997; Firestone 1970; Jeffreys [1985] 1997), yet Dallas's analysis did not extend this far. She was thinking about the pleasure she got from falling in love with a man who was "tall, dark, and handsome." We both laughed at this point because we recognized it was a line from the script of fairytale love.

Being Captivated by "The One"

Many people find fairytale love so enchanting because the banalities and complexities of life are nowhere to be found (Sternberg 1998). With its happy-ever-after finale, the curtain usually falls on fairytale love stories at the point of marriage. Not only does this shroud our understanding of how such relationships are sustained, but it also re-inscribes the belief that marriage will deliver lasting happiness.

In the story called "That Was My Role," Cecilia talked about the views she held when she married her first husband in her late teens and describes her past attempts to emulate the classic script for "The Good Wife and Mother" (Westlund 1999):

> That was my role: being feminine, caring and *succumbing*. And then beyond all of that, that would be good because someone would look after me. If I did all of those things and I was *good* if I was a *good woman* and a good person then I'd find someone to look after me.

When she was a young woman, Cecilia believed that if she were "good," she would be rewarded by someone loving, cherishing, and protecting her. Now, as a woman in her forties, however, she believed that this was a sweet but naively optimistic view for her to have held. Yet at other times in the interview, she was not so critical of romantic ideals. Take, for instance, the story she told me about falling in love with her first husband:

> It was like he was "The One" because I admired his musicianship. He taught instruments and I admired a lot of things about him. I admired that he was so handsome and so tall, and so, um, a very gentle personality.

Cecilia's use of the term "The One" is culturally loaded and historically significant. In Anglo-American cultures, the discourse of "The One" is predicated on the idea that destiny unites lovers who are meant to be together. This discourse is most closely associated with romantic and chivalrous expressions of heterosexuality (see Langford 1999). For Cecilia, the discourse of "The One" was useful because it combined the admiration she felt about his musical talents with the pleasure she got from him being "so handsome and so tall." As she spoke, I anticipated that she was going to tell me how Warren was a "gentle[man]" who made her happy, but I was wrong.

Yet, as Cecilia tried to emulate the role of "good wife and mother," she found happiness elusive. Instead she felt isolated and depressed, and not because Warren had been mean or cruel to her, but more diffusely because their marriage was failing to deliver the life that she had hoped. We talked quite a lot about this. For Cecilia, marriage represented an emotional haven, one that she desperately wanted, especially since most of her childhood had been so emotionally impoverished. For Warren, however, marriage was meant to offer him a stable home, one that he could return to without feeling under pressure to perform. It would be a place where he could relax rather than engage in emotional discussions, which to him seemed unnecessary and foreign. Over time, these differences created a gulf between them. Separating was not easy. I got the impression that both of them had trouble giving up on their relationship because there was no abuse, not even hostility. Instead, there was sadness and shame. For Warren, it hinged on the fact that this was his second marriage and he had yet to turn 30. For Cecilia, it was due to the fact that she had cast him as "The One."

Cecilia was not the only woman I spoke to who had trouble severing ties with someone cast as "The One." As I have suggested in previous chapters, the discourse of love conquering all is often used to reinforce gender-specific sexual scripts that urge women to demonstrate hope, loyalty, and endurance. Often reinforced by religious doctrines, the scripts for "Love Conquering All" promote the idea that when women display enough love, they are able to change their spouses and their situations so that they can enjoy a happy ending (Hey 1997;

Pipher 1995; Ussher 1997). However, as Langford (1999) contends, many of these discourses not only encourage women to surrender to love, they also call for them to surrender themselves to their husbands' authority (see Doyle 2000).

In Search of a Happy Life

Although many of the participants in this study did not surrender themselves to the authority of male intimates, many were captivated by fairy tale love, at least for some period of time. Many were captivated by the promise of leading a happy life, and some reported that they had experienced exactly this. For some women, such as Karen and Linda, the love they shared with a sexual partner enabled them to feel blessed. Others evoked the cliché of "just knowing" that he or she was right for them, and noting how it had grown over the years (also see Chapter 9). Vera, however, struggled to sustain this feeling. In the story called "A Happy Life," Vera reflected on her marriage to Dan:

> I think everybody thinks that when they get married they're going to have a happy life. We had such a happy life to begin with. It was sad it ended up the way that it did. I think circumstances changed us. I always hoped that he could get over his alcohol problem. Um, like most people, I went to Al-Anon to learn how to cope with it, but basically the alcoholic has to learn how to do it for themselves.

Vera's assumption that everybody thought that marriage would deliver lasting happiness was one of the reasons why she felt so sad that her marriage "end[ed] up the way that it did." I listened quietly at this point because I was aware that many women feel uncomfortable criticizing their partners publicly. I am also aware, as Jamieson (1998, p. 145) wrote, that many women "work at suppressing their discontent in order to sustain their marriage." Notably, Vera blamed the deterioration of their marriage on "circumstances," not on her husband. This was telling given I already knew that Dan frequently resorted to violence in his attempts to dominate her and their children.

Like Dallas, Vera blamed Dan's drinking for their marital discord. She had hoped that he would have been able to "get over his alcohol problem" because, in her view, this was the source of their unhappiness. This never happened. With no mention of his violence, she then revealed how responsible she felt for his drinking. It motivated her to go to Al-Anon even though he had no interest in attending Alcoholics Anonymous.

The more I inspected Vera's transcript, the more I found stories about high levels of felt responsibility, irrespective of whether the dilemmas or problems were within her control. For instance, in the story "Making It Better," she said:

> I used to get depressed, but I felt sad that I couldn't make things better for everybody. That was the sad part that I couldn't make things right,

that I couldn't make the children feel happy with their father. I couldn't make them feel happy with their friends, not feeling embarrassed by their father. And I couldn't make him feel happy with his life. And all during this time, all I could do was pay the bills and go to work, like I was sort of a machine.

Vera correlated her sense of responsibility for trying to "make" Dan and their children "happy" with her feelings of depression. She remembered feeling like this "all during this time," which I knew from other stories lasted for more than a decade. Compared to the halcyon days of their courtship, her depressive feelings corroded the hopes she had about the situation changing and destabilized her faith in romance, reminding me that:

> ... depression might be regarded as a potent social metaphor that directs attention to an emotional state in which it feels impossible for one's unhappiness ever to be transformed, acted on or acknowledged within the dominant discourse. (Astbury 1996, p. 29)

Vera's depression related to the impotence she felt at not being able to effect the necessary changes in her family life, even though she was working like some "sort of a machine." Running counter to the image of romantic love, these dehumanizing and lonely images fit neatly with her attempts to service the family unit. They also relate to two dominant theories of love that continue to circulate.

Servicing Love Relationships

In Western capitalist societies, people often use a mixture of economic and mechanical metaphors to represent the social organization of love. Many speak of love operating through a series of exchanges, deals, and transactions (Langford 1999). Accordingly, quite a few believe that after the initial honeymoon phase of falling in love, relationships are sites of investment and work (see Duncombe & Marsden 1993).

In many popular accounts, gambling metaphors are used to locate love within the discourse of the free market. In this discourse, love is often seen to contain many opportunities, but also costs. Lovers are often portrayed as those who play the odds, are lucky or unlucky, winners or losers, and who sometimes cheat or are cheated on. Encouraging people to be strategically competitive, this set of discourses often holds individuals responsible for love that has gone wrong. Sitting closely beside these metaphors are those based on a system's perspective of love. From this perspective, individuals are urged to use love to maximize the functioning of their family unit, yet they are also expected to prevent love relationships from breaking down or becoming too costly (Westlund 1999).

A Labour of Love

Underlying both the exchange and systemic perspectives of love is the assumption that relationships need to be serviced and managed. Although it is possible to use either frame to advance a democratic model of love, they are most often used to endorse conventional heterosexual relations that are based on gender asymmetry (Jamieson 1998; Kingston 2004; Langford 1999). Ironically, asymmetrical gender roles are not seen to negatively impact on the negotiating power each party will be able to exercise. Instead, mainstream psychological texts, along with many popular self-help books, usually assume that heterosexual love relationships will be staged fairly and brokered by roughly equal partners (see J. Gray 1993, 1996). With this assumption in place, these perspectives have a tendency of obscuring love's relationship with power (Jamieson 1998; Langford 1999). On the occasions when power differentials between the sexes are identified in mainstream accounts of romantic love, there is the tendency for gender asymmetry to be re-inscribed as a functional product of the "naturally different" roles that men and women are "meant" to occupy (see Baines 2004; Jackson 1998).

From a structural functionalist point of view, both men and women are allegedly advantaged if they complement each other's different areas of expertise (Oakley 1981; also see Chapter 4). Traditionally, this system of complementarity involves men assuming responsibility for activities in the public realm and women assuming responsibility for managing activities in the private sphere (Greer 1999; Segal 1999). As I have already indicated, this model emerged in many of the women's stories, yet it was Vera who pointed to it most poignantly when she told me how her relationship with her husband changed when she stayed home to look after their small children.

> I had no rights then because I wasn't working. I had no voice. I couldn't—we were going to buy a house together and we had one wage and the wage earner had made the decision. It was a bit hard for me to accept because I was used to being able to share in decisions.

Vera was not the only one to believe that voting rights in families were earned through the financial contributions made through paid labour. This idea stems from the cultural discourses about citizenship and property ownership. In line with much orthodox thinking, Vera defined work as income-generating labour. When she stopped receiving a salary her rights were revoked and she lost her "voice." As the only wage earner, Dan would now decide where they would live and which house they would buy. From Vera's choice of words and also the tone that she used, I understood that Dan's decisions were final.

I have already suggested that Vera internalized more than her share of responsibility for her family's needs. Again, she was not alone, especially when she was not a wage earner. In varying degrees, many of the women I interviewed in Australia and Canada believed that it was normal for women to behave in this way. Consider, for instance, Kim (33 years old) whose first husband told her that while he was the breadwinner, their finances were none of her business. Her protests fell on deaf ears. Arguably, she and other women tolerate these conditions because,

> Growing up as a woman in modern Western societies involves learning a language of the emotions, sensitivity to cues about others' feelings, and a fluency in emotional storytelling.... Women are not only expected to care for and care about those they have intimate relationships with, they are also expected to take care of the relationship itself, to perform the "emotional labour" necessary to ensure its continued viability. (Jackson 1998, pp. 59–60)

Making a House a Home

Culturally, women are expected to display high levels of emotional fluency. This is why many heterosexual women across the Western world continue to assume more responsibility than their male spouses for making their relationships work (Jamieson 1998; Langford 1999; Young 1997). Most visible when it is not performed—or not performed well—emotional labour is often associated with being cast into the role of the "backstage person" (Burns 1994; Langford 1999; Waring 1999).

Traditionally, women have been scripted to be the person behind the scenes. They have been encouraged to pay special attention to the emotional and physical interior of their homes. During modernity, in particular, women were expected to create a warm, nurturing, and well-organized home that allowed family members to retreat from the hostilities of the outside capitalist world (Millett 1971). In postmodernity, these expectations have continued to circulate despite the much greater involvement of women in the paid workforce, and even among women who have few happy memories of home during childhood (Young 1997). Deangelis (2001, p. 362) echoed this sentiment in her text, *What Women Want Men to Know*, when she claimed that "Women think of love as our job. So the more information you give a woman the more we can make an effort to fulfil your desires."

From the 84 interviews I conducted, I heard that, to a large extent, family homes were still idealized as places where family members are able to rest and recharge, yet, given the disproportionate amount of duties that women are still expected to carry out in their homes, it is not a place of rest for many women. Take, for instance, Chloe, a 30-year-old woman in Winnipeg in full-time employment, who described herself as happily married for 15 years, but still said,

> I guess I probably do 75 percent of home stuff, family stuff.... I think that he should probably pick up more of the slack, but I know it's not

really gonna happen. Like, his dad did zero, so I think I've made him progress a lot more, just 'cause his dad was very old school.

Unlike Chloe, who resigned herself to doing more housework, Monica, a 50-year-old woman who recently divorced, talked about how this double standard became intolerable, particularly when her husband stopped making any contributions at home, including the minor repairs around the house. She said:

> If you do enough on your own for long enough when you're in a relationship, you'll eventually wonder why you're in it, especially if you're doing most of the housework.

Unfairness was not Monica's only concern. Her husband's refusal to help out around the house coincided with his emotional withdrawal from their relationship and her escalating sense of loneliness. She was angry because in her view, she did not expect him to be very active on either the domestic or emotional home front anyway. Monica's gnawing isolation eventually precipitated her decision to leave. During the dinner she served me while the tape recorder was playing, she talked about preferring to be on her own rather than be lonely with a spouse. In part, she was talking about the relief of no longer having to shoulder the lion's share of the emotional work (also see Burns 1994).

In her classic study, Hochschild (1983) coined the term "emotional work" to refer to the work that is often unpaid, invisible, and unrecognized. Using Hochschild's (1983) ideas, Frith and Kitzinger (1998, p. 300) contended that:

> The concept of "emotion work" maps readily onto women's allegedly greater facility with emotions the feminine capacity to console and comfort, flatter, cajole, persuade and seduce and reflects women's purportedly greater emotional sensitivity and responsiveness.

Hochschild (1983) built her analysis across the paid and unpaid labour divide. She argued that "emotion(al) work" is a code name for "women's work." It is not easy work to perform given it involves "soothing tempers, boosting confidence, fuelling pride, preventing frictions, and mending ego wounds" (Frith & Kitzinger 1998, p. 300). With no guarantee of success and a good chance of being held responsible for emotional interventions that fail, many women understand all too clearly that it is they who are most likely to be blamed if domestic discord eventuates. Many women were also well aware that the traditional family home is commonly a place in which women may need refuge (Jackson 1996; Jamieson 1998; Kingston 2004; Langford 1999; Scutt 1990; Westlund 1999).

Most of the women I interviewed—of whom very few identified as feminists—said they did a lot more than 50 percent of the emotional and domestic labour in their homes. About 15 of the 84 reported some kind of abuse (physical, emotional, financial, and/or sexual) in current relationships. Many more had experienced violence in childhood or in previous relationships. For the women who had been subjected to physical violence from spouses, most noted that it followed a longer process of being emotionally shut down, devalued, and discredited. Emily provided a good example of this in a story called "Away in the Camper Van for Eight Weeks":

> I went to Brisbane with him in a camper van with seven kids. My youngest was only six weeks old when we left. It was his long service leave and he wanted to go there. All I did was clean the kids and feed them. I had two in nappies [diapers] well, three really, that would stay with me. He'd take the others and I'd have to stay home. I had to wash. I had to do all this. You can just imagine, with all the nappies. Anyway, he couldn't understand why I didn't enjoy it.

Emily's repeated use of the expression "I had to" indicated that she felt compelled to abide by her husband's authority. In spite of her protests, Lester refused to budge on how the "holiday" would be spent. If she "bucked up," she knew she ran the risk of him being physically violent.

Similar to Emily, Colleen (36 years old and from Winnipeg) talked about her husband returning to the trailer in which she and their three boys lived while he was away working. After he was away for more than a month at a time, and often without sending any money home, he would return, expecting her to do little more than nurture him. She said that if she refused, it would take only a couple of days before he would abuse her, both physically and sexually. Sometimes she plucked up the courage to challenge his behaviour. She said that at these times he would lash out at her, claiming she "induced" the violence by not being "a good enough wife." It was a statement that would ring in her ears for many years to come. Eventually it prompted her to divorce him before developing a much more equitable sexual relationship with someone else.

Wanting the Load to Be Shared

The vast majority of the women I interviewed longed for the load to be shared, particularly as they got older. However, I noticed that this was much easier to achieve for the younger heterosexual women who had formed relationships with male partners who did not subscribe to traditional gender roles. The most promising democratic, fairly shared, and emotionally engaged relationships seemed to eventuate when male partners did not assume—even inadvertently—that certain tasks *should* be carried out by women, or vice versa. Bette (28 years old) talked about this at length.

Bette told me stories about striking up a fair and equitable relationship with her partner, but then finding that "cracks" began to appear. She cited the example of her partner expecting her to take care of all the birthday and

Christmas cards for his relatives as well as her own. She said that while appreciative of her partner's openness to gender equality, she was disappointed that she had to explain to him why this expectation was not fair. Yet, her disappointment melted away when he accepted what she said without argument or fuss, and stopped assuming that gifts and cards were women's work. Given the non-verbal language she used to tell this story, I think she was also underlining the point that change is possible, even change that faces obstacles and setbacks.

At least 20 of the 84 women I interviewed told me stories about how they actively resisted the traditional role of women needing to be responsible for others' emotional needs. Annie (30 years old) talked about how she would boycott certain activities if they became designated as "women's work." Lou (28 years old) and Lisa (24 years old) did similarly, holding their positions until partners and relatives got the message. Sasha (21 years old) reported far fewer problems:

> Like, we kind of just—somehow everything gets done, but there's no, like, specific division of labour. There's no, like, "You have to do this. You have to take out the garbage. You have to cut the lawn. There's not really a division of labour there. Like, if I need help with something, he'll help out. And if he needs help with something, I'll help him out.... It's flexible.

Other women told me that while not all protests were victorious, some attempt to stand up for their rights was productive, if for no other reason that it helped to remind family members that they were human beings who also needed space and time to explore their own interests. Forty-two-year-old Donna from Ottawa spoke to this:

> You let it go. You let it go. You let it go. But sometimes you just have to stand up for yourself because otherwise no one notices.

Not having domestic work noticed was a regular theme in many of the women's stories. Over and again I heard stories about how women protested against unfair domestic responsibilities. I also heard how often they were not always successful in achieving the complete redistribution of labour that they had hoped. Yet, most found that, to varying degrees, improvements did eventuate. In other words, most of the women who engaged in such a struggle said it was worth it. A couple of women even talked about being pleasantly surprised about how their partners and children started to pick up some of the slack. One woman said she was kicking herself for not insisting earlier that they share the load, noting that when pressed, her husband took responsibility for his share of dropping off and collecting the children at their respective schools. She was particularly delighted at the way he so cheerfully integrated it into his schedule and how much pleasure he and the children derived from it.

Being Stonewalled

Unfortunately, not all women reported having partners who were willing to hear their claims of unfairness, whether they related to domestic or emotional labour. For some of the women, their partners (male or female) were depicted as "cold," "stony," or "distant." While some found this meant they had to work hard at improving communication, others found such stances were nearly impossible to penetrate. Annie, a woman in her twenties, experienced this in the first year of her marriage:

> In the first year we were married, I would get really mad when Jeremy [husband] always stalked off when we were having a fight. It would make me really mad that he would leave because I had more to say.

Unlike Annie, who was later able to engage her husband in emotional discussions, Diana, a woman in her thirties, found that over time, her husband refused to talk about their relationship. At first she tried to attribute this to his gender:

> It's very difficult. Men just seem to have a totally different mindset when it comes to love and relationships. They look at it so different. It's almost like they're emotionally detached. Well, my husband is anyway. He just doesn't like to discuss the emotional aspects of relationships.

Attempts to engage in relationship discussions are often illustrative of a deep commitment to making the relationship work. Emily, a woman in her fifties, reported a more extreme situation in which her husband would refuse to discuss the violence he was perpetrating against her and the children:

> I used to say to him, "Just come and sit down and let's talk." And he'd sit down and I'd say, "Can't we talk about this?" And he'd shove the chair back like that and he'd get up, stomp out of there, slam the back door as he'd say, "I don't want to talk to you!" And that's how it would go, *for years*.

Like so many women I interviewed and have worked with as a social worker, Emily wanted the violence to end, not her marriage. The problem was how she would do this. She told me she knew she had failings and could be annoying. She realized that these relationship talks were not always easy. She often felt scared that she would provoke his violence if she persisted with her attempts. It was only after her relationship ended that she could see how, paradoxically, how these attempts could obscure his responsibility for violence. Through the domestic violence support group she attended, she came to the conclusion that by trying to get him to talk in this way, she had inadvertently allowed his violence to be framed as *their* relationship difficulties. Yet, even through this framing of the situation, her husband would not talk. By refusing to talk to her and then subjecting her to lengthy periods of the silent treatment, his behaviour used classic tactics of stonewalling.

From her research in Britain, Langford (1999) noted that many heterosexual women complained about their husbands' or partners' emotional unavailability, especially their refusal to talk about the relationship. Along with discussions about the sharing of domestic labour, many methods were deployed. Some of these methods included: deferring or stalling discussions, minimizing the women's complaints, making promises that they had no intention of keeping, using these complaints at a later date to suggest that the women were "nagging," and/or accusing them of being mentally ill (also see Astbury 1996; Langford 1999; McKenzie 2006; Westlund 1999). Taken together, stonewalling tactics can be used to out-manoeuvre partners with less authority or status by discrediting their claims and re-instituting asymmetry (Langford 1999).

Perceptions of Oppression

Over the years, Emily's relationship with Lester became increasingly asymmetrical. In a story called "He Couldn't See It," she was ruminating about the hold she felt he had over her:

> You see, he had this *power*. I don't know what it was. It was like *control power*. He had it with the whole family—the whole lot, even my sister. [pause] Everything I did for him—even though I would have been one of the best housewives, the best mother, the best wife for a husband, and all that—*he couldn't see it*. He could only see ... I'd say to him, "You won't let me out. I've got nothing to talk about. I'm just a housewife that's a boring housewife that's got nothing in common with anyone."

Emily said that she was not the only person to defer to her husband's "power," yet, rather than be infuriated by this, she expressed most annoyance at his refusal to acknowledge that she was doing her best to be a good wife and mother. Without finishing her sentence, I got the impression that she believed that all he could see were her faults and failings. Ironically, her protest came not in the name of liberty but because she did not want to become "a boring housewife."

Expressed in a variety of ways in popular women's magazines and talk shows, the discourse of "the boring housewife" is often used to advise women against "letting themselves go" by becoming uninteresting to men by talking only about the minutiae of their life at home (Ehrenreich & English 1978). Even though such a discourse reinforces traditional gender arrangements, it did not seem to awaken any sympathy in Lester. In Emily's view, this was because his "control power" was built upon her staying at home and making herself available for his service.

Placating others and servicing their needs are themes that emerged in a few stories that Samantha told. In the story "People Call Me the Oppressed Woman," I was trying to ascertain how much domestic responsibility she usually accepted when she lived with men:

> *Samantha:* I did, um, people call me the "oppressed woman." [both of us laughed] I did all the oppressed woman stuff. I did the cooking and the cleaning, the vacuuming and the washing. And I still do [both of us laugh], yeah.
> *Heather:* Did you feel oppressed?
> *Samantha: No, God no!* [pause] But after a while, a little bit.
> *Heather:* Taken for granted?
> *Samantha:* A *lot* taken for granted because he started drinking a lot.

Having studied social work at university, Samantha knew that despite the measured tone I used, the question I was asking was deeply politicized. This was why she decided to pre-empt any negative reaction I might have had by suggesting that when others heard about what she did in the house, they were likely to call her "an oppressed woman." It was an unexpected and provocative comment that prompted us both to laugh, perhaps because we could see the irony in others labelling her as oppressed.

All jokes aside, I was interested in hearing whether Samantha felt oppressed. At first she said, *"No, God no!"* Yet, in the silence of the conversation, she pondered the question a little more and very quietly opted for being "taken for granted" when Tom was "drinking a lot." With Emily, it is interesting that she did not challenge the assumption that she *should* have to do the bulk of the housework. Instead, her demands were far more modest. Mostly, she wanted Tom to recognize her efforts in the household, and when he was drinking, this was unlikely.

For all her feistiness, Samantha joined many other women I interviewed who might be seen to "lapse into being-for-others." Working with some of de Beauvoir's (1972) ideas, Weir (1996, p. 46) wrote that:

> ... women's lapse into being-for-others is typical of romantic love. In love, man reaffirms himself and his own "sovereign subjectivity" through experiencing and being recognized by another; woman does not reaffirm herself, but abandons herself to love, to the experience of loving and of being loved. He remains and affirms himself; she is other, self-less, relative.

By their own accounts, Dallas, Vera, Emily, and Samantha's partners used violence and coercion to regulate their behaviour. Each woman feared that if she terminated their relationship, the repercussions would include more than being socially shunned or financially disadvantaged. Even though the word "oppression" was not one that they either felt familiar with or comfortable using to describe their situations, this is what it seemed to me.

As Mullaly (2002) argued, oppression is a relational concept that describes injustice that individuals suffer as a result of their membership within a particular group or category of people. Typically, oppressed individuals are those who are denied rights that the dominant group takes for granted; assigned a second-class citizenship; blocked from opportunities to self-develop; and excluded from full participation in society (Mullaly 2002). Because all of these forms of oppression are evident in the stories that Dallas, Vera, Emily, Jesobel, and Samantha told, they may be viewed as oppressed, at least at particular times in their lives.

Although questions surrounding the extent or degree to which the women may be seen as oppressed have utility, I believe the concept of oppression is still worthwhile given that few other terms capture the systematic forms of injustice that particular groups of people experience. It is also useful because it reminds us that heterosexual relationships can be exceedingly difficult for women to negotiate.

Not Giving up Too Easily

Many of the women I interviewed told me stories about the abuse they had suffered at the hands of male intimates, particularly after their relationships were cemented through living together or marriage. The fear of being seen as a failure and/or someone who gave up too easily weighed heavily on more than a few. Jesobel, a forty-year-old Aboriginal-Canadian professional woman, provided a good example. She talked about her ex-husband:

> After we got married, it was almost as if I became his property. I remember the first time he hit me.... He had told me that I couldn't talk to someone and I just looked at him and I said, "I think not." *And he hit me.* I was just so taken aback by it that I started to laugh ... and then he hit me harder and then it began to escalate. He used to do really cruel things....

Once she realized that she was embroiled in a violent relationship, Jesobel did what Emily and Vera and some of the other women did not do—she identified his cruelty early on and found that her feelings of love for him rapidly waned. Nevertheless, she felt compelled to endure it for a "respectable" period:

> *Jesobel:* Even though my sister and my friends were so against this marriage, I was willing to work on it for one year.... At this point I couldn't even stand him because I was just so hurt. I think I knew I had let myself down, so I was willing to live with this son of a gun for an entire year so I could say to them, "Oh it didn't work." But after a year.

Heather: Hmm, so you could say, "I gave it a year."

Jesobel: Yeah, but after seven months, two days, that was it. We were in the van driving along and he said, "I could take you out to the country and I could shoot you in the face, and make sure you'd never be found." And you know what? He could have done it.

With fear for her safety overcoming her desire to endure the marriage for at least for a year, Jesobel separated from her husband. While recovering from the violence her partner had inflicted, she gradually felt able to talk to friends and family members about what had gone on. She said she was surprised to learn that others had already seen his potential for violence:

> I never said this to anyone, but my sister told me something really interesting later on. She said that for quite a while after we were married, she used to think that if anything ever happened to me—if I died even crossing the street and was hit by a car—she'd know it was him. She would absolutely know that he had something to do with it. Or if I dropped dead of a heart attack, she would know. She'd want all kinds of tests taken because she'd know that he had something to do with it. She said he was just that dangerous to me.

Caught in the difficult position of not wanting to poison Josobel against her new husband, her sister suppressed her anxieties about how dangerous she felt her brother-in-law could be. However, when Jesobel separated from him, her sister was finally able to speak her mind without fear of condemnation.

Brutality and Submission

As I have indicated, some of the women in this study experienced physical, emotional, and sexual brutality from their male spouses. Westlund (1999, p. 1046) explained that:

> It is not uncommon for a woman to attempt to end the violence by trying, for quite some time, to align her behaviour more closely to the perceived demands of the batterer.

Even when this does not work, women are often loath to reveal the full extent of the problem, and in some instances, attempts may be made to rationalize the perpetrator's actions (McKenzie 2006). Jesobel provided a good example of this. As much as she was able to wrestle herself away from her violent spouse, the time it took her to do so was significant as Jesobel explained:

Well, I was watching TV and went to the bathroom and I lived in a very historic home and they were doing some work on the back stairs, so there was pounding all day, so I didn't pay much attention to it. I went to the bathroom and I was going back to the kitchen and dining room, and all of a sudden I realized it was the door and the door flew open. The next thing, *I'm flying through the air.* He had just got out of jail and was kicking me and punching me. Then he dragged me by my leg into the kitchen and took a butcher's knife and sat on my back and pulled my hair. He was holding my neck up and he had the knife at my throat and told me he was going to kill me. And to this day, I don't know how it happened, but it was like everything slowed down, slowed down totally and I thought of Alice and Alana and Carlena, and all these people, my sisters, who loved me and who'd expect me to be around. And I just said to him in a very calm voice, "Randy, get off my back. I can't breathe." *And he did.* He got off and he went walking into the living room. I got up and I walked out the door. And when I was leaving, there was a plumber coming up the stairs and I asked him to call the police, 911. And he looked at me and I guess my face was pretty, pretty messy, and called right away. I went down in the basement and the plumber stood up in the stairwell until the police got there. And believe it or not, *I went back to him.* After he had broken a bone in my arm and I was in Osborne House [a women's shelter] for about nine days, *I went back to him.* And to this day, I don't know what the hell I was thinking of. *I went back to him.*

Jesobel was still confused about what drove her to return to such a violent man after all that he did to her. Her outrage at herself seemed more palpable than the rage she felt toward the man who held the knife against her throat and threatened to kill her. As she spoke, I knew that she would have preferred to pretend that the whole incident had not happened. Having worked in the field of domestic violence for many years, I also knew that rather than narrate stories about how she was victimized, she would rather concentrate her efforts on her career and other achievements. Yet, here she was, years later and now safely ensconced in a loving relationship, recounting abuse stories to an unknown researcher.

Eroticized Dominance

Jesobel was not the only one to feel ashamed at having been abused. Irrespective of their age, many people feel this shame. For women (heterosexual or lesbian), the act of disclosing abuse by loved ones is complicated by the assumptions often made about them, particularly if they remain involved with their abusers (Burke Draucker 1999). Although they were not necessarily able to name it as such, many women in abusive relationships realized the ease in which they could be described as masochistic (also see Chapter 4). Concerned about how her stories could be interpreted, Samantha talked about the numerous incidents when her second common-law spouse, Michael, was physically and sexually coercive:

> He used to like having threesomes with another guy. It used to turn him on when I used to go and pick someone else up for him.... He was always first. And there was this other bloke and all this other stuff. The first two times it was like *fantasy land* type thing, but he had to keep doing it. He kept wanting me to do it.

Samantha built this story by describing how Michael instigated the threesome. While the other man watched, Michael would be the first to orally and/or vaginally penetrate her. As she spoke, I was reminded of the image of women being sexually "ridden" by men as if they are bicycles (see Chapter 7). In the next few lines the plot of Samantha's story became more complicated. At the start she consented to threesomes because she found them erotic. However, after satisfying this "fantasy," she found herself even more tangled up in Michael's demands.

In the story called "The Birthday Present," Samantha explained why she found it hard to refuse Michael's sexual demands:

> Like, he'd want me to give his cousin a head job for his birthday because he'd never had sex before and stuff like this. And I'm like, "That's really sicko stuff." And the awful thing was I'd do it because I'd get a beating if I didn't later on.

The plot of this story was quite simple: Samantha performed fellatio on Michael's cousin to escape being beaten. Yet the emotions were more complex. While she felt degraded and violated by giving this "gift," she also felt humiliated in having to capitulate to Michael's abusive demands. Even though there was the threat of a beating, she felt confused about how she had become so embroiled in this asymmetrical and coercive love relationship.

Samantha joined many other women, most of whom were a lot older, in her reluctance to categorize a relationship as either loving *or* abusive. Not just for face-saving reasons, she wanted me to see the good as well as the bad. She was one of the first women I interviewed to challenge the love-and-abuse dichotomy that I had, up until that time, been using.

In contrast to hooks (2000), who argued that love and abuse cannot coexist, I found that the two are often tangled up in a single relationship. I say this because very few of the women abused by their spouses believed that love and abuse could be easily disaggregated. In the subtext of some of their stories, abuse disrupted periods of happiness and pleasure that they had with sexual intimates. Sometimes the pleasure they were able to regain after the abuse was shocking, even to themselves. For instance, Emily said,

I'm very sexual, loving with it. Very loving, sort of—oh, how can I say it? With my husband, he was very sexual and so was I. There was nothing wrong there, you know. As a matter of fact, I was thinking, "I'll never get anything like that ever again."

For a middle-aged suburban woman who has a long history of being abused, Emily's assertions about her sexuality were bold and potentially subversive. I say this for two main reasons. First, women, particularly older women, are not supposed to declare their sexuality so actively and unashamedly. Second, women who have been beaten are ordinarily assumed not to derive sexual pleasure from abusive partners.

Yet, from another perspective, other interpretations may be made of Emily's claims. For instance, I noticed how quickly Emily connected her sexual desire to the feminine ideal of being "very loving." Wondering whether this self-characterization prompted her to identify too closely with Lester's interests and desires, I started to wonder whether the idea of Emily and Lester retaining a vibrant sexual life helped her to retrieve from the violence a sense of personal dignity. I know that for many people, good sex does act as some kind of compensation for relationship problems. Given the extent of Lester's violence, if the sex was bad, it was likely to be more difficult to rationalize the fears she had about the relationship ending.

At a much later point in the interview, Emily returned to the subject of staying married to Lester for so many years. In a story called "Why I Stayed So Long," she turned her attention away from their sexual relationship to speak of terror she experienced at the thought of leaving him:

> When my husband was here, I wasn't safe. I was scared all the time.... I always had that fear. He had guns and he always said to me—before we moved here—he used to say to me, "I'll put a bullet through your head one day." *I was always scared he would.* So, when I used to go from his bed to one of the kids' bedrooms and I'd lay there all night. You see, the other house had wooden floors. Soon as I'd hear a creak, I used to go *"Oooh"* all over. I used to think, "It's going to happen." I don't know why I stayed so long. I honestly don't.

It was moving to hear how Emily left his bed to seek refuge in one of the kids' bedrooms; lying there, hyper-vigilant, listening for the sound of his footsteps, convinced that he was going to shoot her, she shuddered. Yet the more she thought about it, the more confused she became about why she stayed so long.

In other stories that Emily told me, I learned of the many times when Lester beat her and secretly audiotaped her conversations. I heard how he would tell her that she was crazy and needed to see a psychiatrist. Then I heard of the time that she tried to escape. In this story she spent a week at a women's refuge, but returned home after he threatened to shoot her and the children. Even so, she continued to question why she stayed so long. It is a question that I examine in some depth in the next chapter as I consider some of the challenges women face as they try to institute changes in their lives that involve creating new stories about love.

Summary

In this chapter I examined some of the stories women told me about how they developed and serviced their love relationships. I honed in on the idea of heterosexual optimism because in most of the women's love stories, hope was a central theme. For some of the women, especially those over 40 years of age, hope was closely tied to the romantic ideals they developed about meeting "The One" and "living happily ever after." For some of them, hope encouraged them to service their relationships in ever more loving ways, even if this meant they ended up "feeling like a machine" (Vera) or fearing for their lives (Jesobel and Emily). Yet, for some of the women under 40 (Samantha, Kate, and Audrey), hope lost its close association with romance and was more actively tied to the everyday experiences of getting by.

With less pressure on them to protect their reputation, women who were raised during the second wave of feminism were more inclined to experiment with their sexuality and modify the sexual scripts that have traditionally governed women's sexuality. Some of the women—notably those who reported no abuse or serious material hardship during childhood—found that their hopes for loving people who would share household responsibilities and respect their individual interests and needs were realized. In the next chapter I continue to explore women's stories from adulthood about love and change.

Cecilia: *I was still fairly unsure, but I could see the possibilities on the horizon. I was getting excited about them, but I wasn't, you know, I wasn't Germaine Greer. I was still a pretty timid little thing.*

10

REVIEWING THE SCRIPTS FOR LOVING
(Not) Losing Hope

IN THE PREVIOUS CHAPTER I FOCUSED ON the development and servicing of love relationships. I gave most attention to the stories women told me about love and abuse converging. From these stories and the ones told by women who reported no abuse as children or adults, I can see how the cultural imperative for women to love is alive and well. Across the board women told me about how they were encouraged to form relatively traditional heterosexual love relationships. Frequently this was done through the lure of romance, which more than a few found enchanting.

For many of the women I interviewed, romance was enchanting not just because of the tingling sensations often associated with falling in love. Often the allure was much more related to what they hoped to get in return for protecting their sexual reputations, seeking out a suitable husband, relinquishing their names on marriage, subjecting themselves to child-bearing, and taking primary responsibility for the home and family care. Yet, across age and political orientation, many women never got to realize the promises they thought would result from hetero-romance. Many never achieved the feeling of belonging that they hoped for. For those who subscribed to fairytale love, many did not feel adored, nor were they treated like princesses. For many women, at different points in their lives, feeling secure, loved, and respected was also elusive. Many women told me stories about conflicts, misunderstandings, and ongoing struggle. For those who separated from intimates that they had cast as "The One," words such as "broken-hearted" and "devastated" were often used to describe the pain of ending the relationships, yet there were also feelings of hope and excitement about future possibilities, as Cecilia describes above.

In the first part of the chapter I investigate some of the difficulties women told me they faced if they were single. I start with some comments about the low social value attached to being single because it influenced whether many of the women were willing to admit to themselves and others any dissatisfaction in their relationships. I then explain that mixed views and emotions often ensued when women tried to pursue new scripts, including those related to being single. I note that as some of the women re-evaluated their ideas about love during these periods of "lovelessness," some became ambivalent about re-partnering and confused about the conventions they wanted to uphold in the future.

Reluctance to Be Single

All the women I interviewed spent time trying to figure out how to "do" love relationships. With experience and over time, preferred love styles often changed, yet the change was not always easy, predictable, or painless. For instance, some of the women who believed that traditional, romantic love relationships alone could deliver lasting happiness were prompted to revise their ideas when their marriages broke down. Most were faced with new questions about how they would now view love. What would they hope for? How feasible were these hopes and what might they need to perform new sexual scripts? These questions were common because across age, sexual orientation, and ethnicity, most of the women still had faith in the notion of love and the prospect of a new love relationship. Quite a few reflected on how their faith in love had sometimes made them determined to make their relationships work even in the presence of abuse. Yet, it was not just their faith in love that made so many reluctant to be or become single.

Social Status of Single Women, Especially Those over 40

The vast majority of the women I interviewed indicated that being single was not their preferred status. Some emphasized the loneliness of being single whereas others concentrated more on the low social value still accorded to single women (also see Ehrenreich & English 1978; Langford 1999; Orenstein 2000). Some women told me that if not in their own eyes, then at least among those around them, being single had less status than being in couple relationships, particularly for women. Tracing the historical treatment of single women, Langford (1999, p. 26) asserted that:

Being in a couple relationship is generally contrasted with the state of being single, something that for women in particular has historically been constituted as a negative identity, connoting undesirability and a useless life.

From the interviews and the four workshops I co-facilitated in Winnipeg with men about love, I know that although it can be difficult for men to be on their own, it can be even more difficult for women. One of the reasons is because such a cultural premium is placed on women loving and nurturing others. Traditionally, this has been established through the terms "bachelor" and "spinster." Unlike "bachelor" (which tends to be positively ascribed to single men who have a good time), the term "spinster" (or other terms such as "old maid," "single mom," or "divorcee") tends to be pejoratively applied to women, particularly those over 40. Some of the women I interviewed told me that although single men over 40 may be pitied and/or assumed to be gay, single women were more likely seen to be "left on the shelf" or have people wonder whether they were going to "turn to other women" because they "couldn't get (or keep) a man."

Unlike men, who were seen to do the choosing, single women were assumed not to have been chosen. For quite a few women, including some of the younger women who enjoyed more sexual liberties, the idea of being left on the shelf was not easy to shrug off. This fits with Greer's (1999, p. 312) contention that

> ... the single state is now less respectable than it has ever been. When people can cohabit informally by mutual agreement, singleness signifies, not a lack of opportunity to pair up, but a failure to pair up.

To learn more about how it felt to be single, I asked many of the women whether they felt negative identities imposed on them when they were single. I also asked them if there were aspects of being single that had or could work for them. Sixty-five-year-old Vera commented:

> There was a stigma if you left your husband.... There was a stigma if you divorced them a very big stigma. I think society still views divorcees as failures.

Vera's experience aligned with Young's (1997, p. 103) contention that "marriage carries an aura of settled respectability."

Kate, a woman 30 years younger than Vera, said that while she did not feel stigmatized as a single woman, she did when she became a single mother:

> *Kate:* You've got the whole stigma of a single mom, but at least you've got a role. You know, you are a *mother*.

Heather: Do you feel that stigma?
Kate: Yep, in a way. But it's also like, "I'm bloody proud of my child!"

Kate's love for her daughter was repeatedly mentioned, especially when she talked about the times she felt under pressure to re-partner. In the story "Get Yourself a Man," she explained:

Kate: Oh look, I've got two hilarious neighbours a 22-year-old neighbour there and a 20-year-old neighbour there. They're in my housing co-op, so I know them really well. And they'll say things like, "Why don't you go and get yourself a man?"
Heather: [laughs] Like going to the supermarket?
Kate: Yeah! And they just say, "Go out and get yourself a man." And it's like, "I don't want one, thanks!"

While affectionately mocking her young neighbours for holding such outdated beliefs, I knew that Kate was annoyed at how their comments could affect her. From other comments made, I understood that she felt most pressure to partner when others reiterated this message. For instance, I knew how annoyed she became when she turned on her radio and heard people discussing "the problems with single mothers" on talk-back shows. Then there were the times that she went to work and heard colleagues professing the need for children to have fathers. If family members and friends echoed these sentiments, it became harder not to internalize the message that she should "get a man" and give her daughter a father figure.

Nevertheless, Kate's ongoing commitment to sole motherhood provided evidence of the postmodern argument that sex, love, and duty are no longer entwined (Giddens 1992; Melucci 1996). However, for the majority of the women I interviewed, this was not the case. Most did not separate their desire to be a mother from their desire to be part of a couple (also see Chapter 9). Most knew that on both counts, these identities are still prized. However, sometimes women became more aware of it post-separation.

Emily talked about how her status dropped post-divorce. She felt it drop even among people who knew that her husband had been physically, emotionally, and financially abusive toward her and the children. When some of her friends, colleagues, and relatives started to typecast her as a "lonely spinster" who was "desperate to get a man," it became particularly hard. Sometimes these messages were conveyed through jokes. At other times it occurred through direct criticism or gossip. On the rare occasions when she confronted people about it, she was mainly dismissed as "paranoid." Making matters worse, couples she had known for years stopped inviting her out. After a few years of this, she found it hard not to feel like the "odd one out" (also see Kipnis 2003).

Across age brackets, many other women I interviewed said that when they were single, they often felt like they were "the odd one out." Sometimes this meant being the odd number in a dinner party, or the person without a partner at a wedding or function. Sometimes it meant not wanting to be "a gooseberry" or "a bump on a log" when in the presence of an amorous couple. Alternatively, it could mean being the subject of others' analysis of why they were still single.

With more than a hint of deviance, feeling like "the odd one out" can be an undignified position to endure, especially in the long term. Embedded in this message is the possibility that you are single (or single again) because you are ultimately unlovable. With this comes the possibility of being pitied or patronized. This is why some of the women cringed when others asked questions about their single status. Women in their fifties, such as Catherine, Barbara, Sula, Monica, Rae, Brenda, and Olivia, told me how they resented being falsely reassured that there was "someone out there for everyone." They also resented being criticized for being "too uptight" or "too fussy." Compounding matters were allegations of older single women being "sleazy" or "a home-wrecker"—that is, a woman who tries to "steal" a man away from another woman.

Mixed Views and Emotions

Yet, from some of the younger women I interviewed, particularly those in their twenties, I heard very different stories. Take, for instance, Elena, who said,

> I kind of lived by the philosophy where it's, like, I'll do whatever makes me happy, so if it means being single, well, that's fine. As long as I'm happy, I think that is what's most important.... I'm not afraid of being alone. I think that's another thing that my mom kind of instilled in me: "Don't be afraid of being alone if it makes you happy."

Christine also believed that being single had many benefits. Associating most love relationships with anguish, anxiety, and stress, she said that she was often "the shoulder for her friends to cry on ... usually those with problems with their boyfriends."

She was so aware of the potential pain of relationships that she was not eager to become part of a couple. Marnie agreed, but was even more scornful of coupledom:

> I don't quite understand why I have to have couple love. Why do I have to have sex with just one person, spending all my time, committing myself to somebody just to get into a pattern—a habit—of security when I can find that security for myself? I can find that through a network of friends or a network of Internet friendships or whatever.

Similar to other women I interviewed, Marnie spent a lot of time deconstructing the politics of love relationships, especially as they were represented through the major institutions of the state, churches, and mass media. Tradition for tradition's sake was something she abhorred, as was the idea of becoming someone else's "property":

> I just find the whole thought of being in a couple sounds very narrowing and squished.... Like, I always thought with a bit of mockery about having to pretend to feel and do things that I don't feel or don't want to do.

I knew that Marnie rejected the idea that men and women are naturally meant to be together. Identifying as bisexual, she sought her ideals from collective living models. Having studied gender politics at university, she was keenly aware of the pressures on most single parents, and mindful of the abuses that can take place in loving, respectable, dual-parent families.

Elena joined the many other women I spoke with who struggled over love narratives and actively resisted the traditional script of the "Little Woman" intra- and interpersonally. Take, for instance, Kate, who said,

> I first moved in with ... Alan after the shelter. It was with his brother and his brother's girlfriend. Well, we didn't have a washing machine. Actually we had fuck all in the house. And we'd be standing in the laundry, washing Mike's jeans and I'd be doing mine by hand, and she'd say, "Aren't you going to do Alan's?" And I'd go, "No! Of course I'm not. He can do his own." But she had this thing that you cook and clean for your man and you do his laundry—and in cold water, you know. I'd just say, "No, if he's going to do mine, then I'd probably do his now and then." It was just like this—she saw it in a different way. I think I've been a feminist from birth. I saw my dad doing dishes and I knew it wasn't a genetic link.

Set in the laundry, this story showed Kate rejecting the cultural expectation that she should "cook and clean for [her] man," yet as she did so, she had to grapple with the possibility that she might sound harsh, bitter, lazy, or defiant. That is why she started to qualify her position. First, she said that she would consider washing Alan's jeans if she felt confident that he would return the favour. Believing that the two women "just" saw it in "a different way," she defended her position by asserting herself as "feminist from birth" before arguing that there was no "genetic link" between gender and housework.

Kate provided other examples of struggling over conventional love narratives:

> When I'm in love, I'm really in love. Like anyone, you *fall* [pause], and you have that whole pit-of-your-stomach thing. Um, it's amazing. But, um, there are times that I'm not. I sort of know that I'm not.... Stan was so shocked when I said that we'd buy things separately and I just thought it was common sense. I've been accused by many friends of being not romantic and not spiritual, as having this practical attitude.... It's seen as a criticism, but they're completely wrong in a lot of ways.

In this story many of the hallmarks of heterosexual romance are examined. Lovers fall in love. They experience times that are "amazing." They know that over time, they are meant to demonstrate a deepening commitment to one another. A central way of doing this is to live together (preferably in marriage) and becoming a single unit of consumption (Jamieson 1998; Langford 1999; Young 1997). So well established are these conventions that Stan was "shocked" when Kate suggested they do otherwise. When her friends heard of it, they were similarly perturbed. That is why they "accused" her of "having a practical attitude" that was not conducive to romance.

Despite all her efforts to renounce fairytale love, Kate found these criticisms stung because she had some lingering hopes that love relationships could last forever:

> *Heather:* You said that sometimes you wished that you could believe in the forever thing. What's that about?
> *Kate:* I think that's the complete ideal—*Woman's Day*, ads, TV, bullshit, crapola—that we get stuffed down our throats as women. All the crap that they have in women's magazines....

According to Kate, it was impossible for women to disassociate themselves from "the complete ideal" because it was continually "stuffed down [women's] throats." Kingston (2004, p. 162) referred to it as the "woman-wanting-to-be-vanquished scenario ... where he pursues. She resists. He overcomes. His sensuality is dangerous, aggressive and forceful. She is swept away."

As I have previously suggested, love can induce contradictory emotions, such as excitement, euphoria, contentment, fear, ambivalence, dissatisfaction, resentment, regret, rage, and despair, and sometimes all of them simultaneously (see Chapters 1 to 4). However, through the interviews and workshops, I came to understand more about how existing ideas about love can alter. Through the hundreds of hours of discussion, I know that there are times and circumstances that precipitate the jettisoning of some views and the (re)institution of others. I also know that there are times when complicated manoeuvres are undertaken to manage ambivalence and reconcile paradoxes (also see Hey 1997; Walkerdine 1984; Ussher 1997). In a story I called "Romance as Feminine," Samantha provided evidence of this:

> Romance is on the feminine side of things, which means that men aren't really taught much about what it means to be romantic. But they're taught enough so that their women are interested in them! [laughs] ... Dirk's told me. I've said, "How come you don't open the door for me anymore?" And he says, "I've got you now. I don't need to do that anymore." And I'm going, "Oh, thanks very much!" He says, "Well, I'm being honest. That's what most of us blokes do."

In Samantha's view, men were not close to romance, but most knew enough to use it as a strategy to seduce women (also see Langford 1999). Dirk, her partner, confirmed this when he told her that he was just one of many "blokes" who "didn't need to do that anymore." From the light-hearted tone she used, I knew she was not offended. Yet, on further reflection, I wondered if this might also be due to the ambivalence she felt about romance:

> It's interesting enough and I watch it, you know. But I see the movies and things like that as pure entertainment, not as things to base your life on.... You'd be setting yourself up for disappointment every time, I reckon.... I realize it's pure entertainment.

In this story Samantha echoed arguments made by some third wave feminists about women's consumption of popular romance; notably, that women who enjoy romance stories do not necessarily condone sexual inequality nor believe that the stories represent "real life" (see Currie 1999; Radway 1991). Other women I interviewed agreed and persuaded me:

> It is not necessary to deny the pleasures of romance or the euphoria of falling in love in order to be sceptical about romantic ideals and wary of their consequences. (Jackson 1999, p. 114)

Like Samantha, many women in the study realized that as they got older, fictional characters were not going to resolve their disagreements in the same way as ordinary people. In contrast to fictional characters who used one single discussion to resolve conflict in intimate relationships, real-life women spoke of the need for protracted discussions, particularly if change was to occur with long-standing patterns of behaviour. They also spoke about containing expectations:

> *Alexandria:* ... you can't be looking for someone to complete you. You are supposed to be two wholes walking together. You can't be two halves looking for each other to make a whole. That's ridiculous. It puts way too much responsibility on the relationship, so it's bound to fail.

Hanging on

While most of the women in this study were willing to scrutinize popular stories about romance for their tendency to trivialize relationship problems, not all believed that lengthy discussions would precipitate sustained behavioural change. Some women found these talks interesting, whereas others seemed only vaguely interested, if not bored. I also noted significant variations in the levels of optimism the women displayed about love, and the extent to which they were willing or able to positively evaluate themselves in their love relationships (also see Chapter 9). In part, this explains why some of the women accentuated the themes of strength, resilience, and autonomy in their stories, whereas others pursued stories that were filled with more ambivalence, vulnerability, and self-criticism. To some extent, the differences depended on how satisfied they were with their own behaviours.

In the story "Hanging on," Emily conveyed a mixture of regret, despondency, and self-blame as she talked about her marriage to Lester:

> I mean when I left 20 years ago—when I first left—that's when I should have left and not gone back. Most of these women do that. What I've seen when I was at my support group—what I seen—is the women stay and stay and hang on and hang on and hang on. What the heck for? To just hang on? I wish I had of left 20 years ago. I reckon I would have been better off.

With hindsight, Emily believed that she should not have returned to Lester after the week in the women's refuge. It was not easy for her to admit this because she knew that she and the other women in the story might appear tragically optimistic. According to her, they did not just stay out of fear. They hung on to the hope that their relationships would improve. Now, seeing the futility of the non-abusive spouse single-handedly trying to make violent relationships work, she concluded that there was little chance of rekindling love once women leave and then come back.

Similar to at least 40 other women I interviewed, Emily moved back and forth between conventional love discourses and feminist criticisms made of them. Throughout the series of moves, I noticed her trying to reconcile her desire to be loved with the hazards of coupledom. From what I could see, she did this by concentrating on how she might choose the right man. In the story "You Can't Tell," she explained her dilemma:

> You can't tell men.... They look okay, but then you think, "They are divorced. Why are they divorced? What's happened in their marriage? Have they been out with other women and that's their reason?" ...It's really scary. Oh, I don't know. It's just that it's scary because it's nice to be loved.

Emily was anxious that she would continue to be a poor judge of character. Having been married to a man who was ostensibly handsome and charming, she knew that appearances could be deceptive. This was why she said that although a man "might look a picture," he might also be concealing secrets from his past. It was a really "scary" thought because she knew how much pleasure she derived from being loved and was aware that her hopes for this pleasure risked seducing her into accepting another abusive relationship.

Shortly after she told this story, Emily started to differentiate herself from other, more assertive women she has known:

> I think women stand up for themselves now. Um, I think, though, when you've got the background that it has an effect on ya. How—when you're a kid—I don't care what anyone says, I'm sure it has an effect on you, on your whole life. I try not to let it. When I turned 40, I said to myself, "That's it now. I'm grown up."

In this excerpt three main cultural discourses were evident. The first was predicated on the view that women are now more likely to "stand up for themselves." Because it is a popular view, it did not require an explanation. The second related to women who have a "background" in trauma (see Saakvitne et al. 1998). Two lines were needed to defend her position because past experiences of trauma risked women being seen as playing the victim. The third set of discourses related to how people might recover from abusive relationships. Three lines were needed to spell it out because, try as she might, the memories of childhood trauma interfered with her resolve not to let the past affect her future.

Resolving to Change

As many women in this study have indicated, change can produce much excitement and many opportunities. However, whether it is at an individual, organizational, or societal level, change is often experienced as threatening. The idea of change can generate fear even when current social practices are found to be wanting, new practices are envisaged, and the climate for change appears to be conducive to success. In less optimal circumstances, change can be even more anxiety provoking.

Breakwell (1986, p. 166) explained that many people become trapped into the continued use of "sub-optimal coping strategies" because "it is no simple matter to anticipate what will be the optimal strategy." As she suggested, people who experience constant threats to their identities may find it particularly difficult to institute change (Breakwell 1986, p. 170). Sometimes people who do not have the space or support to do the "identity work" that is usually required for individuals to "self-enhance." Some try to cope by using physical, emotional, and social forms of withdrawal (Breakwell 1986, p. 176).

Paradoxically, the use of sub-optimal strategies may also persist because individuals are encouraged to represent themselves as consistent and coherent. Because change can rupture narratives of self-consistency, it may be delayed or deferred until an individual has the chance to incorporate the changes into her or his identity. Sometimes change involves turning points (Saakvitne et al. 1998).

Turning Points

Most of the women I interviewed illustrated that there were many possible turning points in people's lives. Many of their stories reminded me that unexpected events such as an accident, illness, or death sometimes evokes turning points. This was evident, for example, when some of the women's partners died, left them for other people, or endured serious health problems. However, turning points were also prompted by happier events, including positive changes in fortune (such as winning money, being offered a new job, or discovering a long-lost relative) as well as conscious decisions that individuals instituted. For example, this was evident when some of the women initiated separations, applied for a divorce, moved to other provinces or countries, enrolled in university courses, and/or retrained for different forms of work. So, while some turning points occurred suddenly and spontaneously, others took a long period of incubation before they were realized (also see Saakvitne et al. 1998).

For some of the women I interviewed, turning points sometimes emerged after long periods of gestation. Sometimes they were painful, while at other times relatively pain-free. Take, for instance, Vanessa, a 33-year-old Métis Canadian woman, who told me about how she tried to leave her husband, a man she loved very much, but one whose drug taking meant that his behaviour had become so out of control that she feared for the safety of their children. Recalling the time when she was in her twenties, she said:

> It was not that easy just to get up and walk away. Like, I knew at that point when things were getting bad, but now I just couldn't live like that anymore. I did have goals for myself, but I couldn't do anything in my life because everything sort of hinged on how he behaved.

I wondered about how Vanessa dealt with such a precarious home situation and she said:

> I couldn't progress. I couldn't get a job. I tried to get a job and then, you know, I knew that he was taking pills and stuff, and he was okay for a while, so he was okay for a couple of months, and I thought, "I can get a job now," you know. "I'm going to work and get a little bit of money for us." But then I got a call because I asked my neighbour to keep an eye out as well. I got a call saying, "Well, you should know that your kids are outside." It was 7 o'clock and I knew they shouldn't be outside

playing just like that. So I came home. He was passed out on the couch and there were pills on the floor and my kids were there, and, like, my little boy came up to me, and he said, "Here's the pills. Those are the bad things that you told us not to eat." Because I had talked to them already and said, "If you see this, don't eat it. This is very bad and it will make you very sick" that kind of thing. So I remember just hugging him and saying, "Oh, I'm so proud of you that you remembered what I told you." And then I had to quit my job.

Living on tenterhooks, Vanessa was horrified that her children were exposed to their father's drug taking:

I couldn't leave them with him [their dad] anymore. It was hard, you know. I could never—like, I wanted to go to school, but I couldn't go because of the emotional roller coaster. There was just no stability. Like, who could I leave them with? And when I'd gone, I kept thinking "Is all my stuff going to be pawned or whatever?" Life was too uncertain.

The situation proceeded like this for some years. The turning point came when Vanessa arrived home to find her husband passed out on the floor and her young son handed her some of the pills that his father had taken. The gravity of the situation sunk in. First, she realized that her efforts to concentrate at school were futile given that she was constantly worried about the security of their possessions. She knew that she had to take some drastic action to safeguard her well-being and the children's.

Unlike Vanessa, who broke away temporarily from her husband until he sought help for his drug use, Dallas confessed that she had trouble leaving a partner until she had set up a new relationship: "I seem to have fallen into some trap where I never ever cut off a relationship until I had another one on the go."

Like so many of the women I interviewed, Dallas was remarkably candid, so much so that she was willing to reveal her pattern of compulsively re-partnering. By her own account, she did this because she was frightened of being on her own:

I can only imagine that I would have shrivelled up and I would have died. [pause] *Literally.* I *had* to have at least one person. And I suppose I can take that back to—no matter how crappy my childhood was, I always had Dad there to love me at the end of the day.

Referring to herself when she was in her twenties, Dallas feared that without a heterosexual love relationship, her life might have been literally threatened. This might sound odd given the abuse she had already suffered from ex-lovers (also see Campbell 2002). Yet, for Dallas, her perpetual hope that the next relationship would be better led her to assume that she would have "shrivelled up and died" if she was not loved by "at least one person."

Dallas was not the only woman I interviewed who talked about the fear she felt in leaving an abusive relationship for life on her own, yet she was unique in that she attributed this yearning to the relationship she had with her father. In her mind, the last 40 years of his love had helped her to enjoy moments where she could feel good about herself. Feeling this love within an otherwise abusive family, she was accustomed to experiencing love and abuse all mixed up together. As a result, she did not want to relinquish what she believed was a potential source of happiness for her life (also see Chapters 12 and 13).

Waking up

Dallas's appetite for love appeared to have been stimulated by two popular assumptions: (1) that coupledom was "normal" given that everyone else seemed to be in couple relationships (which is an intriguing belief given the increasing number of women who do not live with a spouse or partner); and (2) that unreconstructed heterosexual love relationships have the capacity to create "a just and humane society" (Langford 1999, p. 151). For Langford (1999, p. 151), both assumptions were erroneous because they constricted women's ability to envisage a more expansive and less privatized social organization of sexual intimacy. For Dallas, however, monogamous coupledom made perfect sense.

With love often evoking fear and confusion, Langford (1999, p. 152) argued that many women are "gripped by compulsions which they do not understand." While not agreeing with Langford's appraisal of heterosexual love, Dallas provided a good example of being gripped by compulsions that surfaced most when she was single:

> It all seemed to open up everything. I just went from the sublime to the ridiculous in all psychological ways. So many compulsive disorders just started flooding out. And it was *absolutely horrible!* But then, I don't know, something happened one day. This seems to happen periodically. I just wake up and something is different. It's, um, real weird. I wake up and something's different.

It did not seem fair that Dallas suffered such an overwhelming disintegration of her psychological state after she finally became free from the exacting and abusive demands of her former love relationship. Yet, according to Saakvitne et al. (1998, p. 280), this is not unusual. Many trauma survivors find that they can start to recover only when the full extent of the horror has had a chance to register (also see Campbell 2002). For Dallas, the horror registered only when she was on her own, safe from ongoing abuse. It was then that "everything ... opened up" and she was "flooded" with "compulsive disorders." Not surprisingly, she panicked, wondering whether she would ever find an escape from this torment. Then one day she woke up feeling utterly "different." It was so sudden and "weird" that she was not able to explain it. All she knew was that this kind of change happened to her "periodically." Almost like a weather pattern, it just lifted and she was able to get on with another phase of her life.

Although not many other women experienced such cataclysmic changes that came to them through the night, quite a few other women I spoke with told me stories about how they experienced a radically different sense of themselves when they were away from their spouses. Take, for instance, Samantha, who talked about the changes she instituted during the three months that her partner, Michael, was in jail:

> I was going to uni[versity]. I was going to school. I was changing. I was getting better. I was getting strength. I was learning. I mean it was only year 12, but he knew that I wanted to go to uni after that.... I had plans—m*y own plans*.... If he didn't want to be there, then he didn't have to be. Um, he saw how much it changed the relationship because we couldn't go out and drink every day and whatever. I had to study. I had to do all this stuff. I was growing a brain and he just didn't like it at all.

Similar to other women I spoke to who entered education or training courses as mature-aged students, Samantha found that her studies were not just a vehicle for improving her labour market opportunities but a major source of strength and personal growth. By her own estimation, it helped her to gain the confidence she needed to create her "*own plans*," which, in turn, helped her to focus on her own aspirations rather than her partner's demands, especially after he was paroled. On his release from prison, he found that Samantha was not just able to resist his pleas to join him in his daily drinking sessions, but that she had other activities stimulating her interest, namely her interest in "growing a brain."

Had Australians Samantha and Dallas sat and talked with Canadians Vanessa and Jesobel, I think they would have had a lot in common, especially when it came to thinking about defining moments. For Jesobel, the change was first precipitated by a comment made to her by a friend while they were having coffee together, and then realized when her partner announced to her that he intended to plead "not guilty" to the assault he had inflicted on her (see Chapter 9):

> I was having coffee one day with a friend—one of those days I would sneak out [from Randy, her violent partner]—and I told him something that Randy was doing. All of a sudden he [the friend] stared at me and talked about how far I'd come down and why. And he looked at me and said, "Oh, you need to be rebooted." And they were like magic words. I recognized it. *I was rebooting*. I waited. And I waited for this to happen. And when I found out that he was going to plead "not guilty"

to assaulting me, it all changed. Because I had thought, "Okay, we'll go to mediation, he'll go into therapy." You know, do this and that. So, that's the line he crossed.

"Rebooting [her]self," as a computer does, came after Randy had "crossed a line." It was then that Jesobel decided that "enough was enough," or, as the Canadians say, "enough already!" Randy's refusal to admit that he assaulted her was such a defining moment that it spurred her decision to leave the relationship:

> So, when I found out he was going to plead "not guilty," I told him, "I'm leaving." And he was doing one of his little tricks about packing up all of my stuff and leaving it outside. Like, he'd do that quite often. *But I packed up all my stuff and I left.* And then he would call me and finally I called his lawyer and told him, "Tell this guy to stop calling me or I am going to call the police." Then I went back into Osborne House [a women's shelter] willingly. From Osborne House one day I called the police and I said, "You have an unsolved crime. There was a man who was stabbed at a restaurant such and such a time and I know who did it."

Pumped with courage and determined not to suffer the indignity of him "packing up all of [her] stuff and leaving it outside," Jesobel not only instituted the separation but decided that while she was at it, she would inform the police about her knowledge of a stabbing that she believed he had committed. She did this despite the profound impact it would have on her life:

> It took nearly three years to get through the whole court process. During that three years he called the Civil Service Commission looking for me. He had other people do it too. I had to change my entire life. I had habits I could no longer follow. I had lived in Osborne Village for years and I had to move out. I'd have these patterns on Saturdays—get the paper, have a second cup of cappuccino, later in the afternoon go to the used bookstore, stroll through the Village, go window shopping. Well, that all had to change, and it took me, oh gosh, until I was 40 when I was fine with Wayne, when I was fine with other men. That's when I was okay. But any man who was single, it was, it was horrible. I couldn't be alone with them. I would shake. I'd get nervous. I'd have panic attacks.

As Jesobel described, it was not easy to testify against her violent ex-partner. It was even worse because the court case was long and drawn-out, yet she believed it was central to her loving and respecting herself after separation. In the story called "I'm Perfectly Content by Myself," she said:

> Then one day, I was busy puttering around and I had a very good job that paid extremely well; I had a granddaughter; I'd been to California twice—I'd actually moved there for six months and came back. And it was, like, I was happy. I was putzing around and I recognized it. My daughter was in the living room, my granddaughter was playing with something, and I recognized why I was happy and I thought, *"I don't need a man to be happy. I'm perfectly content by myself."* I can go wherever I want and do whatever I want. I can shave my hair off tomorrow if I felt like it.

In this story it is apparent that Jesobel enjoyed her work and loved her daughter and granddaughter. Feeling safe and secure, she was alive with the freedom that she could do as she wished. When she recounted how she had been able to "reboot" herself, her face radiated with pride. She was so proud because her life had not been easy, right from childhood:

> I had read so many books by then because of my childhood, because of my relationship with my ex-husband, the dysfunctions between my mother and my grandmother and now us. I'd read a great deal and I understood what it all was. I think I finally arrived at that place where I was sort of at peace with myself and I knew that there was never going to be that great passion … that the storybook love wasn't going to happen.

Part of Jesobel's process was to relinquish the idea of "the storybook love." By giving up this idea, she was able to find "peace" in herself. It was ironic then that a couple of years later she would develop a relationship that certainly sounded like it contained "great passion" (see Chapters 11–12).

Breaking the Habit

With Jesobel and Emily, Samantha also found it hard to break away from a violent spouse (also see Fraser 2005). In the following story she tried to explain why:

> Michael was just, um, he was a habit basically, and I didn't know how to break it. Because I knew that basically he was violent and drunk as well. And when you're scared of someone the way I was scared of him … even though you know that it's better to go, it's very hard. *Very hard.*

Initially, Samantha simplified her situation by describing her relationship with Michael as "a habit" that she did not "know how to break." A few sentences afterwards, however, she was more willing to admit that leaving a love relationship could be more complicated since it involved resigning herself to the fact that the relationship (or the spouse) was not going to change. As many women and men have discovered, by the time one arrived at this conclusion, she or he may well have submitted herself or himself to what Langford (1999, p. 138) described as "a most insidious form of governance." It is insidious because it is not unusual for lovers to submit themselves to the governance of the people they hope will one day love them as they have always hoped they would be loved.

Similar to Samantha who embarked on a new pathway when Michael was in jail, Cecilia started to conceptualize the changes she would later make when her first husband was working away from home. In a story called "Wondering How I Got There," she explained that:

> One day I kind of looked at my life the way it was and thought, "God, hang on a minute. Here I am with all these things I want and I don't know how I got here. Who am I anyway?" I've been swept along and there's always been these things around me. Things that I thought I wanted and thought I understood. But who's that? You see, it was like a big confrontation.... I was being swept along in this dream for several years. But you know, if I thought about it—about the love thing and what I wanted—and what I needed and what I thought was the best thing for me.... It was shattering that it wasn't real anymore. I couldn't live with that idea.

Cecilia's story illustrates how one's faith in fairytale love can unravel. No longer swept up in the whirlwind romance that offered her special male attention, a home, and a legitimate avenue for sexual expression, she started to pose existential questions about the direction her life had taken (also see Fraser 2005; Langford 1999; Wolf 1997; and Chapter 9). Her questions were radical because by envisaging an alternative way of living, she threatened the viability of her family life. This was borne out when she said that "It was shattering that it wasn't real any more" that it was "like a big confrontation" that she could no longer "live with."

Jackson (1999) explained that as heterosexual love relationships become routinized through commitment, women's subordination often becomes more obvious. Cecilia's stories support this idea. In the story "Deciding to Leave," she said:

> I remember sitting in my house—in this house—the day thinking to myself as a 28-year-old and saying, "No, I can't do this. I can't be 28 and be doing this. *No, I can't.*" That was the day I made my decision, I

can tell you. I knew that night that when he comes home, this isn't going to be, you know.... It was a pretty hard thing for him to hear.

Cecilia found it hard to break the news to her husband about wanting to separate because she knew that it meant rejecting him and reneging on the vow she had made to stay with him "until death do us part." In the next story she described how he reacted:

> What I started to do was kind of refer to, "Oh, there's a voice of mine, you know. *I actually have a voice somewhere.* I'm starting to get it and I'm going to have to start using it." And he said to these people around me at a party—he said it with this real tone of sarcasm, which was so unlike him, but I guess it was just pain that he was just having to face what was going to happen. And he said, "She's like that these days. She's got this thing. She's her own person." I remember hearing that and it was like validation. "That's right, that's right. I'm seeing things now. My eyes are opening up and I don't know where I'm going, but it's not here!" [laughs] You know, I was on this mission.

Finding her "voice," Cecilia recalled how her eyes opened up, she could see that she must actively pursue her mission. Determined to create change but unclear of the destination, she joined Jesobel in the search for scripts to help her alter the direction of her life.

Summary

In the early part of the discussion I explored why it is not always easy to be single, especially for women over 40 years of age. Mostly I pointed to the discomfort the women said they felt when cast as the odd one out. However, I also made references to the ongoing stigma that many single women experience. Wanting to avoid this stigma is part of the wide range of reasons why so many women, across age brackets and other demographic divisions, pursued love relationships with such energetic commitment. Unfortunately, this energetic commitment often meant they found it very difficult to dissolve relationships that they believed were not happy or healthy for them and/or their children. Many women struggled over the kinds of love relationships they thought they should have. Sometimes the incongruence between their hopes and lived experiences created such tension that epiphanies or turning points would occur. As I discussed, the themes of "hanging on," "waking up," "rebooting oneself," and "breaking the habit" were common to many of the women's stories about the dissolution of committed but violent intimate relationships.

The next chapter considers how women revise scripts for loving over the years. I consider how they move on from intimate relationships, how they alter conventional scripts, or create new ones for future relationships. This material seeds the final two chapters that examine the kinds of hopes women have for the future and the implications these findings might have for professional practice.

> Vera: *If I ever got remarried again and I was treated in a cruel manner, I would move on. I would leave. I wouldn't stop. Even verbal abuse. I wouldn't tolerate any sort of abuse now. I would move on.*

II
REVISING THE SCRIPTS FOR LOVING
Trying to Move On

IN THIS CHAPTER I CONCENTRATE ON women's stories about rebuilding post-separation. I am particularly interested in understanding how the women's ideas about love and abuse can change in light of personal experience and new cultural norms. Because social workers work mostly with oppressed and abused groups, I give most attention to how abuse victims/survivors renegotiate, renounce, and/or reform their ideas about love relationships. As I suggest, the stories used to convey these changes provide insights about how new ideas about love, gender, and sexuality are possible, even within circumstances where there are significant social and material constraints. A discussion of self-help recovery narratives follows because they underwrote many of the women's stories. Recovery scripts for moving on are highlighted since they offered some of the women a way to express their future aspirations for themselves and their love relationships.

Self-Help Recovery Narratives

Many tales about recovery are told in Anglo-American cultures, particularly if one considers the assortment of daytime television talk shows, self-help texts, and other popular sources of advice (Plummer 1995). However, even though comments are sometimes made about the need for political change, the more dominant set of recovery tales gives most, if not all, their attention to personal change (Plummer 1995).

If You Stay with an Abusive Partner, Are You Addicted to Love?

Plummer (1995) noted that popular programs for recovery are often framed around the notion of addiction. Referencing Norwood's (1976) *Women Who Love Too Much*, he said that people are usually recommended to (1) go for help; (2) make their recovery the main priority of their life; (3) find a support group of peers who can empathize; (4) develop their spirituality through daily practice; (5) relinquish any tendencies to manage and control others; (6) learn how to avoid becoming hooked into the games; (7) confront their problems and shortcomings; (8) cultivate whatever needs to be developed in themselves; (9) become selfish or self-identified; (10) share their experiences and knowledge with others (Plummer 1995, p. 100).

At first glance, this kind of recovery program seems relatively innocuous since it provides "addicts" with a series of sensible steps to follow. However, on closer inspection, some notable problems are evident. For a start, it takes for granted the idea that all "addicts" are in a position to incorporate these strategies into their daily lives. With scant attention paid to the socio-political constraints, radical transformations are expected to eventuate from individual change alone. Should recovery efforts not succeed, individuals are, therefore, liable to be seen as uncommitted or personally deficient (Plummer 1995).

Because mainstream recovery scripts rarely incorporate a critical analysis of gender, little attention is given to the way love addictions may be culturally induced. In other words, little attention is given to the possibility that women are expected to love too much and, in some instances, disparaged if they do not. The absence of gender analyses also means that most recovery programs fail to appreciate that some tasks are easier for men to accomplish than women. For instance, even though gender conventions might make it easier for women to seek help and find a support group, it may not be so easy for them to prioritize their recovery over other demands, particularly those of their children. Also, because mainstream recovery narratives often imply that the central route to happiness involves "forgiving those who trespass against you," they have the potential to encourage women to uphold or return to traditionally feminine behaviours.

Must You Forgive Your Abuser?

As Langford (1999) argued, when women are hurt by loved ones, they are commonly expected to forgive and forget so that they can love again. The imperative of loving anew is so widespread that even Dowrick (1993, 1997, 2005, 2007) a popular feminist author of self-help books in Australia, recommended that women relinquish their anger, forgive others for any wrongdoings, and look for ways to love more generously so that they can move on. And by moving on, she meant being able to embark on a new love relationship, one that may result in an "almost perfect marriage." In an interview with a newspaper journalist, Dowrick is quoted as saying that:

> Cultivating a sense of injury is deeply unsustaining. It keeps your mind fixed on what's wrong; it falsely strips you of your power to see what's right. Moving on from that sense of injury ... does not mean condoning what has been wrong, or pretending what has happened did not happen. (Hawley 2000b, p. 27)

Inferring that there is a right and wrong way of surviving trauma, Dowrick suggested that there are only negative effects to be had when survivors emphasize what is wrong (Hawley 2000b, p. 27). Apart from putting too much pressure on survivors to remain ever hopeful that such an injury will not occur again, this type of recovery discourse may also be used to deny the "long-term impact of trauma by urging victims to 'get over it and get on with it'" (Saakvitne et al. 1998, p. 280).

Cecilia was one of the women who survived abuse and then found that for her to move on, she needed to deal with the abuse rather than forgive her abuser:

> I think I was saying it to you on the phone that day: You can't deny lived experience. It's *always* part of you, only somehow you have to try and not let it dominate you. And if I hadn't gone through the years of psychotherapy and depression, I'm sure it would have still dominated me. How could I possibly be, you know, have another normal relationship and be a practitioner and all the rest of it if I hadn't done some dealing, dealing with it?

Cecilia's first comment is important because it showed her refusal to ignore the possibility that past trauma can cast a long shadow over an individual's life. Using the externalizing language of "you," she nevertheless generalized the need for women to somehow prevent the legacy of child abuse from dominating them. By her own account, this was not easy since it had taken her "years of psychotherapy" to "deal with ... [her] ... depression."

Re-partnering with Men Who Take Charge

As I have intimated, there is some utility in constructing love as a set of stories so long as it involves an exploration of the social, cultural, and historical conventions for loving. These conventions are important to consider because they constrain the choice of love story that women are likely to pursue and influence the type of love story that they are likely to end up in (Jamieson 1998; Langford 1999).

In a story called "The Head of the Household," I asked Kathleen, a 75-year-old Canadian, to comment on this traditional script:

> *Kathleen:* Well, some ladies like men who take charge.... I think because it lets you feel like a lady, someone who's special and cherished.
> *Heather:* So there's some delight that can come from someone else being in charge?
> *Kathleen:* Yes, there can be. Well, if you have the right man in charge. Not all of them can be trusted with the role and many of them think it's how it should be in a marriage.

Vera, another older woman, expressed a similar sentiment:

> *Vera:* We like the model of the man being in charge because we *like* the man to have to make the decisions and do things. Be able to fix things, and organize things, and drive us around.... we *like* that situation.
> *Heather:* Um, err, why? [laughs]
> *Vera:* I think it, err [starts to laugh], I think—oh, I don't know. Maybe when you get to 65 you will like the idea of somebody taking charge of your life. And when you've been a widow for a while, you get sick of being in charge.
> *Heather:* So there's a sense of comfort in someone else being in charge?
> *Vera:* That's right, that's right. But there would be, um, there would be—oh, it doesn't always work out that way because most women that are older that meet gentlemen that are older than them, and they end up having to do all the running around for the gentlemen. Because the gentlemen end up being sick.... That's when the model falls apart.

Well aware that this model of relationship conflicted with the one I endorsed, Vera defended her position by relating its appeal to her generation of women. Also using the term "being in charge," she described how lonely and exhausting it could be at 65 to do everything for oneself (also see Chapter 12). However, as she reflected further, she started to point out some of the disadvantages of women forming relationships with men who are older than themselves, and who were likely to have health problems that obstructed their ability to actually perform the role of being "the head of the household."

Because I was intrigued at the way Vera prized a relationship model that, at least in her case, had fallen far short of its promises, I asked:

> *Heather:* But that idea that two people might come together as equals, what do you think about that idea? [pause] Share the decision making and—
> *Vera (interrupting):* *That's the best way to go.* That would be the best way to go, but I don't know whether that works out with a 60-year-old, the 60- to 70-year-old gentleman.

In contrast to her earlier defence of asymmetrical love relationships, Vera now entertained the idea of a democratic model of love being *"the best way to go."* Apart from wondering whether she was just trying to appease me, I noted that her lack of interest in the equality model was also tied up in her sense that was not likely to appeal to "the 60- to 70-year-old gentleman." Quite simply, she did not believe a democratic relationship was likely to be an option with her generation of men.

Trying to Institute New Conventions for Loving

Living in the twilight of convention and change can be difficult. Without a well-articulated set of sexual scripts to assist, many women become confused about where they might draw the line in their love relationships. Recognizing that familiarity with particular styles of relating can make one susceptible to falling into old patterns, many women feared they would repeat past mistakes, including those for which they had limited responsibility (see Chapters 7 to 10).

Making a Break with the Past

For instance, Dallas indicated that while she wanted to form another love relationship, she was unclear as to how she might orchestrate one that would radically break with the past. In the story "Not Knowing What to Do," she explained:

> *Dallas:* That 13 months that I had here of total relationshiplessness, well, I don't know what made me do it. I was just looking through the paper, you know, those *Connections* ads [personal columns] and something just focused in.
> *Heather:* You just decided to call?
> *Dallas:* Yeah. We spoke on the phone for about the first couple of weeks. We had quite a few conversations on the phone. Then we met for coffee and that was nice. And then he invited me to his house and we had afternoon tea and that was nice. And I kept on waiting. I thought, "No,

I'm going before he gets any ideas." I'd say, "Well, I have to go now" and I'd all but run to the car. [her voice rises and she starts to laugh] *I would all but run to that car.*

Intrigued about what was running through Dallas's mind at the time, I signalled for her to continue. She said:

Dallas: I'd get around the corner and I'd sit there and shake. And I thought, "What did you get up and go for? Go back! No, I can't go back!" [both smiling] How embarrassing! What am I supposed to say? That I've left something behind? [Heather laughs] So then I'd wait for his call. I never once thought of imposing in any way—in any way. And then he'd invite me over to dinner and to the movies and dinner and all this. There's something wrong. Is he gay? And I couldn't—I couldn't work out what was wrong, but there was nothing wrong. He was just being a gentleman. And maybe he didn't want to go falling into bed in the first stages of a relationship. But to me, that just wasn't *normal*. There was something not right and I couldn't work it out. Well, Tony and I laugh about it now.

In forging a love relationship with a man who was not abusive to her, Dallas still had to wrestle with her own inner dialogue about what she was meant to do. Similar to many people who are dating, especially people who have survived abuse in the past, her self-talk was filled with confusion, embarrassment, and self-deprecation. Underneath this dialogue are the themes of trust and suspicion.

Knowing that intimate relationships usually require a level of trust for their development, Dallas's prior experience of abuse meant that she must suspend her disbelief that the new man would respect her. From other stories she told me, I knew that she was often caught in this trust/suspicion bind. It was a bind because although suspicion can be a form of self-protection, it can also block or stifle opportunities to connect with non-abusive others.

Dallas's experience of being sexually coerced explains why she was so surprised when the new man made no sexual overtures toward her. It was such an uncommon experience that she wondered whether he was gay. It took some time for her to accept that he was "just being a gentleman" who did not want to become sexually involved with her so early in their relationship. Having been raped so many times, she had trouble accepting that this was "normal." However, through the counselling she had with Tony, she tried to shake off this self-defeating idea by "laugh[ing] about it."

Dallas further elaborated the difficulties she confronted as she tried to author a new kind of love narrative:

Dallas: So where do you go from there when you're almost 45 years of age?
Heather: To get lessons? [smiling]
Dallas: Yeah!
Heather: Do you—have you known people who have relationships that you consider to be effective?
Dallas: [pause] No.
Heather: [laughs] Really?
Dallas: Well, I'm just trying to think. There's always been some major part of it that I wouldn't put up with. I couldn't put up with. But they seem to plod on happy enough.
Heather: Well, how do you think people learn to behave in relationships? [pause] Other people?
Dallas: They learn how to give and take. But I don't know the limits of give and take. I don't know where I should set the limits of what I'll take. Yeah, so I don't know.

Positive Role Models for Future Possibilities

Unlike Kate, Cecilia, and a good number of younger women I interviewed in Canada, Dallas did not have a feminist role model or a progressive sexual script to help her to negotiate a democratic love relationship. Confused by the mixed messages she received about love in popular culture, and without an example of a love relationship that she wanted to emulate, she had trouble knowing "the limits of give and take." At middle age, this was a disorienting place to be as it risked her returning to old sexual scripts that she had vowed to discard, yet this was only part of the story.

Even if Dallas did have a democratic script from which to work, she had to try to meet a man whose views would be compatible. This was not as straight-forward as it seemed given the reputation Western heterosexual men have for rejecting democratic love stories (Jamieson 1998; Langford 1999; Sternberg 1998). The relative scarcity of compatible and available heterosexual partners in her immediate orbit may explain why Dallas turned to the personal columns.

Although these commercialized meeting places tend to re-inscribe gender conventions through the way individuals are encouraged to market themselves (Jagger 1998), personal columns offered Dallas the chance to contact a more extensive array of men than she might otherwise have met. Routinely involving communication media such as the telephone and Internet, some women gravitate toward these sites because they allow them to make their initial assessments from the perceived safety of their homes, workplaces, or local libraries (Jagger 1998).

Dallas went on to provide more details about the relationship that arose from the personal column:

> I was in this relationship with a guy for about eight months and I was, I was scared shitless. I was scared shitless for about the first two or three months. I never realized, but I was sabotaging the relationship because I thought he was too good for me, because he'd never been a ratbag. Tony, my shrink, he had to really talk me through it to stop me sabotaging everything. I didn't know that just gentle love and being respected in bed—I didn't know what that meant.

Bluntly put, Dallas was "scared shitless" because she was attracted to the idea of a new love relationship, but terrified of being re-abused. Doubting her worth, she talked to Tony, her counsellor. Using mainstream love discourses, he helped her to see how she was sabotaging the relationship. Encouraging her to trust that her new lover is not a wolf in sheep's clothing, he was fortunate that his advice did not backfire. Dallas went on to experience the pleasure of being loved in the ways she had always wanted to be loved: gently. For the first time in many years, she felt "respected in bed."

Eroticizing Gentle Love

Dallas was not the only woman who was striving to be loved in a gentle and respectful manner. Similar to many other women whom Sternberg (1998) researched, she was attracted to "travel love stories" and "gardening love stories." Yet, in contradistinction, most of her male partners were attracted to asymmetrical love stories that revolved around pornography, sacrifice, and surveillance (see Chapter 2).

Jackson (1999) provided another way of understanding how women's desire for heterosexual tenderness can leave them open to men's brutality. She said that:

> Although the concept of love in some senses carries connotations antithetical to violence, in its passionate, romantic form it is not a gentle feeling. It is often characterized as violent, even ruthless. (Jackson 1999, p. 117)

From many of the women's stories, I learned that "gentle love" was most likely to develop when women asserted their interests, not when they surrendered themselves to men or other women. For example, in the story "Creating a Bottom Line," I asked Cecilia to talk about power in love relationships:

> During those 14 years that I was on my own, I started to get a sense for it and I really liked it. Really, there was a bottom line—some very clear bottom lines for me entering into another long-term, committed life with someone. And it was very much around my power.

Tapping into her "power" while she was "on [her] own," Cecilia established "some very clear bottom lines" for her projected re-entry into a "long-term, committed" relationship. It was a useful period that helped her to redefine herself as someone who would not always be submissive. In the next story she illustrated her point by repeating the conversation she had with her prospective second husband:

> *Cecilia:* Let me say it now: I have a life here and I have two daughters. I understand what you're saying, but I'm not saying that I will always go where you go. I will not always drop everything and go where you go, no.

From her previous marriage and from many popular songs and films, Cecilia knew that men are scripted to lead whereas women are meant to follow. Refusing to "drop everything" to go "where [he] go[es]," she was, however, aware that this was not the reaction she was meant to have with her prospective husband. That is why she felt pressured to make it clear to him before they got married. Nevertheless, she used the qualifier "always" to indicate that she may accompany him, but it would depend on the circumstances. It was a complicated manoeuvre because it challenged her to find a way to represent herself as an independent but flexible woman who was loving enough to him and her children that she would do her best to accommodate all their competing needs.

In the next story called "Power Can Be Attractive," Cecilia started to distill her ideas about love and power more clearly:

> *Cecilia:* The thing that occurs to me is that you can actually be using— you can actually be having power—personal power for yourself. It can actually be something that is appealing and attractive to a potential person who loves you. Even though if I think about it, back then I'm sure that never entered my mind. I was such a passive, placid little person. And also because that's not what I learnt either.

Raised to be "passive, placid [and] ... little," it took many years for Cecilia to realize that women's exercise of "personal power" might be "appealing and attractive" to men after all. A few minutes into this story, she then said:

> *Cecilia:* So, I s'pose what I'm getting at the long way around is that the power thing—I can say now that perhaps what I've learned is that you know, um, *it can be a very important part of the love relationship.*
> *Heather:* That it doesn't have to be unsexy?
> *Cecilia:* It *doesn't* have to be—that's right. That can be the appealing thing.

Cecilia's comments illustrate how feminist ideas have infiltrated ordinary women's lives, yet they do not lend support to the contention that sexual equality has already arrived (see Mann 1994). Actually, less than 10 of the 84 women I interviewed presumed the existence of sexual equality. Although a few reported being in a democratic love relationship—and although many women hoped to experience one in the future—most heterosexual women did not tell stories that depicted sexual equality as the underlying norm. Instead, most pointed to the absence of, or struggle for, equitable love relationships, while a few illustrated the difficulties they faced trying to sustain them.

For anyone committed to sexual equality, these findings are disturbing because they reveal the persistence of gender asymmetry in ordinary women's lives, at least as the women themselves perceived it. Despite the rhetoric surrounding the transformation of intimacy, I found limited evidence that men's and women's expectations about love and sex were converging around "mutual self-disclosure" (Jamieson 1998, p. 482). From this I agree with Jackson (1999, p. 121), who argued that:

> Given the lack of evidence that women's demands are currently being met, claims that a more egalitarian form of love is emerging seem absurdly over optimistic and wilfully neglectful of the continued patriarchal structuring of heterosexuality.

Summary

This chapter illustrated some of the difficulties women faced as they attempted to institute changes in their love relationships. After examining why few women were attracted to a single life, I explored some of the mixed views and emotions produced when women try to renegotiate conflicting love narratives. Central to this discussion was the argument about hope, ambivalence, and confusion. Encouraged to be self-sacrificing and submissive while at the same time assertive and decisive, some of the women—particularly those over 45 were confused about the "limits of give and take" (Dallas).

From the stories that Samantha, Emily, Dallas, Jesobel, and Vera told, I noted how confusing it can be when a spouse was intermittently loving and aggressive. For this group of women and others, such as Karen, Kate and Linda, I could also see that in "real life," love and abuse are not so easy to dichotomize. I noted that when love and abuse co-exist, the results were often disorienting and distressing, yet some of the women's stories also suggested that even the most dominating love relationships are not permanently fixed or stable. In some way or another, they indicated that their own actions were not always rational, coherent, or intended.

As Walkerdine (1984, p. 181) noted, women are *not* always selfless "good girls" who "slip painlessly into their roles as women." As I will elaborate further in the next chapter, women as a group do not slavishly adhere to or totally reject the cultural prescriptions for heterosexuality. Instead, they are more accurately portrayed as people who, like many men, are involved in an ongoing process of re-evaluation and revision as they decipher what these discourses might mean for their own lives.

Sasha: *He's my high school sweetheart ... my shoulder to cry on ... a great person to lean on ... he's my best friend.... You know, if you're going to be in love with someone, he might as well be your best friend.*

12

STILL WANTING LOVE, BUT NOT WANTING ABUSE

IN HIS TEXT *LOVE, WHAT LIFE IS ALL ABOUT,* Leo Buscaglia (1979, p. i) quoted Kierkegaard, who said, "To cheat oneself out of love is the most terrible deception. It is an eternal loss for which there is no reparation, either in time or in eternity." Neither Buscaglia nor Kierkegaard are alone in their belief that love is the ultimate source of meaning for human life; that it is so profoundly important that it is a universal phenomenon prioritized in all cultures across the globe (see Jankowiak 1995).

Yet, as I have argued in the early chapters of this book, love may feel natural and organic, but it is governed—or at least mediated—by the cultural conventions that dictate how people should love. These conventions are neither timeless nor innocent. As I have indicated in Chapters 2 to 11, love has many faces, and not all of them are pretty. Many historians, philosophers, sociologists, and critical psychologists alike have argued that over the centuries, the dominant discourses of love have, for the most part, been male dominated. They have shown how laws, informal and formal, have been used to foster, harness, and direct people toward patriarchal love styles. At the same time, these laws, written and unwritten, have been used to thwart, subvert, and/or penalize other love styles, especially those based on sexual equality, "queer" relations, and/or non-monogamy (see Irigaray 1992; Ireland 1988; Sternberg 1998; Wilson 1998; Wood 2001).

While patriarchal love styles vary to some degree, they all share the expectation that women should be the primary guardians of love. Whether it is from traditional fairy tales that invite lovers to enact the roles of rescuer and damsel in distress, or from more pragmatic structural functionalists who promulgate the roles of breadwinner and mother, the message is clear. It is women who are scripted to ensure that love is nurtured every day (see Chapters 4 to 5 and 8 to 11).

Feminists critical of women having fewer rights than men in love relationships but many more responsibilities have gone to great lengths to show how these sexual scripts have disadvantaged women. Langford (1999) spent her entire book doing just this. Ultimately, she argued that while love promises to revolutionize women's lives, it instead returns them to positions of subservience. In her view, so many women subscribe to hetero-patriarchal love styles because they mistakenly believe that their main source of happiness will come from loving men:

> Despite everything, we believe in love. We have faith in love. We have a blind faith in love. Because of this we see love as a means of salvation without noticing how it is a form of re-becoming. If we loosen our attachments and begin to see love for what it is, we cannot but face a crisis of faith for if not love, what then would we place our hearts upon? (Langford 1999, p. 153)

Kipnis (2003) could not agree more. Believing that monogamous hetero-coupledom was deeply flawed as well as unjust, she argued that conventional love relationships, even those built on more contemporary values such as mutuality, were more likely to produce anxiety than happiness. Her basic argument was as follows. For women to "qualify" for love, they must be deemed lovable. Being deemed lovable required "an acceptable level of social normalcy," often achieved by hiding one's abnormalities (Kipnis 2003, p. 71), yet this was not all:

> ... normalcy just gets you in the door ... lovability will also require a thorough knowledge of *mutuality*.... Mutuality means recognizing that your partner has *needs*, and being prepared to meet them. This is largely because modern intimacy presumes that the majority of those needs can and should be met by one person alone: if you question this, you question the very foundations of the institution.... [As a result] intimacy will be, by definition, a rather fraught and anxious scene. (Kipnis 2003, p. 71, original emphasis)

Certainly many of the women I interviewed indicated that their love relationships were sometimes, if not often, fraught and anxious, yet almost none adopted the views put forward by Langford (1999) and Kipnis (2003), who ultimately suggested that love relationships with men were doomed. While open to the question myself, relatively few women were interested in questioning whether love enslaved or liberated women. Instead, the vast majority of them wanted to help me to understand how they had understood and experienced love, irrespective of age, religion, or sexual orientation. That is why I pursued questions about the premium they placed on loving others, what they were aspiring to, and how they were negotiating the pitfalls and dilemmas that so many of them had narrated in their love relationships.

From all the conversations, stories, and analyses carried out for this book, I found that irrespective of their sexual orientation, almost all the women believed that love's trials and tribulations were *worth the effort*. As I will show, many said that love was their primary reason for living. Some told stories that showed me that their faith in love was critical to their future well-being, even if their current experiences of love were a health hazard. For quite a few women and some of the men I talked with, love *could* be a balm, a salve, and a remedy to past suffering, especially suffering caused by abuse. A few even said that without love they would have—and be—"nothing." This is why this chapter is designed to explore why women "bother" to love, particularly given that outsiders might see their faith in love as misguided.

I have organized the material in relation to age, clustering the responses of women who grew up during similar cultural eras. Again, I am not trying to assert that there are some watertight generalities that can be deduced here. Rather, I am suggesting that this material can be used as one more piece of the genealogy of love sewn together for social workers and other health and welfare practitioners to consider as they reflect on how their own fields and modes of practice understand and/or ignore, dismiss, or trivialize stories about love and abuse.

Having stressed the importance of language throughout this book, I have taken a keen interest in the words women used to define love, but also abuse. I asked them directly what words they associated with sexual love, as well as what they were hoping to experience through their love relationships now and in the future. While I acknowledge that we may frame our interests and definitions in ways that we do not live out or believe deep down, I still think that it is important to discern the words that the women chose—at that point in time—to represent good love relationships. This is what they said.

Words That Women Aged 18–29 Years Associated with Love

As Kamen (2000) found in her North American study of post-baby-boomer young women, most of the younger women I interviewed said that while they were sometimes open to casual sex, they preferred to have sex with people they loved. And unlike stereotypes often promulgated about their grandmothers, many of them loved to have sex. This may be due not just to the easing up of sexual restrictions that have long denied women the right to sexual pleasure but also to the licence that the language of love gives women to explore their sexuality in physical and emotional terms. For most of the 26 of the 84 women I interviewed who were in this age range, the language of love, and the feelings associated with it, helped them to feel closer to their partners, and more respected.

Respect, Equality, and Closeness

Katrina and Emilie, the only 18-year-olds in the study, respectively associated love with "family, commitment, security, and closeness," and "respect, equality, and communication." Slightly older, Emma associated love with "stability, fidelity, and support." Erin honed in on "shared values, physical attraction, and intimacy." Holly thought love was about "communication, trust, respect, and admiration." She advised other women to:

> Ask the hard emotional questions, but be prepared for the range of possible answers. Value yourself. Love yourself most of all. Walk if you need to, but don't declare an ultimatum if you're not going to follow through.

Samantha wanted love to be about "trust, care, and sexual desire," yet she went much further than some of the other women (who did not identify experiences of abuse) to suggest that love can provide people with a sense of meaning in their lives:

> *Heather:* What do you think your life would be like if there wasn't love?
> *Samantha:* Oh God, very empty. I'd have this little void of a person. I'd just be walking around with nothing.
> *Heather:* So, it gives your life meaning?
> *Samantha:* Yeah, *it does.*

For Samantha, "a life [without] ... love" would be so "empty" that she would "have this little void of a person." And she was not alone when she said that without love, she would feel as if she was "walking around with nothing."

De-emphasizing sexual desire, and not representing love as the leitmotif of living, Stephanie used the words "trust," "respect," "shared values," and "equality" to outline the love relationship that she hoped for in the future. Similarly, Elena prioritized "respect, trust, shared values, equality, and teamwork." She told me that she grew up with a sole mother who taught her about feminism and had a poster on her bedroom wall that said, "Girls can do anything!" Bette focused on "warmth, closeness, support, and reliability," adding that:

> Both people in a relationship are not necessarily happy every moment, but that they're supported by each other so that they can each, like, achieve goals that they want to work towards, and that if one person needs more support at that time, the other person is there.

Honesty, Fidelity, and Good Communication

With Bette, Bethany spoke of her desire for "trust, respect, and honesty" in a sexual love relationship, and Sarah echoed "trust, respect, honesty, and fidelity." For Sasha, love was—or at least should be about—"commitment and sacrifice," whereas Merryl hoped for "financial security, status, and family."

Stepping away from the customary associations of financial security, status, and family, Carla, Lou, and Kelly all mentioned equality, respect, and communication. Rose used these words, but added the term "kindness" to the mix. Tamara did likewise and connected kindness with "consideration." All of them sought to be valued as equal partners, ones who would have equal rights and privileges in their relationships, "even when a baby came along" (Lou). For some, equality hinged mostly on the division of household labour and access to leisure time, whereas for others, it had more emotional connotations where "communication" was used to signal the shared effort both parties would contribute to making the relationship work.

Sometimes the women's aspirations for love relationships were placed in opposition to the relationships they had with their fathers or past lovers, even when they were with partners who would or could not oblige. Kelly provided a good example of this when she said:

> I definitely don't want a relationship with a man like my father. Um, I think the relationship I am in now he's probably a bit like my father and I think it's probably all those qualities in him that I don't like that are similar to my father. My father is just not a very, um, he's not very connected, I don't think, with myself or sister or my mom really. He doesn't seem to take an active interest in any of our lives, which was something that was frustrating that I was younger and I wanted, you know, I wanted him to be interested, but now that I think of it, I can see how you sort of get used to it.

Echoing Kipnis's (2003) sentiments about mutuality, many of the younger women I interviewed wanted to be emotionally connected to their partners so that they could share their dreams, hopes, and past hurts. Using the language of "connection," Lisa defined "compatibility" with "sharing a similar intellect" and "having similar interests." Gill saw that having "shared values and goals" and being "empathic and compassionate" with one another was the most likely route to happiness. And for most of the younger women, happiness included sexual satisfaction. One of the benefits of being emotionally connected to a lover is the sense of entitlement that many women felt as a result. For many, their sense of sexual entitlement allowed them to shake off the historical expectation that they should be "the exclusive guardians of the moral order" (Kamen 2000, p. 235). Not having to be the exclusive guardians of the moral order gave them more space to explore their desires, including those that might otherwise be viewed as naughty, dirty, or sinful.

Love without Commodification

Preferring to associate love with "connectedness, respect, honesty, and tenderness" Marnie said she wanted "love without commodification." By this I understood her to have meant that love was not about dedicating oneself exclusively to another person, privately or publicly. Nor was it about the joint ownership of property. Instead, it was about joining with a person—or persons—in emotional and sexual experiences that would be rich and gratifying to all involved. I say "all" rather than "both" because Marnie was loath to be seen as part of a couple. For her it involved inhibiting her desire and curtailing her freedom, especially her freedom to express herself sexually:

> My sexuality is bound up in my individuality. It's not a commodity. It's not something that I think of as a bargaining chip or as, um, a means of owning someone or being known by somebody for the purposes of some kind of long-term, um, compensation. To me, um, I am an individual. I go through life as an individual. And right now I identify as a single, polyamorous person. So I don't like to have just one primary partnership. At the moment I do have one person I consider a lover, but I don't really, um, it's sort of weird.... I just mostly call him my friend. And, uh, I don't want to be identified as being part of a couple.
> *Heather:* Mmm, can you tell me why?
> *Marnie:* ... it's like I see these little clusters of castles—little nuclear families—their own little unit. To me, they're all separate and all alone. Scary things happen behind closed doors.... Terrible things happen and people are so afraid of losing faith, so afraid that the world will see what terrible things are happening, so they hide this stuff....
> *Heather:* What would you like to see happen?
> *Marnie:* People being open, not wanting to have that kind of closed door. It's also my way of saying to the world I am going to make sure that I, um, I am not hiding any secrets, that nobody's going to be able to lock me up and keep me there. Um, I don't know, I don't know how to put it exactly.

Part of the reason why Marnie was not sure "how to put it exactly" was due to the paucity of precedents or role models that she could use to explain what she meant. As I noted in Chapters 6 to 8, working from conventional sexual scripts can be much easier because the road to travel is well mapped and worn. Given the potential penalties applied to those who do not conform, not having a clearly identifiable sexual script to use can be confusing and scary. It was a dilemma facing other women, especially those who did not identify as straight and who did not seek to base their relationships on monogamous coupledom, such as Rachael and Fiona.

Words Used to Describe Love by Women Aged 30–39 Years

Of the 84 women I interviewed, 21 were aged 30–39 years. Rachael and Fiona were two of them. Similar to Marnie, they defined themselves as polyamorous (wanting many loves) rather than monogamous (just one love). This was informed by their definitions of love. For Rachael, love was associated with "respect and growth" and for Fiona, "freedom." Hoping to throw off the shackles they associated with monogamous hetero-coupledom, they told me how they tried to "play fair"; how they tried, as a couple, to engage in multiple sexual liaisons in an ethical manner.

Polyamory: Love without Limits?

It was Rachael and Fiona, the very first Canadian women I interviewed, who prompted me to read Anapol's (1997) *Polyamory: The New Love without Limits*. They also urged me to read Easton and Liszt's (2002) *The Ethical Slut*. Both books encouraged readers to consider engaging in sexual possibilities that moved beyond or outside conventional monogamy. They were possibilities that did not divide the world into gays or straights or singles or couples. According to Anapol (1997, p. 27), polyamory, which literally means "many loves," can serve as a vehicle for personal and spiritual growth, but only if subscribers realize that it is:

> ... a demanding lovestyle. The challenges of relating intimately to more than one partner at a time will certainly accelerate your own development. This can be an asset or a liability, depending upon your motivations.... Nothing will bring your "stuff" to the surface more quickly than involvement with several intimate partners at once. Nothing will open your heart and activate your fears more intensely. If you welcome the chance to work on yourself in this way then polyamory maybe for you.

Both Rachael and Fiona, who identified as lesbian, were keen to promote the benefits of polyamory, patiently answering my questions, such as "What do you do about jealousy?" and "How do you sustain the primacy of your first relationship?"

> *Rachael:* We've committed to only love each other. We don't, um, want or seek out any emotional connection to the level that we have, we just like the friendship level, um, with other women, and sex and dating and whatever. Like, I mean we have our guidelines—our sexual guidelines—as to what we do, what our limitations are. We will only *love* each other, but we also acknowledge that we are attracted to other women, and that we like to have fun. Whether we're getting together with friends and maybe it's a little bit more or you meet somebody new and go on a date and they become a friend instead of a lover. Or maybe you know one person for years that you see them once in a while who's a lover. Those kinds of things.

I learned that part of the way they dealt with this was to be honest, open, and upfront, and, most importantly, to talk about it often. Rachael explained:

> It's something that we talk about constantly too because our ideas about it can change as we experience different things. Maybe we'll experience something and not be so comfortable with it. Or maybe we haven't really acted on it, uh, say we haven't been non-monogamous in a year or whatever, and we want to check in and make sure it's all still good to go....

"Check[ing] in" with each other that they were "still good to go" (ahead with multiple love liaisons) was just part of the process spelled out. There were many other dimensions to loving if more expansive possibilities were to be realized.

More Expansive Possibilities?

Fiona and Rachael dedicated much time and energy to enacting this alternative love style in ways they believed were ethical. Strategies and techniques for managing emotional discomfort were part of the process. For instance, both tried to harness the energy of negative emotions (such as jealousy) so often produced by non-monogamy:

> *Fiona:* We recognize we're going to feel jealous.... It's just not necessarily given the weight that other people put on it.... It's not the worst thing that could ever happen. We know we will feel jealous and that's *ok*. We try to eroticize it too, you know. I feel jealous because you're so hot....

> *Rachael:* I think jealousy says more about the person who's feeling it than the situation. If I feel jealous of Fiona going on a date, I get far more information if I sit down and think why is this bugging me? And is that a legitimate reason?

Rachael recounted conversations she had with herself, particularly those used to deal with strong emotions, such as fear:

> Am I afraid she's going to leave me? What does monogamy or non-monogamy have to do with that? It's not a protector either way. There is no protector. Am I afraid that she finds this other person more attractive? Well, she's spending her life with me and I've never felt that she doesn't find me attractive.

They then explained how they dealt with the wider social pressures to conform to established, monogamous hetero-coupledom:

> *Rachael:* It's just kind of reminding ourselves ... that these programmed tapes come from society and flow into us. *But I didn't choose them.* There are other ways of loving that are more expansive. All [our love relationships] have done is to bring really great things into our lives. It hasn't narrowed us or harmed us at all. *It's expansive. It's very expansive* and—
> *Fiona: Free.*
> *Rachael: Free and fun.* It's a wonderful way to love. Yeah, I recommend it.

Freedom came from being able to shrug off the prohibitions against their preferred love style, as Rachael explained:

> I think the biggest thing is that we're not treated as if this is a real relationship, which there's nothing we can do about. But the internal struggle isn't really that big a deal.

Ria agreed.

Effortless Effort?

Ria also identified as polyamorous (but bisexual), and used the words "easy," "open," and "honest" to define the key elements of love. For her, moral conservatives and radical feminists alike were not going to convince her that she had to decide whether she was either "lesbian or straight, not both." Said Ria:

> I have the ability to love more than one person at any one time. The way that I love these people won't necessarily be the same.... I'm able

to love a person not because of their gender.... I believe that there are more than two sexes and I have the ability to love all kinds of people along the continuum.... There are just so many different ways of being in this world.

Ria told me she was sexually involved with a person biologically classified as female, but who identified as male. Aware of how sexual classifications can be used to constrain, if not hurt people, she was careful when she spoke and preferred not to use any categories, including "transgender" or "transsexual." Instead, she tried to get people around her to think about how strict gender categories can be harmful to the health of those who do not "naturally" align. Admittedly, Ria sometimes found it difficult to maintain the patience she needed to help others see beyond the binaries (or divisions) of male/female and gay/straight. She persevered so that she was "not forced to choose between family and [her] relationship."

Tonya was another woman I interviewed who had to figure out ways not to alienate her family while she embarked on (bi)sexual relationships that she knew would be viewed as foreign and unacceptable. However, she differed from Fiona, Rachael, and Ria insofar as she believed in monogamy so long as it was contracted rather than assumed. For Tonya, love was a verb rather than a noun. People acted loving. It was not a possession. That is why she believed her love relationships need to involve "honour, integrity, and effortless effort":

> Love isn't a commodity.... Love isn't grasping, projecting, demeaning, or belittling. Violent behaviours aren't love.... It's about effortless effort.

"Effortless effort" referred to loving others in energetic, generous, reflective, and insightful ways. It was about loving without counting the costs, yet it was not so arduous that it felt like hard labour, nor was it characterized by anger and violence, which she disassociated from love. Love was reliant on trust, support, and friendship. They were bases on which honour, integrity, and effortless effort could be built.

Trust, Support, Commitment, and Friendship

Jen (monogamous and heterosexual) also used the words "trust," "support," and "commitment" to describe the basis of a good love relationship. Miserable as a child from the constant ridicule she received, she never imagined that her life could be so happy. She never thought she would experience the joys that love could bring through the relationship she had with her partner. Vanessa agreed.

Also in her thirties and heterosexual, Vanessa had a lot of faith in love's potential to change a person. It helped her to believe that in spite of much childhood neglect, she might be able to have a relationship not built on pain and disappointment but on "trust, sharing, and respect." Vanessa told me stories about how she had stopped accepting blame for her adopted mother's depression. However, when she was much younger, this was not the case.

To escape the pressures at home, Vanessa married young and quickly had to figure out how she might nurture her children while their father's drug problem was spiralling out of control. She saw many twists and turns in all their lives. Both positively and negatively, she had first-hand experience in witnessing people and love relationships change. In her view, love could act as a catalyst for personal transformation. She wanted other people to think about this, and seriously. She was eager to see health and welfare professionals contemplate the possibility that abusive intimates *could* change. She was more than a little frustrated by the tendency for people to assume that once someone was an abuser, the person would always be an abuser. She knew this was not the case because she had witnessed how her husband had eventually been changed by love, how their relationship stopped being dominated by his fears and drug use, and how, over the years, they had developed a relationship in which she felt secure and accepted (also see Chapter 11).

Feeling Secure and Accepted

Many 30–40-year-old women wanted love relationships based on "trust, stability, loyalty, and commitment." While most still wanted sexual passion, they honed in on the need to be able to get along with partners in an everyday kind of way. With delight rather than smugness, quite a few said they had achieved this. They included Chloe, Kim, Ria, Su, Colleen, Annie, and Felicity. Take, for instance, Felicity, who appreciated how she and her partner, Keith, valued each other's love of life, as well as their love for each other. She told me that she and Keith shared a similar sense of humour, and that she appreciated their playfulness. Most of all, she was delighted by their uncritical acceptance of each other's physical appearance:

> For me, it always has to—always has been—it has to be somebody funny. You know, quick-witted. I'm not one huge on looks, like, it doesn't really matter. I mean Keith is, you know, 5-foot-5, bald, with a big truck-driver belly. It's not a physical kind of thing for me at all....

Kim, 33-year-old communications worker from Winnipeg, also liked the idea of being with a man who could see a woman's inner beauty. She was tired of having her value measured through her looks. She said the pressure to keep slim prompted her to overeat. When criticized for putting on weight, she would feel low. It was then harder for her to believe in herself. It was also harder to maintain faith in her preferred love style, one in which she could feel secure and accepted.

Similar to some of the older women I interviewed, especially those smitten with the idea of chivalrous romance, Kim found it took some time for her to develop the kind of relationship that she had been hoping for. Referring to her second husband, she said, "He still thought I was the most beautiful woman in the world even when I weighed 210 pounds."

Feeling Emotionally and Sexually Connected

Annie was another heterosexual woman in her thirties to feel sexually and emotionally secure with a male partner, and one with whom she had developed an egalitarian relationship. Noting how comfortable they were in each other's company, she attributed their solid basis to the years spent sharing a house as students. Without romance clouding her vision, she had been able to get to know him as a friend and housemate first. Only after they had established a strong emotional connection did she fall for him and marry. Passionate about her husband, she nevertheless distinguished what she described as "the hubba-bubba, let's get it on kind of passion" with another kind of passion evoked from the "little touches." These little touches included the times her husband called her from work to say "hi," or when she watched him laugh with loved ones, and play with young children. She also made it clear to me that this emotional connection was central to her sexual satisfaction.

Now in a common-law relationship for two years, Mary also prioritized sexual and emotional connectedness and derived great pleasure from doing so. She said that "trust, happiness, respect, equality, and communication" helped her to feel loved and accepted. She explained that she needed to "walk a different path" to build a relationship of this kind. From her previous experiences, she had learned that while sex was important, having a solid friendship and shared vision for the future was even more so. Ever practical, she advised women to keep a little money aside for themselves, "just in case things change, or there is an emergency."

Maree provided a degree of contrast to many of the women in her age bracket. Having been married to her childhood sweetheart for 10 years and having recently found Christianity, she believed love was about "respect, acceptance, appreciation, and the laying down of self." She told me about the epiphany she had one day when she stopped expecting her husband to meet all her needs, and when she stopped "looking at what [her] husband didn't do" and instead tried to see "what he is, and what he does do."

Words Used to Describe Love by Women Aged 40–49 Years

Not one of the 19 women whom I interviewed, aged in their forties, rejected love out of hand. Actually, women in this age bracket did not define love in distinctly different ways from the younger women I interviewed. Take, for instance,

Polly, Lynne, Cindy, and Dianne all foregrounding the importance of "sharing, respect, trust, and commitment." Many told me how they were trying to instill these values in their children. Alongside the younger cohorts of women in this study, most of the women in their forties—across sexual orientation, class background, educational level, and body shape—derived happiness and satisfaction from their love relationships. Most reported that despite the bumps in the road, loving others was something that they would continue to value. Dianne, from Winnipeg, was a case in point.

Everyday Respect, Care, and Togetherness

After being sexually and physically abused by her father, and then raped at knifepoint as an adult, Dianne told me that she wished that every woman, especially women who had survived abuse, could develop the kind of love relationship that she had with her husband. Another woman, Jesobel, agreed. Both women shared a childhood of abuse and the painful legacy that can ensue, yet in adulthood, both had long-standing love relationships that soothed their souls. Both told me how they had honed in on prospective partners who shared similar values. They sought out people whom they could respect as well as feel respected by. Both pursued relationships in which they felt a general sense of care and togetherness.

> *Jesobel:* When I read it [the advertisement for the research] I thought, "Ahh, that's so important to talk about." But I also thought, "No one has really examined it, not like this." I've never read any books, especially when I was going through a therapy that dealt with love after all of that, love after all of the nightmares and the self-loathing and this and that. Everything you go through after a relationship like that [an abusive one], and coming out on the other side and meeting someone, you know, how delightful that is. To think, "Gosh, I don't have to go through life alone. Even when you're comfortable with the knowledge, you're fine being on your own. There *is* something to be said for somebody getting up in the morning before you and making coffee. It's all those wonderful *little things*. Now I've got to get home to that wonderful man. I promised him I'd come home tonight not too late....

Patience, Shared Vision, and "the Little Things in Life"

Iris and Libby could see what Jesobel was talking about. Love *could* be wonderful. Libby and Iris felt so strongly about one another that Libby migrated from Australia to Canada so they could be together. Neither woman expected it was going to be easy having immigration officials positively assess a newly formed, international lesbian relationship, particularly given the tighter border-control measures instituted post-9/11. They also recognized how difficult it was for them to both get great jobs in the same town. Patiently, they persevered and weathered some storms. A few years into their relationship, both women remained adamant that it had all been worth it. As well as love, they also shared their vision.

Sharing a future vision with a partner was also important to Natalie. She stressed the importance of valuing partners equally. She also stressed how great it was to be able to share intellectual pursuits. Sam agreed. She defined love as "happiness, trust, respect, sharing, and equality." Alexandria said love was about "walking the same path together and sharing the same vision." Ana added how she needed a "true companion." A true companion was someone with whom she would want to share the minutiae of daily life.

The three Australian sisters I interviewed, all aged in their forties, also emphasized the importance of the minutiae (or small things) of love in everyday life. Karen said this was how people showed "respect, fairness, and kindness" to each other as they went along. Noticing the small things was one of the reasons she believed her marriage had lasted for the long haul. In relation to her own marriage, Linda agreed. She, however, stressed the importance of "closeness, connection, and support." Cecilia preferred to emphasize the words, "respect, sharing, and shared values." In contrast to her sisters, whose constructions of good love relationships had not altered much over time, Cecilia's views had completely changed. Instead of basing her relationships on traditional fairytale love as she had when she was young, she prized her second marriage for its respect and shared values (see Chapter 9–12).

In the Spirit of Loving Oneself and Others

When talking about love and respect, women in their forties often mentioned self-respect. Diana, an artist in Winnipeg, was quite direct about the need to respect oneself or risk being trampled on in a relationship. For her, "good love relationships" "bring out the best in each other." Taking stock of this was part of the way women could figure out whether to commit to a love relationship. Married for almost 20 years and with two children whom she loved dearly, she noted how important it was for women to love and respect themselves enough to seek out relationships where they would be valued.

While not necessarily using the same words as Diana, Evelyn, Olivia, and Shelley all told stories where they prioritized love relationships that involved partners showing grace and goodwill to one another. Evelyn emphasized "trust, commitment, and sharing," and Olivia put a high premium on "real companionship, shared interests, and sexual connectedness." Shelley, a 44-year-old administrative worker from Winnipeg, spoke of "equality, respect, and being with someone you can rely on." Married now for 21 years, she was delighted to be able to say that "He [her husband] helps me make my dreams come true."

Polly shared Shelley's view, but only in relation to her second husband. While she described her first husband as cold, emotionally detached, and controlling, she nevertheless accepted that he might not have been like this with someone else. Philosophical about what she could learn from her divorce, she said:

> ... the relationship dynamic was very unhealthy for *both of us*, for *both partners*. I learned a lot from the experience, took a lot away. Hopefully I have been able to encourage my daughter to be more independent, but still understand that *love is a tremendous force in anyone's life, male or female, and that it's not the—it doesn't have to be the controlling aspect and the negative.*

Faye displayed a similar degree of optimism about the ways in which love can change people. Associating love with "care, concern, being one another's confidantes, and respect," she talked about the changes she had undergone through the dissolution of her first marriage:

> How you love yourself makes a big difference on how you love other people. I'm just learning more and more about me and how I view love. It was very different from how my [first] husband viewed love. You know, I would always say to him, "You can tell me that you love me, but actions speak louder than words." He would profess that he loved me, but his actions didn't show it. That's why my perspective is that you have to show a person that you love them. You just can't say that you love them.

With so many of the women I interviewed, Faye sought emotional intimacy with her partner, hoping that he would *show* that he loved her, not just say "I love you" from time to time. Like many of the women, she hoped to see love in action, and by this she did not mean receiving gifts or having fancy dinners. Instead, it was the acts of kindness, the little actions woven into the week that were done with a semblance of grace and joy (rather than duty or burden) that made all the difference. Many women told me that it was when these little actions dropped away or became notably absent that they would start to lose faith that their relationships could last the distance. Perhaps because many of them had been married, had children, divorced, and re-partnered, it was the women in their forties who seemed most keen to tell me this. They also tended to tell stories about how their views of love had altered over the years.

Not So Convinced about Fairytale Love

Not all the women in their forties were enamoured with fairytale love. In earlier chapters I explored how some of the women modified their views about love, particularly after experiencing relationships that soured or became abusive. Brenda provided a good example of this. She altered her views about conventional romance stories after she separated from her husband. She was particularly skeptical of the notion of finding your soul mate, and of the possibility of mutuality, as expressed only with one person:

> I like looking at the romance industry. I like looking at the concept of what we're sold. I think a lot about gender and roles and feelings and what makes people connect to other people. You know, intimacy is many things. We get it from many sources, but we're sold a bill of goods about having it with one person. Then the other day I passed by a stand that had *Psychology Today* on it. The cover was something on *soul mates*. They said it was the single most damaging thing that had ever happened in the last 10 to 20 years. They said that this concept of a soul mate creates so many unmet needs. Why not see that you need to get things from so many different sources rather than just one soul mate?

Brenda told me that her long-term marriage had worn away to the point that both of them felt as if they had nothing left, yet she said she hated having to deal with the identity of being single again. Others around her kept urging her to get out there again. Reluctantly she started reading the personal columns and Internet dating sites. As she flicked through people's lists of hopes, desires, and testimonies, and reflected on the many dates she'd had, she concluded:

> Everyone wants the same thing.... They all want someone who's *really sincere*, someone who *communicates*.... They say, "I really want to meet someone who, you know, is just really comfortable with who she is." You know, someone who isn't into game playing.

Earlier associating love with "shared values, respect, and a common vision," Brenda had become jaded. This was not surprising given most of the dates had amounted to little more than a quick coffee and a hefty dose of embarrassment, with mumbled excuses made at the end for why they should not meet again. However, what I found interesting was that she *persevered*. She kept on trying even when she felt so cynical about the prospect of meeting a man with whom she could create the kind of relationship she so clearly wanted. And she did so even though, by her own admission, her pride was high and she was deeply fearful of rejection.

Brenda's stories reminded me of the stories Dallas told about Internet dating (see Chapter 10). She also reflected on Brenda's comments about lots of people wanting someone who is sincere and can communicate. In spite of, or perhaps because of, her experiences of abuse, Dallas spent a lot of time trying to reject the popular fairytale that with enough love, all obstacles may be overcome. She had so wanted to believe that with enough love, abusive behaviour would disappear:

> I've always wanted a real sense of *belonging*—always—so in a way I think maybe I was looking and hoping that their arsehole behaviour would

> go away if only I could make them love me enough. Yeah, but I had to make them love me enough and care for me enough to let go of their erratic behaviour.... The more I failed, the more I thought, "There must be something dreadfully wrong with me if I keep failing." ... It just reinforced everything that I was told when I was a child—that I was plain and stupid and ugly and all the rest of it.

Still plagued by the voices of ridicule carried from childhood, Dallas struggled not to believe that she was personally responsible for love relationships that did not turn out as she had hoped. Hope was plentiful because she sincerely believed in love. Her faith was so strong that when troubles came, she tried even harder. Only when she was much older was she able to see this pattern and notice how self-defeating it could be.

Dianne also survived chronic child sexual abuse and wrestled with fairytale love through her adulthood. Thinking about her twenties, she could see that she had held onto the idea that "you will know who you're meant to be with when you meet him."

> When I was much younger, I had this crazy idea that I would know the man that I was supposed to love and be with for the rest of my life by the way we were together sexually. I would just know. It would be some sort of intuitive realization based on the big O or something ... but inside there was this, "I can't do this" kind of feeling. There was also an enormous, an enormous amount of guilt because [when] I was with my dad I had an orgasm.

Dianne told me that she was able to create a happy, safe, and sexually pleasurable marriage of 15 years only because she had given up the romantic ideal that "you [will] just know" when a love relationship is right or meant to be. Instead, she took her time to develop trust, build respect, and explore sexual compatibility. She did this a man with whom she would have previously dismissed because he was not heroic, nor tall, dark, and handsome.

Ricky was another woman in her forties to challenge conventional claims of romantic love. The first related to the requirement that sexual infidelity would signal the end of her relationship. She said that after being married to a man in the armed services for 20 years now, she was prepared to accept that he might have a fling when working out of town. Distinguishing a fling from an ongoing affair, she said only an affair was likely to spell disaster. For her and many other women, especially older women, the romantic feelings associated with being passionately in love were lovely, but they were like the icing on the cake. They were not something that could compensate for "the lows" if the rest of the relationship was missing a more substantial and sustainable intimate base. Alexandria explains:

Intimacy is, is letting your guard down—when you take off everything. I mean, not that you're just stripped naked in physical body. An intimate relationship means that you've stripped yourself and you stand before someone with all your faults, with all of your fears, all of your inadequacies, and you stand there and they accept you anyway. That's true intimacy.

Words Used to Describe Love by Women Aged 50–59 Years

Of the 13 women in this age range whom I interviewed, all believed in love. Most reinforced the need for love relationships to have a solid basis, stressing their desire for monogamy and a real sense of family. Take, for instance, Monica, who emphasized "sharing and respect," or Barbara from Toronto who associated love with "trust and companionship" before underlining their need for sexual fidelity. Catherine agreed. She associated love with "companionship, trust, and respect." Freya did likewise, using the terms "shared lives, emotional connectedness, and respect" to define their preferred love styles. Rae emphasized "family and being there for one another." However, Catherine told me that she wanted "monogamy without ownership."

Having been married to her husband for 12 years, but now having been divorced for 18 years, Catherine said she wanted a relationship where she could express her emotions without her partner recoiling in discomfort or disapproval. This became a priority after her husband said he had lost interest in her because of her emotional insecurity, yet at the same time, she said he resented her attempts to be an independent person.

Wanting the Whole Thing: The Sex and the Love

Cutting across those who sought a sense of security and family were those who foregrounded their needs for sexuality and sensuality. Freya did this when she associated love with "closeness, desire, and skin touching skin." When Joy noted "passion, delight, and pleasure being in one another's company," her references were also sexual. Scarlet (who deliberately chose that pseudonym) said that she needed to be with someone who also thought that sex was important. She said that was the only way it worked with her because she was a "very sexual" person. Open to long- or short-term relationships, she judged the quality of her relationships not on longevity but on displays of respect, care, and sexual compatibility. Playfully, she said that "For my epitaph, I'd like it to say, 'She was good at her job and loved by many men.'"

Emily had more in common with Scarlet than their single status. Choosing to define love as "trust, care, and sexual compatibility," she agreed that the quality of the relationship was more important than duration. When I spoke with her many years after her divorce, she was still hoping to meet someone who would love and cherish her. Yet, for Emily, sex was impoverished if it was not tied to love. It was a view held by many of the women I interviewed, irrespective of how comfortable they were with casual sex, yet it did not mean that all aspects of conventional romance were accepted. More provisional and circumspect, Emily joined lots of women in her age range to question particular dimensions of monogamous heterosexual marriage, saying, "I don't think marriage is a good idea because when they marry you—when I married my husband, he said, 'Now you're mine. *You're mine!*' Now to me, that's *sick*."

Lori was similarly circumspect about marriage. Prioritizing "respect, equality, emotional availability, and care" in love relationships, her reservations with marriage related to the tendency of married couples getting in a rut. Post-divorce, she hated the idea of re-enacting the role of the dowdy wife, one who was expected to cook, clean, and look after children.

Lori explained what she was hoping for after she left her husband and met someone else:

> He was at grad dinner and he's sitting across the table from me, and the next thing you know, we're having this mad, torrid affair. And I thought, *"This was what I want!"* ... I had love like that. [snaps her fingers] It was just so chemical.... Whatever it is, it's a chemical high. I swore I could *fly*. You know it was *incredible*. It was traumatic for the kids, but they got over it. We talked about it. They understood and once they realized I wasn't going back, and I didn't say, you know, what I thought was the problem. I just said, *"Look I can't do this anymore. I'm not going to stay with your dad, and so this is my life."*

After 25 years of putting her husband and children's needs first and sublimating the desires she had for herself, Lori now felt entitled to explore herself and her sexual desires.

The Thrill of Sexual Passion

Similar to some other women in their fifties, Lori was enthralled by sexual passion. I could see it when she recounted stories about times when she told friends and colleagues about her new life:

> It was great to have him [boyfriend] there that first summer. We saw each other as often as we possibly could. *It was wonderful.* If everybody could be in love like that ... you just break out laughing at the stupidest time. I couldn't wait to tell people.... If I met somebody in the parking lot where I worked, they'd be, "So, how's your summer?" I'd say, "*Great!* I left my husband, I bought a condo, I bought a car, I have a new boyfriend, and I'm happy. And they'd go *"Wow!"* [laughing] You

> know, one of my friends actually said, *"You're living my dream."* And I thought, *"Yes, I am. It was just so exciting. It was so exciting.*

It frustrated Lori if people reacted cynically to her tales of delight:

> Some people would say, "You know, that won't last, those feelings, that incredible high, *it won't last.*" I just thought, "Oh pooh you," you know, "Just leave me alone." *It did last.* It lasted, like, three-quarters of the year and it was just totally exciting.... It was so wonderful, but eventually it got comfortable. It does get a little bit more predictable and, you know, things kind of calmed down, but it's still a nice place to be.

Lori was not the only woman adamant that relationships could be joyous, wonderful, and fun. Many women over 60 also thought so.

Words Used to Describe Love by Women Aged 60 and Older

Of the 84 women I interviewed, only five were over 60. That is why I have clustered their views, not because I have assumed that they grew up in exactly the same era. All five women in their older years used words such as "respect," "trust," "commitment," and "communication" to characterize good love relationships.

Not Forcing Love But Using It as a Guide

For Marcie (64 years old) and Amanda (59 years old), the love they shared was best summarized by a card that one of their children had given them after they told them about their contemplation of marriage:

> *Marcie:* How do you like this for a card from your daughter?
> *Heather:* [reading from the card] "It's a never-ending journey of discovery of how much two people have grown in love for each other. It is wonderful how happy you have been together. Recognize this and hold it close. Keep on listening to your hearts. Let your love continue to guide you every step of the way and you'll find life's journey more exciting, wonderful, and fulfilling than you could ever imagine." [Now reading the message written by their daughter] "I am so happy you've finally decided to get married."
> *Amanda:* See the kind of attitude the kids have? As the kids grew up, it was their choice, whoever they brought home.... Our daughter said it in several letters that we have too—that she is so grateful for having the parents that allowed her to bring home whomever she liked without any repercussions.... Martin [their son] said he feels the same way.

Having been together for so long, and having overcome some of the long-standing difficulties that stem from the social prohibitions against same-sex love relationships, Marcie and Amanda were eager to point out how important it was to love others in their community as well as themselves. Marcie also added that when it came to loving others, it was important for women to use their intuition to decipher how they wanted their relationships to unfold:

> I think women have a lot of intuition that we don't use and they should listen to their inner self to know whether this combination is good for them or not. And don't force it. Don't force love. Don't feign love in the name of security and not living the rest of your life alone, which I think drives a lot of people to make alliances that have no substance.

Forming relationships that had "no substance" concerned Marcie and Amanda, mostly because they believed it was likely to hurt women. However, they were also concerned about the pressures often placed on people, especially women, to form and remain in unhealthy love relationships because of fears of living alone and going against couple convention.

Love's Transformative Powers

Sixty-four-year-old Vera was concerned about women getting hurt in love relationships and also about them moving too far away from love. Having been married to a man who physically and emotionally abused her for much of their 37 years of marriage, she said that she had experienced this reluctance herself and had observed many other women, including much younger women, shy away from love. In her view, shying away from love was a problem because it meant barricading oneself from a source of potential joy. Instead of denying oneself this pleasure, she was interested in how people might embark on new love relationships that would be healing, transformative, and enlivening:

> *Vera:* Love can heal people. I've seen it with my friends. I've seen it with Lindell and Jack, now married and living in China. I've seen the difference since her husband left her. When she married Jack, she really blossomed.
> *Heather:* Has she?
> *Vera:* Mmm. I've seen it with Patricia now that she's got Dick. She's really *happy*. She's got somebody who phones her every day to see how she is.
> *Heather:* Has she come to life?
> *Vera: Yes*, she *has* come to life. Morag with Andy—she's another one.

With other women such as Brenda (who criticized the idea of the soul mate) and Ricky (who was not convinced that the feelings associated with being in love could be sustained), Vera was critical of the idea that true love comes only once:

> I don't think there's any one person in this world for, for you. I think that's a fallacy. This "You're meant for each other"—I think it's a fallacy because the world is such an enormous place and there are so many people in it. There can't be just one person in the whole world for you. There's got to be a big selection. It's all a case of time.

Denouncing the discourse of "The One" as a "fallacy," Vera appealed to rationality as she figured that since the world is "such an enormous place" and that it contains "so many people," there must be more than one love match possible per person. This thinking gave her hope that future love was possible since it must "all" be a question "of time." As an aspiration, the desire to love again fits with Langford's (1999, p. 150) contention that "the cure prescribed for love is more love—'don't worry, you'll meet someone else.'"

Love Can Make Life Rich and Exciting

Eighty-year-old Kathleen quite simply believed that

> love … is important. It is joy and happiness … the kind of love that I had with Jimmy. Every day was a sunshiny day even though it was cloudy sometimes.… Love has made my life meaningful and rich. I wouldn't have had it any other way. (80-year-old woman in Winnipeg who retired from the armed forces)

And Kathleen believed this despite being "the other woman" to a married man for 26 years and initially being "his plaything." She said: "I could do without the passion as long as I had the love. The kind of love that I had was Jimmy. He eventually loved me and that made life even more exciting."

Also aged 80, Lillian shared some of Kathleen's ideas about love, but zoomed in on companionship, comfort, and reliability:

> *Heather:* When the word "love" comes up, what sort of words spring to mind?
> *Lillian:* Companionship is one of them. Being with someone that you're comfortable with and you trust. It's sort of a very overwhelming sort of feeling in lots of ways. It covers so many aspects of your life, just ordinary everyday things, but also holidays and celebrations and things like that. It's a constant throughout, at all of those things.

Having been married for 57 years and still mourning the death of her husband just the year before we spoke, Lillian told me many stories, including stories about their wartime courtship. The story "Waiting to Hear the Doorbell Ring" was recounted when I asked the following:

> *Heather:* What were the feelings that you had when you were in love?
> *Lillian:* Oh, *excitement*. It was just so *exciting*, looking forward to him coming over each night and looking at the time and waiting to hear the doorbell ring. The *anticipation*, opening the door, and there was a big hug.

After almost 60 years, Lillian could remember not only how she and her husband had met but how she had felt when they first dated. Not really going anywhere and without the space they needed to fully explore their sexual desire, they nevertheless felt the electricity of the love and sexual passion that they would go on to feel for each other for many more decades. From this story and many others, I knew that Lillian felt emotionally rich and fulfilled.

Summary

As I have shown, almost all the women in this study, albeit women who volunteered to be interviewed about love, believed that love was critical to them enjoying their life and feeling fully human. While embodying different norms about how love should be and what love relationships should look like, this was true of women irrespective of whether they were heterosexual, bisexual, or lesbian. It was also true irrespective of whether they placed a lot of stock on monogamy or opted for polyamory, or negotiated something in between.

While not all women thought that love was a remedy for past suffering, and although a couple of women were not interested in love relationships, the rest were broadly optimistic about what they believed love had to offer them in their lives. Most expended a great deal of energy trying to rebuild, reconstruct, and reform their love relationships. Even those women who had yet to experience fair and respectful love relationships believed that it was possible to do so and that it had the potential to make them happy. Elegantly simple but so often elusive, the desire to be happy motivated many of the women to keep trying to love their spouses, or to try to love again.

In the next chapter, this commitment to love provides the impulse for me to consider how we might think about love and abuse in social work practice. As I have suggested throughout this book, while love relationships have the capacity to produce such joy and happiness, they should not be sites where abuse can reign supreme.

> *We human beings are social world makers, though
> we do not make our social worlds in conditions of our
> own choosing.... We work and worry, pray and play, love
> and hate; and all the time we are telling stories about our
> pasts, our presents and our futures.*
> (Plummer 1995, p. 20)

13
CHANGING WORLDS
Future Possibilities for Professional Practice

GIVEN ALL THE STORIES THAT ARE TOLD about love and abuse, how might we move forward? What changes might we hope for? What hopes might we have for love, and how might we approach its study? If we connect the world of love with the world of abuse, what are the benefits, opportunities, and risks? Are there projects that have already brought love and abuse together? What might they tell us? And what other research needs to be undertaken? These are the guiding questions for this chapter.

In an attempt to offer ideas that are not just interesting but also useful in practice, I sketch some possible ways forward (also see Madigan & Law 1998). I do this on the basis of what I have learned from this study and also through observations and insights acquired from teaching social work students, and my ongoing work with counsellor/advocates in sexual assault and domestic violence agencies. The comments I make are directed mostly to those who work in the areas of health, welfare, and education, and whose work brings them in contact with people at risk of, or affected by, intimate abuse. To this broad array of professionals I reiterate the reasons why we should take love seriously. I encourage the study of love and its contradictions, including those that are abusive. I summarize my rationale for using a critical, postmodern, feminist perspective to understand some of these connections. As will become evident, however, I am not suggesting that love and abuse cannot or should not be distinguished. Rather, I am suggesting that more attention should be given to *how* they are distinguished, not just by professionals but also by women in everyday life.

Scanning across a range of fields and modes of social work practice, I highlight some of the programs and campaigns that have already taken place. I then look at future possibilities. My basic premise is that there is no single way forward. Across all modes of practice (individual, group, and community work, as well as social policy and research), a web of pathways and yet-to-be-experienced resources and alternatives are required if we want to live in worlds where intimate abuse is not a regular feature in any form.

Connecting the Worlds of Love and Abuse in Practice

In this book I have examined many claims made about love, and the relationships enacted in its name. From the wide range of narratives analyzed, I have argued that love is a complex social phenomenon in physical, psychological, emotional, and material worlds. Resistant to definition and measurement, love relationships are influenced by historical events, cultural conventions, and systems of governance. At the same time, they are subjected to individual modification and socio-cultural change (see Kipnis 2003; Lindholm 1995, 1998). The women who participated in this study certainly knew this.

Reasons for Health, Education, and Welfare Professionals to Study Love

All the women I interviewed recognized that individuals, as well as groups and societies, played a role in the construction of love relationships. Differences were expressed in how this could and should be done. Some women were proud to have made love their life's work even when their love relationships had not transpired as hoped. More than a few looked back with hindsight and changed their ideas about love. Anger was sometimes expressed at loving foolishly or without discretion. Some women felt frustrated at themselves and others for subscribing to love narratives and styles that, in their current view, were never going to work. All agreed that social workers and other health and welfare professionals would benefit from studying love. In the table below I reiterate these reasons.

As indicated in Table 13.1, love sources many stories that are used to script a wide range of experiences and emotions. Love takes place in physical spaces that elude the borders of public and private (Jackson 1996, 1999; Kipnis 2003; Summers [1975] 1994; Young 1997). Productive of much human happiness but also misery, love relationships are the sites where individuals exercise control and may be subjugated, if not abused (Butler 1997; Jamieson 1998; Langford 1999; McKenzie 2006; Rose 2000).

Table 13.1
REASONS TO STUDY LOVE

Social/Cultural	Physical/Material	Emotional/Psychological
Love narratives are so ubiquitous that they constitute an important site for group and cultural meanings.	Love is corporeal and liminal; it is embodied by individuals and enacted in physical spaces.	Love involves many intense emotions and influences a wide range of psychological states, including those that are not pleasurable.
Love narratives are crucial to the reproduction of gender and the performance of many roles that are culturally scripted.	The performance of sexual scripts cuts across public and private domains and affects how men and women use space.	In the absence of social research, many of the emotions and psychological states attributed to love will feel natural, instinctual, and/or genetic.
Love narratives and sexual scripts are used to justify many forms of governance.	Stories about love, sex, and romance are used to differentially regulate and monitor specific subsets of bodies.	Many people's feelings of (un)happiness and (dis)satisfaction revolve around their love relationships.
Love narratives are used to decipher the distribution of income, the composition of many households, and the classification of work.	Love stories teach us more about social problems such as domestic violence, sexual assault, and child abuse and relate to many concerns about health and well-being.	Love narratives help us to develop a more intricate understanding of many mental health problems, including those associated with substance abuse and behaviours classified as obsessive and/or compulsive.

Connecting the Dots between Love, Abuse, Hope, Confusion, and Despair

Many of the women I interviewed talked about the hope they had for ex-partners, especially those who ended up being abusive. Some searched for reasons why they had adopted particular love stories and styles, vowing never to do so again. Some women berated themselves for their naivety, especially in relation to promises made immediately after abuse. Some linked their hopes to prior relationships with fathers, mothers, or siblings. Others told me how family members, teachers, and other authorities influenced the hopes they had for a brighter future. From all of this talk I learned that it was precisely because love and abuse *could* co-exist that women often found it hard to know what to do when abuse began (also see Fraser 2005). For some, abuse threatened their worlds (see Kaplan 1995).

From many of the women I learned that when love and abuse co-existed, it could be confounding. Quite a few of the women who had been abused by intimates were confused about why it began, why it sometimes stopped, and then started up again. Some women told me how they had great experiences between the abusive episodes. Some shook their heads at the ways they would try to block out the abuse, feeling relieved when the post-abuse "honeymoons" started. Others felt themselves go so numb that they shut down the future possibility of good times. Some found themselves resenting, even detesting, their partners. Often these angry feelings rebounded negatively onto themselves. Over time these feelings could turn to rage that they felt was destructive.

Most victims/survivors of intimate abuse anguished over what to make of bad love experiences (also see Domestic Violence and Incest Resource Centre 2006). Some asked what they did to deserve it. Some wondered whether they were not good enough for anything more. Some believed they should have had the foresight to see the relationships were doomed. Some, post-separation, were baffled by the loving behaviours they saw their ex-partners display toward new spouses. Some despaired that they were the common denominator if they were subsequently abused in another intimate relationship.

More than half the women believed that being abused—or, for that matter, being abusive—would not necessarily recur in future relationships. As outlined in Chapter 11, many women expressed great hopes for love in the future. Most hope was dedicated to respectful love styles (see Chapter 12). Nevertheless, many believed that in this day and age, abuse could become a regular feature of intimate relationships if one wasn't careful.

Some women said they hoped for the best, but planned for the worst. When it came to figuring out whether a formerly passionate but now abusive relationship could or should be saved, women often battled with optimism and pessimism, or hope and despair. For some women, this battle lasted many years. For some it took decades, and for a few, it never ended.

Examining Love Stories, Styles, and Social Contexts Fertile for Abuse

Across age ranges, women expressed confusion about what to hope for, and whether it was realistic. Changing social conventions were felt with mixed effects and the family was often experienced as uncertain and risky (also see de Beauvoir 1963; Maeve 1999; Overall 1998; Perkin 1999; Plummer 2003; Ristock 2002; Walker 1989). Many younger women spoke of their deep longings to be connected to partners without becoming someone else's property (see Chapter 12). Others longed for the right and freedom to be lesbian, bisexual, or non-monogamous (see Chapter 8). Some of the older women wrestled with wanting a masterful husband who could be the head of the household, but also one who was gentle, kind, and fair. Still others wanted love relationships that were both romantic and democratic.

Straight and queer, some women said they wanted equal love relationships, but could not find them or sustain them. Some said that even when they had forged equal and respectful love relationships, family members, friends, colleagues, and social policies conspired against them. Some felt stigmatized for not emulating the conventional scripts of "the good woman," while others were prompted to take on the script of "bad girl," shrugging off others' disapproval. While many women found the social contexts of love relationships difficult, some found that they could be abusive, particularly women who identified as lesbian, bisexual, and/or polyamorous (also see Overall 1998).

From all this talk I noticed that the risk of abuse was highest when relationships were often (1) based on "object relationship stories" (Sternberg 1998); (2) riddled with emotional volatility; and/or (3) located in contexts that were begrudging of—if not hostile to—sexual equality. When all three converged the effects were often poisonous.

As discussed in Chapter 3, object relationship stories are those promoting the value of having one partner more dominant than the other. They are stories about the righteousness of patriarchy. They assume male domination is natural and inevitable. They produce rigid gender roles that cast men as masters, deciders, and protectors. Scripted to be the head of the household, they have the right to govern all family members and police their movements (also see Overall 1998). In some communities, men are considered aberrant in their duties if they fail to do so (see Chapter 4).

Emotionally volatile relationships are those where emotions run high much of the time. There are frequent interpersonal dramas that produce conflict and anxiety (also see Domestic Violence and Incest Resource Centre 2006; Eisikovits et al. 1998). Over time, and if familiarity sets in, the conflict can become entrenched, multifaceted, and traumatizing (see Chapter 2). Nevertheless, these domestic relationships might be euphemistically described as fiery, passionate, or stormy (see Chapter 3). They were most likely to be portrayed like this if family violence was dismissed, tolerated, or accepted as part of "real life," especially violence that is not expressed physically (see Chapters 4–5 and 7–11). For women in any or all of these circumstances, it can be difficult to know whether to give up an intimate relationship, or give it more of a chance (also see Eisikovits et al. 1998; Johnson & Ferraro 2000).

Deciding Whether to Give It up or Give It More of a Chance

Across socio-economic and political locations, many of the women I interviewed, including some who identified as radical or alternative, worked hard to transform unsatisfying and unhealthy relationships into those that more closely resembled their hopes (see Chapters 9 to 11). They seemed especially keen to do this if their courtship was romantic and/or passionate, and if they had then declared that their partners were "The One," their "Soul Mate," or their "Other Half."

Other incentives to try to transform a bad or decaying relationship included being young, poor, and/or stigmatized as an ex-ward of the state (see Chapters 7 and 8). Young women who had experienced care systems with little support, limited education, and few labour market opportunities were especially vulnerable (see chapters 8 and 9). However, even middle-class girls and women were not always spared. Many were keen to transform rather than end their relationships if it meant not having to institute drastic changes to their living environments or face being alone. Consciously or subconsciously, some women persevered with unhealthy, if not abusive, relationships if they knew they could not afford to buy out the mortgage or cover the full rent. Some could not face the prospect of being separated from children and/or companion animals, and relying on an abusive ex-spouse for their care. Some feared separation would involve them relinquishing education or training opportunities.

Having internalized the message that people should work at love relationships, many women persisted, often by searching for ways to placate and keep the peace. None believed they were perfect, or perfect at keeping the peace. Many women were quick to detail their imperfections and deficiencies. Some did so to save face. Some women told me how they tried to ensure they were home on time, kept the house clean, or the kids quiet, often suppressing comments that might be interpreted as antagonistic. Others paid close attention to their appearance and made themselves sexually available even when they were not aroused. Some immersed themselves in new interests in the hope that it might make them more appealing to their partners. However they did it, many fought for their relationships (also see Eisikovits et al. 1998).

Some women told me that they persevered because they attributed their partners' abuse to alcohol and other substances, health problems, or because they thought they were going through a really rough time. In other words, some women attributed the abuse to external factors and difficult social contexts (also see Johnson & Ferraro 2000). Among these women were those who feared recriminations and possible alienation from friends or family if they were thought to have given up on the relationship too soon. Some feared that in years to come, they might regret not having given it more of a go. And then there were the fears about what partners might do to them if they dared to leave.

Amid these fears, many women, at least initially, denied the existence of the abuse and/or minimized its impact. Some told elaborate cover stories to deflect attention from abuse and keep the relationship alive. Some looked back with regret, noting the dangerous ease with which they could start to believe their excuses, or those offered by abusive "loved ones." Some said that after a bout of violence, their partners would make grand promises that they feared or knew would be broken. Nevertheless, some women hung on (see Chapters 9–11).

Even those women most determined to leave abusive spouses once and for all were not immune to doubts. Some women who were able to kick out their abusive partners expressed guilt at displacing a person they had once loved, and perhaps still loved. Shared memories and commitments could make an emotional glue that was strong enough to make some women feel wracked with guilt after separation about whether they had done the right thing. Shared experiences of hardship or oppression could compound the situation (see chapters 7 to 10).

Some women sought help from professionals such as GPs and social workers. Some went to psychiatrists and psychologists. Some consulted priests, rabbis, aunts, and mothers. Some went to psychics and others turned to yoga. Some got drunk or tried to find some other way to escape. Almost all of them taught me that only when hope was exhausted were most of them able to give up and walk away (also see Fraser 2005).

As I discussed in Chapter 10, hope is like oxygen to love. Without this oxygen love relationships *are* doomed because hope fuels trust, faith, and connection. Across age, ethnicity, and sexuality I heard this message. From it I learned that exploring and assessing the role of hope provided a rich conversation source for abused *as well as* abusive spouses. Many women told me how much they valued being able to think about hope. Some women expressed how much they would have liked professionals to help them think about hope, and think about it in relation to love and abuse. Some wanted the chance to experience the different facets of hope, including the ways in which hope can wax and wane, sometimes unexpectedly, yet few said they had had the chance to do so in professional settings. More than a few felt pressured to make quick decisions about whether to stay in the relationship or go. As I elaborate later in the chapter, many women indicated to me that when it came to deciding that a relationship was abusive, they wanted to draw their own lines in the sand and do so in their own time.

Existing Examples of Projects That Connect Love and Abuse

While they are unlikely to have studied it at universities, many professionals have learned from experience that love and abuse can co-exist and can be confounding. Some have helped to produce work that conveys this understanding. Their work shows how knowledge-in-and-from-practice (praxis) can provide many theoretical insights, especially in the area of intimate abuse.

Over the last decade, practice wisdom about love and abuse seems to have expanded. From hallway conversations and observations of front-line practices, I have noticed that people are becoming more interested in learning about love and abuse and considering their possible connections. From the Critical Social Work classes I coordinate for MSW students and the monthly narrative feminist peer review sessions I facilitate with a local Centre against Sexual Assault, I have witnessed more openness and curiosity about love and abuse. From all of these sites, including the supervision sessions I have with a feminist social worker in a hospital setting, I have also witnessed a much greater sensitivity in appreciating women's diversity, including those who identify as queer.

In Table 13.2 a diverse range of policies, programs, campaigns, projects, and exhibitions are identified across the five modes of social work practice. All of them connect love and abuse in some way.

Table 13.2
EXAMPLES OF WORK DONE TO CONNECT LOVE AND ABUSE

Individual Work	Group Work	Community Work	Social Policy	Research
Counselling for Love Addiction, Toronto (2002–)	*Is This Love?*, feminist high school theatre project, Victoria (1998)	*Love Makes a Family*, same-sex photo exhibit, Amherst	*Tough love social policies*, Britain (mid-1990s and ongoing)	*Social Work and a Love of Humanity*, Morley, L. & Ife, J. (2002)
Learning to Love and Nurture Yourself, tips from Advocates for survivors of child abuse, Sydney (2007)	*Love class projects*, primary school, Maui (2005)	*Have I Told You Lately That I Love You?*, child abuse prevention campaign, Victoria, Australia (mid-1990s)	*Equal Love*, gay and lesbian rights lobby's campaign for relationship recognition, Melbourne (2005)	*Why Love Hurts: Measuring Beliefs of Spouse Abusers*, UBC, Vancouver (2007)
Getting the Love That You Want, counselling directory, New York (2007)	*Men and Love workshops*, Winnipeg (2005)	*When Love Hurts*, domestic violence prevention program for young women, Melbourne (2008)	*Money Can't Buy You Love*, monitoring policy making at the United Nations, New York (2006)	*When Love Hurts: A Woman's Guide to Understanding Abuse in Relationships*, New Westminster (2007)
Breaking the Chains of Painful Love, Spiritual Institute of Australia, Frankstonia (2007)	*Alternatives*, responding to love and hurt in families in western Nova Scotia (2008 and ongoing)	*Don't Walk Away from Love*, community art project, New York (2006)	*All Love is Equal*, gay and lesbian rights lobby, Melbourne (2006)	*Love, Hate, and Welfare*, Froggett, L. (2002)

By no means an exhaustive list, the examples of policies, programs, campaigns, projects, and exhibitions in Table 13.2 indicate the breadth and depth of possibilities. Most have Web sites that allow readers to quickly and easily learn more about them. All illustrate ways of connecting love and abuse. Most show us how we might understand the connections between personal troubles and socio-political problems. Take, for instance, the material developed by the Gay and Lesbian Rights Lobby in Victoria, Australia, used to argue that *All Love is Equal* (see Table 13.2). In some detail it showed that the social conditions facing "queer" people are often hostile and discriminatory. Nevertheless, it joins many of the other policies and projects listed in the table, which indicate that for all of the risks and costs, there is much to celebrate about love.

Photographic exhibitions such as "Love Makes a Family" remind us of this by celebrating the love that is shared in same-sex families in spite of heterosexism and homophobia. The "Men and Love" seminar series did similarly. Also promoting a respectful love approach, the 1996 child abuse prevention campaign in Victoria, Australia, was broadcast on popular television stations through the song, "Have I Told You Lately That I Love You?" And in more recent years, programs led by Art Fisher at Alternatives, in Halifax, Nova Scotia, have been offered to individuals, groups, and communities alike, operating from perspectives compatible with those underpinning this book (see Fisher 2004, 2005).

There are many other good examples of how love and abuse can be connected in practice, including the "When Love Hurts" domestic violence prevention programs and research in Canada and Australia. In my view, they are good because they engage with ordinary people's lived experiences. They do this with care and respect. While challenging myths and misconceptions, they try not to take away all the magic of love. They do not pretend that love relationships are always good or rational. They give attention to the strong emotions that love and abuse can evoke. They do not try to demolish women's faith in romance and passion. They recognize that women often connect their aspirations for romantic love relationships with their feminine self-esteem. And they know that the goal of sexual equality is not desirable for many women if it means relinquishing hopes for love. Put simply, they try to engage ordinary women as they strive for social change.

Changing Worlds of Professional Practice

As indicated throughout this book, working in a professional capacity with other people's experiences of love and abuse calls for an interest in and knowledge about how love relationships may be formed, sustained, processed, refashioned, and dissolved. It calls for us to appreciate the diverse psychological processes that come into play, as well as the prevailing social conventions that affect decisions made (also see Johnson & Ferraro 2000). Recognizing the philosophical, anthropological, sociological, and political aspects of loving are important if we are to avoid de-contextualizing people's love lives and pathologizing them for the ways in which they perform intimacy.

Studying Love Lives from a Critical Postmodern Perspective

As I have argued in Chapters 2, 4, and 5, if we are to demonstrate a full understanding of love, and if we are to really join with others in empathic meaning-making processes, we need to move across the intrapersonal, interpersonal, and cultural dimensions of people's relationships. This helps to circumvent the tendency to either overpsychologize or oversociologize sexually intimate relationships (see Fraser 1998, 1999, 2003, 2004, 2005).

I found a critical postmodern feminist perspective helped me to do this. It helped me to see the intrapersonal, interpersonal, and cultural dimensions of women's love lives. In Table 13.3 I clarify my understanding of this perspective, and its relationships to structural feminist and postmodern feminist perspectives.

Table 13.3
THREE FEMINIST APPROACHES TO WOMEN, LOVE, AND ABUSE

Structural Feminists	Postmodern Feminists	Critical Postmodern Feminists
View power mostly in possessive terms (that is, people are powerful or powerless) and examine structural inequalities using concepts such as patriarchy and oppression	View power as fluid and relational, honing in on the ways in which language creates meanings for different groups of women and men	View power in possessive and relational terms, and use the concept of heteronormativity to highlight the valuing of male and heterosexual identities
Use the categories of men and women as they foreground the ways in which women are pressured to love men and prioritize men's interests	Question the ongoing viability of the categories "women" and "men," and explore other sexual constructions such as transgender and intersex	Defend the use of categories "men" and "women," but problematize overarching generalizations made about any members of sexual categories
Use meta-narratives to explain the causes of women's oppression and fight for macro-political change	Deconstruct personal and cultural narratives and accentuate women's subjectivity, agency, and performativity	Use meta-narratives and personal narratives to cautiously prefigure cultural and individual change
Concentrate on ongoing patterns of women's material and sexual disadvantage	Concentrate on women's desire and relationships of sexual pleasure, including those described as romantic	Attend to questions of desire, but concentrate on women's struggle for sexual equality in and beyond intimate relationships

Structural Feminists	Postmodern Feminists	Critical Postmodern Feminists
Foreground women's commonalities and celebrate acts of solidarity	Underline women's differences, diversity, and individuality	Theorize women's commonalities and differences, and consider multiple and contradictory identities
Dichotomize perpetrators and victims of violence, and use statistics to argue that most perpetrators of domestic violence are male	Shy away from discussions of abuse and assault, especially those using terms such as "domestic violence".	Prefer to use terms such as "intimate abuse" or "violence" and argue that while most perpetrators of violence are male, women may also be abusive
Catalogue and condemn acts of abuse as well as accounts that pathologize women as weak or masochistic	Entertain the possibility of personal pathology and explore women's desires that others may describe as perverse	Are skeptical of accounts that pathologize women because such accounts usually divorce problems from their social contexts
Defend women-specific services, especially those related to domestic violence and sexual assault	Contribute little to discussions about the provision of services and material support for women	Promote women-specific services as one of the many types of services that are needed

Initially, I decided to use a critical postmodern feminist perspective because it could accommodate the study of love *and* abuse. It also made sense to me to understand power as possessive *and* relational. I liked the way it considered women's commonalities *and* differences. It did not call for me to abandon class analyses, yet it urged caution when generalizing.

A critical postmodern feminist perspective reflected my observations that multiple and contradictory identities were possible, and that people could feel torn and conflicted. It offered me concepts, such as hetero-normativity, to describe the valuing of male and heterosexual identities. It did not mock calls for social change, nor was it contemptuous of the idea of solidarity. Neither ridiculing nor exalting queer politics, it was open to questioning the ongoing utility of gender categories.

A critical postmodern feminist perspective helped me to understand a diverse range of women's stories without totalizing or atomizing their lives. It helped me to see women's diverse sexual desires without losing sight of questions about sexual equality. And it helped me to see how meta-narratives *and* personal narratives can be used productively to prefigure (not dictate) cultural and individual change.

As complex, ambitious, and convoluted as it can be, it is an approach that does not deny or minimize women's material needs, including their need for women-specific services. It accepts that for all of its shortcomings, the concept of needs can be used strategically. As suggested in Table 13.3, it also accepts that women-specific services are an important but not exclusive service possibility.

Yet, a critical postmodern perspective is not without its limitations. Because it draws from so many disciplines and tries to pay attention to the individual, interpersonal, cultural, and structural dimensions of life, it is very ambitious. It is also ambitious in the way it tries to democratize knowledge and develop strategies in consultation with a wide range of women. Arguably, it is quicker and easier for professionals to occupy the role of expert and devise interventions *for* rather than *with* ordinary women. It is also easier to hone in on one dimension of love, such as the psychology of love, than it is to pay attention to multiple dimensions, including those that require long-term systemic change.

A critical postmodern feminist perspective can also be hard to use because it takes time. With new public management strategies adopted by so many state-sponsored social and community organizations across the Anglo-American-dominated world, the time needed to carefully examine and respond to complex situations is often not made available (see Baines et al. 2007). Regressive social policies, the under-resourcing of public infrastructure, and work-intensification processes have all put pressures on workers to process more clients more efficiently, sometimes using prescribed checklists to ensure accountability. These regimes are not conducive to critical postmodern feminist perspectives. Instead, they encourage workers to cut to the chase (or get quickly to the point), especially if they want to go home on time.

Resisting the Inclination to Cut to the Chase

Many domestic violence practitioners already know that women do not always discern the borders between love and abuse quickly and efficiently. Some know that women can find it hard to come to grips with the idea that intimate/domestic violence had infiltrated their relationships. They understand that most need time to process whether their partners' particular actions were abusive.

In this study I found that most women hesitated, if not recoiled, from immediately alleging abuse. Many needed to exclude a range of other explanations before they felt confident that it *was abuse in their eyes*. Some processed their thoughts and feelings through lengthy conversations they had with girlfriends, sisters, or mothers, often over the phone. Some bemoaned the bad advice they had been given. A few spoke of their gratitude to counsellors and therapists who had taken the time to enable them to express their anguish and arrive at their own conclusions. More women felt empowered by the having the chance to critically appraise their relationships than when well-meaning others jumped in with quick declarations and crisis-oriented solutions.

Of those who sought professional help for issues relating to intimate abuse, some felt they were given short shrift in exploring the real nature of their problems. Some said they felt that professionals were too keen to end messy, time-consuming conversations in favour of more concrete, goal-oriented plans for the here and now. Some came away classified as "depressed," "anxious," or "unstable," or as having some kind of syndrome, such as battered women's syndrome, hostage syndrome, or post-traumatic stress disorder. A few said they were sent away with prescriptions for antidepressants, but no other support. Some said that while the pills might have helped them manage their depressive symptoms, they did little about domestic abuse.

Cutting to the chase, whether by a GP, a child-protection officer, a school welfare officer, or a counsellor/advocate working in a sexual assault centre, often means that workers will draw premature conclusions. It can mean that too much energy goes into slotting people into categories, using instruments and assessing risk. While I understand the need to assess people for the risk of self-harm, suicide, or the risk of re-offending, at least in certain roles and agencies, the impact of inadequate housing options, below poverty-line welfare payments, and the increasing costs of child and elder care should not go unnoticed. It is all part of the context of how victims/survivors of abuse feel about themselves and their relationships, including how they decide whether to leave or stay.

Understanding That Separation Can Mean Poverty for Women

Too often, leaving an abusive spouse runs the risk of women falling into poverty. Although some programs have worked hard to evict the abusive family members, most women realize that addressing the violence could require them to relocate from their homes, their children's schools, and local communities (also see Johnson 1999). Most women knew that getting child support from ex-spouses could be fraught with difficulties, as could access. Women over 30 were particularly aware of the difficulties other women faced as single women after separation or divorce. They also knew that if they want primary care for their children, they might have to fight it out in the family court. More than a few knew that they would have to do this while juggling casual, low-paid work with child-care, and perhaps elder-care, responsibilities. Some women assumed they would have to do this for years on end. Some told me about their fears of not being able to endure such conditions. Some were frank about how they hated the fact that money was an important consideration in what they did about abuse if it emerged in their intimate relationships.

It is naive to say that money is not a factor for women when deciding what to do about a violent spouse. Money sits alongside other factors, such as the emotional vulnerability that can come from losing one's mate and protector. Without an adequate alternative income source, and usually quite a few dollars behind them for bond and rent in advance, most of the women knew that they would be vulnerable in an underfunded public welfare system that can be hard to experience. Some expressed relief that they had credit cards to use or family members to give them loans, so that they did not have to rely on public welfare. Many understood Plummer's (2003, p. 145) contention that:

> Intimacies are lodged in worldwide inequalities of class, gender, age, race, and the like. These inequalities structure on a daily basis the debasement and degradation, the patterns of exclusion and marginalization, the sense of powerlessness that, in one way or another, many people experience as the inevitable backdrop of ordinary intimacies.

Some women indicated that they found issues relating to money, identity, and emotions hard to separate. Some described feeling so financially and emotionally dependent that leaving did not seem to be an option. Some had wondered how they would manage and how they would be seen. Many feared falling into poverty and becoming stigmatized. Labels such as "single mom," "divorcee," and "spinster" did not sit comfortably. Many felt these labels undermined their self-esteem and denied them the right to be sexual. Although a few women embraced (hetero)sexist labels and tried to reinvigorate them with new meanings (such as "bitch," "slut," "queer"), most resented having to battle the stereotypes.

Given the social, cultural, material, and psychological incentives to be in monogamous, committed (preferably heterosexual) relationships, as well as the barriers confronting those who try to disentangle themselves from relationships that are abusive, it is not surprising that women may be loath to recognize intimate abuse. Even if they do recognize it as such, many feel pressured to dismiss its impact and try to justify why it occurred. If it recurs, additional pressure may be felt to hide it, often out of shame and confusion. If pressed, there may be denials that it took place or was serious.

Men are not the only ones taught how to minimize and trivialize abuse in families. In subtly different ways, many women are taught this as well. They/we are taught to turn a blind eye to many acts of male aggression (also see Wood 2001). We are taught that "boys will be boys" and that a family without a father "isn't a real family" (also see Young 1997). Some are forced to marry early and respect their husbands by demonstrating subservience. In some groups and communities, gender fundamentalism is so strong that women who dare to challenge male authority, including its excesses, may find more than their group membership in jeopardy.

From some of the women I interviewed I learned how hard religious fundamentalism and other patriarchal regimes can make it for women with children to deal with abuse. Bombarded by narrowly prescribed "pro-family values," many women knew that other family forms, including women-headed families, were classified as deviant. They also knew the perils of removing children from their fathers, homes, and potentially all that is familiar to them. For those who had vowed to honour and obey, rebellion could seem even more daunting (also see Wood 2001). It is one reason why, at least at first, the abuse will be cast as an aberration, a bad patch, or a phase.

Many women told me that after the abuse started to set in, they tried to negotiate changes with their partners that did not involve separation. Ultimatums were sometimes made, but not always with conviction. Outright endings were usually left as the last resort if all hope had been exhausted. Hope was often tied up with fear. Some feared losing their sense of family. Some were scared of their partners, while others were not. Some were convinced that they could stop the violence. Some reported success, while others found themselves subjected to more extreme violence, especially if they were seen to be pandering or cowering (also see Johnson & Ferraro 2000).

Keeping Optimism and Skepticism Alive But in Check

Psychologically and socially, I have learned that when women have been subjected to abuse, especially from partners they say they deeply love, it can be important for professionals and others to engage in careful, measured, and thoughtful talk, where the inclination to show too much optimism or cynicism is resisted. This can mean resisting the urge to totalize the situation, cast it as "hopeless," and assume that there is only one dignified course of action to take. Similarly, it calls for people to resist dismissing the acts of abuse as something that just happens when couples fight, that they can be solved if they kiss and make up, or some other clichéd recovery plan.

Talking carefully with others about the connections between love and abuse calls for us to resist the urge to become bleak and conspiratorial or, conversely, superficial and "pop psychological." It means helping others to engage in open explorations of their love relationships, assessing what, if anything, they need to change. Such relationship work can be hard to do because it requires patience, discipline, and dedication. It is much easier for us as workers to discharge whatever emotions emerge. It is can also be more tempting to be self-righteous and arrogant than it is engaging in more measured, reflective talk about the possibility of change (also see Jenkins 1990).

Conversations about love and abuse may be inspiring as much as they might be confronting or disheartening. They do not have to end up promoting a radical separatist agenda any more than they have to end up colluding with perpetrators of violence by trying to return women to traditional feminine scripts, especially those that encourage women to be long-suffering. If conducted with curiosity and political intelligence, discussions about love and abuse have the potential to connect personal difficulties with cultural and social patterns. They have the potential to allow people to explore how their lives might be influenced by (hetero)sexism, classism, racism, ageism, and ableism (also see Baines 2007). These explorations may or may not bring back painful childhood memories. This will depend on the time and the nature of the service or program.

When done with care, conversations about women's hopes for current and future love relationships offer the opportunity to explore dreams as well as differences. They can be critical and inspirational at the same time, and they can help women to move from small steps to breakthroughs as they (re)discover themselves and their hopes for a sense of belonging and community.

Many women reiterated the old adage that it was not the relationship that they wanted to stop, but the violence. For those who ended up deciding to leave, some did so only temporarily. Some women left for a few days and stayed with family or friends (usually with their children but not always) until "it blew over." Some did so for clearly identified safety reasons. While apart, some women found that it was only when they had taken the bold step of leaving the house that they had greater leverage to lobby for and get agreement from their spouses that the terms of the relationship had to change.

If you work in a job related to domestic violence, you are likely to know that women may need to leave abusive partners over and again before their separations will be permanent. As I've suggested, women can take years to lose hope. Along the way they can find periods apart very useful. Time spent at friends' and relatives' houses, motels, and, in some case, hospitals, can be required to take stock of what has just happened and feel confident in tackling it. Periods spent in refuges with others facing similar challenges can be crucial for women, young people, and men alike.

Depending on how they are resourced and run, refuges can be great short-term solutions to problems of obtaining food, shelter, and safety. With the support of refuge staff, they have the opportunity to have the impact of their suffering recognized. Refuge staff can also take the load off overburdened extended families. Yet refuges and other public welfare housing solutions can be stigmatized places where people are denigrated and the connections between love and abuse are not well recognized or are actively scorned.

Opening up Our Worlds of Understanding

From the many conversations I had with women, I know that a lot of time and frustration can be spared if there was less emphasis on either (1) categorizing abuse and laying out trajectories for women to leave abusive partners; or (2) minimizing the abuse, shifting blame, and/or helping people to figure out how to avoid "provoking" it. For women to take a firm stand against abuse, many more options needed to be considered, including those relating to socio-cultural change.

Exploring What It Can Mean to Become a Welfare Recipient

Some of the women I interviewed knew that taking a firm stand on abuse could mean becoming a welfare recipient. They knew that this could be demoralizing. For the uninitiated, the web of confusing possibilities, all requiring appointments, assessments, and completed forms, could feel like another world and not one they wanted to inhabit.

While we do not often discuss it, most professionals know that public welfare can be difficult to negotiate. It is why many of us privately insure ourselves and our families. It is why we try to save money for a rainy day. As inside observers, we know that "good" government-subsidized programs can be difficult to access because of waiting lists in too few and overburdened agencies. We know that public welfare systems can expose people to further abuse (see Baines 2007; Mullaly 2007). Some of us have seen practices in agencies that could make your hair curl. We have seen co-workers and bosses patronize and chide service users, classifying them in ways we ourselves would object to. We have also seen how hard it can be to qualify for particular benefits, especially those that allow for a life above the poverty line.

Analyzing Whether "Tough Love" Is Victim-Blaming

We know that even when they do not mean to be, programs such as material aid and Workfare (or Welfare to Work) usually come with judgments made about deservedness. The tangle of paperwork often confirms the assessment of someone as either deserving or undeserving, and may require people to serially recount their traumatic experiences.

While it is often easier for people to negotiate public welfare if they have a recognized identity within it (such as an unemployment card or health care card), those seen to be at risk of developing welfare dependence may find that there are punitive attitudes. Sometimes these punitive attitudes are expressed through the euphemistically titled social policies of "tough love" (see Jordan & Jordan 2000).

Although some people might find "tough love" social policies endearing, even if a little old-fashioned, women who rely on benefits and programs governed by it usually find it anything but innocent. For the unacquainted, "tough love" was introduced by England's former prime minister, Tony Blair, a decade ago to describe his government's tough line on welfare dependency. It is a position adopted by many other governments that have followed suit, to the point that "tough love" has been adopted in other countries and settings. It is noteworthy that it was originally designed to advise parents of troubled teens (see http://www.4troubledteens.com/toughlove.html).

Agencies that use "tough love" to prevent welfare dependency concentrate much more on fulfilling contractual obligations with funding bodies than tackling social disadvantage and inequality. Workplaces can be affected by the ethos of "tough love" to the point where those who suffer social problems are held responsible for having them (see Mullaly 2007; Ryan 1976). This can happen to women who leave abusive relationships and become single mothers.

Women reliant on public welfare over the long term are most susceptible to being revictimized by being held responsible for the effects of abuse that they did not commit. Many will have to face the near impossibility of securing decent housing, particularly means-tested social housing. Many will find their parenting work rendered invisible. Some will have to face the indignities of keeping a "dole diary" to prove how often they sought work over the specified period. For those who do get a job, a significant number will have to confront the bitter irony that while they are out serving as wait staff, bank tellers, cleaners, or caregivers of other people's children, they will struggle to secure adequate child care for their own children. They will find that expensive child care, low wages, and lost welfare provisions are not compatible. More than a few women will wonder if they are better or worse off psychologically, physically, emotionally, and financially.

Even when greeted with warm and empathic professionals, victims/survivors of abuse will not necessarily escape the vagaries of being constituted as a welfare recipient. After all, the women will, by necessity, have to join the ranks of the others who rely on welfare in this post-welfare era. They will have to face that this "tough love" era demands that public welfare consumers, clients, or service users show gratitude for the support they receive, even it is delivered with hostility, indifference, and/or incompetence (see Baines 2007). Ultimately, "tough love" can be more like "tough luck"!

Assessing All the Costs of Intimate Abuse

Women across the board knew that when domestic violence broke out, there were many costs. Some said that when a partner first became abusive, they felt shock and disbelief. Some tried hard to bury their feelings and push on with their lives without involving paid professionals. Sometimes they did this because they feared the involvement of child-protection authorities. Others were preoccupied with the shame they felt from being abused. Of those who attempted to hide the abuse, most did so at great cost to themselves and their children. Some regretted not getting professional help sooner. Still others regretted getting help from agencies they found to be unkind, particularly at the height of the drama and the early phases of a separation.

As hard as it might be to believe, some women found that having insufficient emotional and material resources post-separation felt more humiliating than the abuse. It is why many older women, when asked what they might advise younger women to do about love, said, "always keep in touch with your friends," "don't underestimate the support of a mother or sister," and "keep some money aside" so there would be "enough to move away if need be." Some advised keeping a secret bank account "just in case." Some said not to let religion or in-laws "get in the way." Many realized that abuse, in its many guises, is a major social—not just a personal—problem. They knew that abuse in love relationships is especially common, even though it is often not discussed in polite company, and that its impact could be long lasting.

Much research effort has been dedicated to calculating the costs of domestic violence to the economy. Rates of sick leave, workplace accidents, and injuries are sometimes measured. When these rates increase, much publicity can ensue. Consultants may be called in to design labour market policies that will stem, if not reverse, the losses. A variety of organizational welfare programs may ensue, including employer-funded support and counselling. Sadly, a burst of state money is sometimes made available for family violence policies, programs, and services only when lost economic revenue rises or when a critical incident or public inquiry releases findings that are hard to ignore (see Child Migrants' Trust 2001; Goddard 1996; Human Rights and Equal Opportunity Commission 1997).

Nonetheless, many people believe the social costs of domestic violence are at least as important at the economic costs. There are costs to health, happiness, and well-being. There are the costs of being involved in crises and dramas. Victims, perpetrators, their children, and extended family and friends know that these crises make it hard to concentrate. It can be hard to go to work or school when one feels fearful, sleep deprived, sad, and/or angry. It is not an exaggeration to say that some battle to maintain the will to live.

Domestic violence also has costs felt by family and friends. When they are frequently asked for support and advice, they may find that intimate abuse weighs heavily upon them. The costs may be material, emotional, and social. They can also be physical. Family and friends may also seek out support, and not always in ways that are efficient and productive. Under pressure, they may find they return to or increase their substance abuse. Some find mental health problems return or intensify. These costs of abuse are rarely brought to the attention of authorities, let alone measured. Sometimes there is a premium placed on not letting authorities in on the secret, particularly if children are involved.

Even when family members believe they have shielded them from the abuse, children are not always spared. Many children feel the tension, and develop anxiety in response to it, even if no aggressive acts are perpetrated in their presence. Some children have the benefit of being nurtured in other safe spaces. Some, however, have no such refuge and risk becoming hostage to the emotional climate of their homes (see Chapters 7 and 8). School may become their only place to escape.

It is well recognized that children's experience of domestic violence can extend to the classroom and schoolyard. Some children retreat inward into a fantasy world for so long that they become isolated and fall behind in their studies. Other children, or at other times, do not retreat. Some act out and hurt others as well as themselves. More than a few carry their experiences of domestic violence into their adulthood. Some end up with substance-abuse problems, mental health problems, or both. While there is no straight line between childhood abuse and abuse in adulthood, this book provides evidence that exposure to abuse, especially in the younger years, creates many more obstacles to achieving good health and well-being in adulthood (see Chapters 7 to 12).

As I have indicated, the costs of domestic violence can be profound and innumerable, although not always well measured nor understood. There is still much that we do not know. Future debates about the costs of domestic violence need to address the full realm of possibilities, not just those pertaining to economic growth. They need to be addressed not just by politicians and other senior bureaucrats, who admittedly play important roles in shaping and promoting policies, but also by people with first-hand experience. For too long now economic conservatism has permitted economists to dictate the legitimacy and adequacy of social welfare.

Along with service users, many practitioners in welfare, education, and health have this first-hand experience. Some have already incorporated ideas about love and abuse into their practice to prevent, or at least reduce, the costs of abuse. Some realize the importance of critical reflexivity.

Table 13.4
CRITICALLY REFLEXIVE CONVERSATIONS ABOUT LOVE AND ABUSE

Explore	Analyze	Assess	Reflect on
Love, abuse, and the role of hope; try to trace the cultural stories that underpin personal narratives	The types of narratives that clients use to conceptualize love and distinguish it from abuse	The incidence and prevalence of systems abuse, not just interpersonal and self-abuse	The types of stories most popularly promoted about love and abuse
The degree to which the roles that people enact in love relationships are freely chosen	Whether the love stories are mostly built on gender asymmetry and, if so, the implications	The space made available to discuss abuse in all its forms without erasing social context	Whether people are always free to choose if and whom they might love
The constraints facing some groups who try to renegotiate the roles they perform in love relationships	How single women and lesbians are treated; compare and contrast to heterosexual single men and couples	The costs to children (inside the home and classroom), and family members and friends who are drawn into domestic dramas	The extent to which some groups feel able to exercise their basic human rights in love relationships
How intimate abuse can subside or even go away for a while before generating crises that have the potential to upset whole social networks	Whether there are sanctions levelled at people who are seen to transgress conventions through the love relationships they develop or dissolve	The human costs of separations, divorces, relocations, and reconstituting a new family form, sometimes amid threats of violence	Whether there are the necessary supports to alter or dissolve relationships without discrimination or disadvantage

Explore	Analyze	Assess	Reflect on
How hard it can be for people to pretend that everything is okay when their worlds feel like they are collapsing	How victims/survivors of abuse may be more liable to be deemed abnormal or deviant than their abusers	How our privileges, personalities, cultures, religious values, and social locations influence our preferred love styles and our ability to enact them	The feelings of shame and degradation at concealing physical injuries and/or believing that it will never happen again
Possible connections between love, abuse, substance abuse and/or addictions, other obsessive-compulsive and/or dissociative behaviours	How whistle-blowers are treated, including whether they are implicated in, if not blamed for, the abuse and/or scorned for exposing it	Lost opportunities, including those related to psychological, educational, and/or spiritual growth for all affected by domestic violence	How our intimacies have been globalized, digitalized, technologized, medicalized, commodified, and destablized (Plummer 2005)
What this might mean for practice	How different modes of social work might be used	The impact of using particular methods and approaches	What else could be done in the future

Being Critically Reflexive in Conversations about Love and Abuse

Influenced by critical theory, critical reflexivity involves keeping questions about power, domination, and oppression centre-stage (Myerhoff & Ruby 1992; Skeggs 2002). It calls for honest and searching analyses that do not dichotomize (or split) the personal from the professional (see Chapter 6). It requires us to have insight about our own love lives, including how we classify abuse and what we dismiss as troublesome but normal. It prompts us to think about where our boundaries might conflict with others, especially those located in less privileged social contexts (see Fook 1996). And it urges us to open up conversations about love and abuse in ways that do not erase the influence of social contexts and conventions (see Table 13.4).

As Table 13.4 suggests, whether campaigning for safer families, making policies for safer neighbourhoods, or crisis work with individuals, we need to be clear about our own values, preferences, and proclivities. We need to know how our beliefs about love shape how we understand other people's hopes and dreams for loving. This does not mean that love and abuse are indistinguishable. They are not "one and the same." Rather, they are social phenomena that can overlap and co-exist.

Put simply, we need to learn more about how people define love and abuse and determine where abuse begins and love ends. We need to know more about what kinds of abuse are most easily dismissed but may do the most damage. As so many domestic violence workers know, we need to move beyond the assumption that physical violence is the most heinous form. And we need to move beyond the idea that only men can be abusive (see Mulroney & Chan 2005), and that when they are, there is no hope for change.

By joining with others in these explorations, assessments, analyses, and reflections, we will be better positioned to know how to help (also see Fook 1996). It will also help us to figure out whether we need to use different classifications of love and abuse, depending on the client group, the mission of the organization, the aims of the program or policy, and whether clients are (at least nominally) voluntary, mandated, or underage. This is crucial if we are to prevent unintended but negative consequences. It also needs to be done with reference to how the connections between love and abuse can be used for different political purposes (see Table 13.5).

As indicated in Table 13.5, there are many potential benefits, but also risks, in connecting love and abuse. Rather than ignoring the risks, we need to think strategically about how economic and moral conservatives may appropriate some of these ideas for their own purposes. We also need to be aware of how badly some connections between love and abuse might be made if done by people who have insufficient time, skill, and knowledge.

In the current context of economic conservatism and new public management regimes, most professionals are under pressure to be *fast* rather than *useful*. Many are asked to spread themselves too thinly. More than a few realize that engaging and developing rapport with others is not easily achieved in a hurry. They know that if they take their time and focus their attention properly on a situation, they may be able to do some excellent work with clients to create real and longed-for change. Some will encourage a wider range of women and children to avail themselves of the service by giving them more opportunity to voice how the abuse was experienced and help them manage any quandaries.

Yet, many workers also know that if they linger on a client's situation, they may not be contributing to the agency's productivity gains. They may not be working toward some agencies' goal of de-politicizing the work so as to avoid bad publicity that could dissuade funding bodies or donors from continuing their support. Some try to keep under the radar as they enact practices that they know are effective but not necessarily well esteemed. For those who work with women who have been exploited and abused and are now in poverty, there are the added risks of connecting love and abuse in socially regressive ways that could be used to justify further budget cuts.

Table 13.5
BENEFITS AND RISKS OF CONNECTING LOVE AND ABUSE

Benefits	Risks
It validates many ordinary women's belief and experience that love and abuse can co-exist.	Connecting love and abuse could be mistaken to mean that no distinction can be drawn between the two.
More space will be given to exploring how particular love stories and styles can make people more susceptible to being abused and/or becoming abusive.	Anti-feminists might find ways to use the connections between love and abuse as proof that feminists are confused or misguided.
There is less likelihood of dichotomizing abused women from loved women as both may be possible.	Abusive spouses might view this as a way to abdicate responsibility for their actions. Some might push for more attention to be given to the connections than the abuse.
Victims/survivors who want the abuse, not the relationship, to end may feel less pressured to leave and more able to seek professional help.	Workers who are already ambivalent about women's human rights might see this as a way for them to sidestep their responsibilities to work toward women's safety in and out of the home.
Recognizing the connections between love and abuse may mean that abused women become better understood and less stigmatized.	Social agencies could assume that the connections between love and abuse make it impossible to develop policies and programs to prevent and/or redress the effects of abuse.
It is more likely to reach the abused and the abuser in intimate relationships, which, in turn, could mean more opportunities for non-violent intervention across the board.	Rather than increased funding for domestic violence programs, it may be spread ever more thinly, threatening the viability of some women-specific agencies.
Intimate abuse can be examined in light of prevailing social conventions and pressures, including those promoting military power and other forms of hyper-masculine aggression.	It can invite us to use old clichés, such as "There is a fine line between love and hate," to normalize rather than deal with abuse in intimate relationships.

Demanding Adequate Public Policies, Programs, and Benefits for Women and Children

Whether it is in Canada, Australia, England, Scotland, Ireland, Wales, the United States, or New Zealand, many of us realize that domestic/family/intimate abuse hurts women and their children most; that in New Zealand alone, about 10 children are killed every year from it, and that one woman is killed by her partner or ex-partner every five weeks (New Zealand Police 2007). Across the Anglo-dominated world, we know that family violence is common, affecting as many as one in four women (Women's Aid, Until Women and Children Are Safe 2005). We know that family violence occurs most when dominant family members—usually the men—abuse their positions of power (Department of Justice Canada 2007; Women's Aid, Until Women and Children Are Safe 2005). We also know that the risk of abuse rises when people have been subjected to dislocation, colonization, racism, sexism, homophobia, disability, poverty, and isolation (Department of Justice Canada 2007). And we are aware that when people are sent to state institutions, abuse can be rife (Department of Justice Canada 2007; Human Rights and Equal Opportunity Commission 1997; Indian Residential Schools Resolution Canada 2007; Parliament of Australia, Senate 2001).

Many of us are familiar with how social institutions operate. We realize that not having adequate social and physical infrastructure affects what women do when they are abused. Many direct-service workers on the front line, as well as researchers, policy makers, and planners, know that the chronic shortage of public housing, inadequate forms of income support, and decaying public education systems can dissuade people—mostly women and young people—from leaving violent homes (also see Weeks 2000; Young 1997). We know that without public support and a new, safe home to go to, intimate abuse can be very hard for individuals to tackle. Yet these resources are often unacknowledged or sidelined. It is far easier to focus on individual women's psychology than it is to confront the inadequacy of public infrastructure (also see Baines 2007; Mullaly 2007).

To reduce domestic/family/intimate abuse, much public infrastructure is required (Department of Justice Canada 2007; Women's Aid, Until Women and Children Are Safe 2005). Whole societies and communities need to be involved in designing, assessing, and redesigning this infrastructure. Given the multitude of messages that encourage men to "remain dominant" and women to "surrender," ongoing awareness campaigns are likely to be needed. Most needed are campaigns that do not ignore power differentials between spouses or blame victims, but connect people to information and resources.

If we are to create policies that are genuinely family friendly, many changes are required. As many second wave feminists understood so well, more critical attention needs to be given to the problems of monogamous heterosexual coupledom (see Bell & Klein 1996). However, as many third wave feminists have taught us, changes should not straightjacket people into rigidly prescribed love styles, yet the pursuit of sexual equality must remain central. Family forms that do not revolve around monogamous heterosexuality cannot continue to be written off as "deviant."

To seriously address intimate abuse, communities, groups, and individuals need to be encouraged to reflect on the assumptions they make and the stereotypes they hold when trying to explain how abuse emerged in a love relationship. They need to spare a thought for the people most likely to be abused—that is, those who own the least and have lower social status. More support and resources need to be allocated to victims/survivors of abuse, and in ways that are not stigmatizing. Ongoing support is also required to work with perpetrators of intimate violence who acknowledge their abuse and are seeking alternative love stories and styles for the future. And the funds needed for programs for perpetrators should not be taken from those needed for victims/survivors (see Mulroney & Chan 2005).

Quite simply, workers need more time to help women think through the implications of leaving. These conversations should not shy away from discussions about the state of public welfare. Apart from bringing to the surface some of women's deeper concerns, these conversations can remind us that when women are abused, they can find themselves caught between a rock and a hard place. In turn, they can remind us to keep agitating for more adequate public policies, programs, and benefits. These provisions are crucial if individuals are to have a real choice about staying or leaving.

Summary

As Plummer (1995) explained at the start of this chapter, human beings engage in meaning-making activities that help to shape the world in which they live, but not always in the conditions of their own choosing. We can love, but not always in contexts that we most desire. For some women, the contexts for loving are as abusive as their love relationships. For too many, the world of abuse is hidden from public view and becomes dangerous. When perpetrated by people they love(d), and who claim(ed) to have loved them, abuse can become even more confounding and dangerous.

However one looks at it, it is hard to dispute that in spite of gains achieved in the name of sexual equality, women are still more likely than men to be on the receiving end of intimate abuse. As a group, they are expected to perform roles where love and care are central. They are still more likely to accept most of the unpaid responsibilities in the home, making them more vulnerable to poverty and other forms of financial disadvantage should their relationships break down.

A simple but important point I learned from this study is that women were not "doormats" if they persevered with love relationships, nor should they be assumed to have developed learned helplessness or battered women's syndrome. Private reflections on the abuse often belied the public sentiments they expressed. Women had much more insight about the abuse than was popularly assumed. Many were fearful of the patronizing indignities that can accompany public identifications such as "abuse victim" or "battered woman." Some found these classifications unintentionally consolidated the threats to their identities. When applied by professionals making too many judgments in haste, the effects could be even more oppressive.

Most importantly, this study has taught me to grapple with questions about how to hear and represent alternative views without relinquishing my right and responsibility to keep questions of injustice alive. It has taught me to appreciate women's diversity without assuming the inevitability of abuse. And it has prompted me to spend so much energy explaining why it can be hard to recognize abuse in intimate relationships and take decisive action.

References

Anapol, D. 1997, *Polyamory: The New Love Without Limits: Secrets of Sustainable Intimate Relationships*, Intinet Resource Center, San Rafael.

Ang, I. 1995, "I'm a feminist but ... 'Other' women and postnational feminism" in *Transitions, New Australian Feminisms*, ed. B. Caine & R. Pringle, Allen & Unwin, St. Leonards.

Astbury, J. 1996, *Crazy for You: The Making of Women's Madness*, Oxford University Press, Oxford.

Atwood, M. 1996, *Alias Grace*, Nan A. Talese, New York.

Bagshaw, D., Chung, D., Couch, M., Lilburn, S. & Wadham, B. 2000, *Reshaping Responses to Domestic Violence, Research into the Needs of Women, Men, and Young People Who Have Experienced Domestic Violence*, vol. 1, Office of Status of Women, Department of Prime Minister and Cabinet, Barton.

Bail, K. (ed) 1996, *DIY Feminism*, Allen & Unwin, St. Leonards.

Baines, D. 1997, "Feminist social work in the inner city: The challenges of race, class, and gender," *Affilia*, vol. 12, no. 3, pp. 297–317.

Baines, D. 2004, "Caring for nothing: Work organization and unwaged labour in social services," *Work, Employment, and Society*, vol. 18, no. 2, pp. 267–295.

Baines, D. (ed) 2007, *Doing Anti-oppressive Practice, Building Transformative Social Work*, Fernwood, Halifax.

Barker, R.L. 1995, *The Social Work Dictionary*, National Association of Social Workers, Washington, DC.

Barrett, M. 1980, *Women's Oppression Today*, Verso, London.

Barthes, R. 1978, *A Lover's Discourse: Fragments*, trans. R. Howard, Hill and Wang, New York.

Baumeister, R.F. & Wotman, S.R. 1992, *Breaking Hearts: The Two Sides of Unrequited Love*, The Guilford Press, New York.

Behrendt, G. & Tuccillo, L. 2004, *He's Just Not That into You: The No-Excuses Truth to Understanding Guys*, Simon Spotlight Entertainment, New York.

Bell, D. & Klein, R. (eds.) 1996, *Radically Speaking: Feminism Reclaimed*, Spinifex, Melbourne.

Bellafante, G. 1998, "Matchmaker, matchmaker," *Time*, vol. 152, no. 25, p. 74.

Benjamin, J. 1988, *The Bonds of Love: Psychoanalysis, Feminism, and the Problem of Domination*, Pantheon Books, New York.

Berger, A. 1997, *Narratives in Popular Culture, Media, and Everyday Life*, Sage Publications, Thousand Oaks.

Berger, P. & Luckman, T. 1966, *The Social Construction of Reality: A Treatise in the Sociology of Knowledge*, Penguin Books, Harmondsworth.

Berger Gluck, S. 1991, "Advocacy oral history: Palestinian women in resistance," in *Women's Words: The Feminist Practice of Oral History*, ed. S. Berger Gluck & D. Patai, Routledge, New York.

Berlant, L. & Warner, M. 1998, "Sex in public," *Critical Inquiry*, vol. 24, no. 2, pp. 547–567.

Bettelheim, B. 1976, *The Uses of Enchantment: The Meaning and Importance of Fairy Tales*, Penguin Books, London.

Blagg, H. 2000, *Crisis Intervention in Aboriginal Family Violence*, University of Western Australia Press, Perth.

Borland, K. 1991, "That's not what I said: Interpretive conflict in oral narrative research," in *Women's Words: The Feminist Practice of Oral History*, ed. S. Berger Gluck & D. Patai, Routledge, New York.

Bowlby, J. 1953, *Childcare and the Growth of Love*, Pelican Books, London.

Bowlby, J. 1969, *Attachment and Loss*, Basic Books, New York.

Breakwell, G. 1986, *Coping with Threatened Identities*, Methuen and Co. Ltd., London.

Brenner, C. 1955, *An Elementary Textbook of Psychoanalysis*, Doubleday Anchor Books, Garden City.

Brontë, C. [1848] 1966, *Jane Eyre*, Penguin Books, London.

Brown, M.E. 1990, "Introduction: Feminist cultural television criticism: Culture, theory, and practice," in *Television and Women's Culture*, ed. M.E. Brown, Sage, London, pp. 11–22.

Brown, R. 1987, *Analyzing Love*, Cambridge University Press, Cambridge.

Brunt, L. 2001, "Into the community," in *Handbook of Ethnography*, ed. P. Atkinson, A. Coffey, S. Delamont, J. Lofland, & L. Lofland, Sage, London.

Bulbeck, C. 1997, *Living Feminism: The Impact of the Women's Movement on Three Generations of Australian Women*, Cambridge University Press, Cambridge.

Bunch, C. 1978, "Lesbians in revolt" in *Feminist Frameworks*, ed. A.M. Jaggar & P. Rothenberg Struhl, McGraw Hill, New York.

Burke Draucker, C. 1999, "The psychotherapeutic needs of women who have been sexually assaulted," *Perspectives in Psychiatric Care*, vol. 35, no. 1, pp. 18–28.

Burns, A. 1994, "Why do women put up with the double load?" in *Australian Women, Contemporary Feminist Thought*, ed. N. Grieve & A. Burns, Oxford University Press, Oxford.

Buscaglia, L. 1979, *Love, What Life Is All About*, Fawcett Columbine, New York.

Butler, J. 1990, *Gender Trouble: Feminism and the Subversion of Identity*, Routledge, New York.

Butler, J. 1997, *The Psychic Life of Power, Theories in Subjection*, Stanford University Press, Stanford.

Caine, B. & Pringle, R. (eds.) 1995, *Transitions, New Australian Feminisms*, Allen & Unwin, St. Leonards.

Califia, P. [1981] 1996, "Feminism and sadomasochism," in *Feminism and Sexuality: A Reader*, ed. S. Jackson & S. Scott, Edinburgh University Press, Edinburgh.

Camilleri, P. 1996, "Into the text: A genealogy of social work," in *(Re)Constructing Social Work*, Ashgate Publishing, Aldershot.

Campbell, J. 2002, "Health consequences of intimate partner violence," *The Lancet*, vol. 359, no. 9314, pp. 1331–1336.

Carver, R. 1988, *Where I'm Calling from: The Selected Stories*, ed. R. Carver, Harvill, London.

Carver, T. 1998, *The Postmodern Marx*, Manchester University Press, Manchester.

Cave, N. 1996, "People ain't no good," *The Boatman's Call* [sound recording], Mute/Reprise.

Chambon, A. 1994, "The dialogical analysis of case materials," in *Qualitative Research in Social Work*, ed. E. Sherman & W.J. Reid, Columbia University Press, New York, pp. 205–215.

Chanfrault-Duchet, M.F. 1991, "Narrative structures, social models and symbolic representations in the life story," in *Women's Words: The Feminist Practice of Oral History*, ed. S. Berger Gluck & D. Patai, Routledge, New York.

Chester, G. 1979, "I call myself a radical feminist," in *Feminist Practice: Notes from the Tenth Year*, Theory Press, London.

Child Migrants' Trust 2001, *Submission to the Senate Community Affairs, References Committee, Inquiry into Child Migration*, http://www.aph.gov.au/Senate/committee/clac_ctte/completed_inquiries/1999-02/child_migrat/submissions/sub132.pdf.

Chisholm, J.S. 1995, "Love's contingencies: The development of socioecology of romantic passion," in *Romantic Passion: A Universal Experience*, ed. W. Jankowiak, Columbia University Press, New York.

Cixous, H. [1974] 1994, "First names of no one," in *The Helene Cixous Reader*, ed. S. Sellers, Routledge, London.

Cixous, H. [1977] 1994, "Angst," in *The Helene Cixous Reader*, ed. S. Sellers, Routledge, London.

Cixous, H. [1984] 1994, "The book of Promethea," in *The Helene Cixous Reader*, ed. S. Sellers, Routledge, London.

Cixous, H. [1987] 1994, "Crime, forgiveness," in *The Helene Cixous Reader*, ed. S. Sellers, Routledge, London.

Cixous, H. [1990] 1994, "Firstdays of the year," in *The Helene Cixous Reader*, ed. S. Sellers, Routledge, London.

Cixous, H. 1991, "The laugh of the Medusa," in *A Reader in Feminist Knowledge*, ed. S. Gunew, Routledge, London.

Clarke, C. [1981] 1996, "Lesbianism, an act of resistance," in *Feminism and Sexuality: A Reader*, ed. S. Jackson & S. Scott, Edinburgh University Press, Edinburgh.

Coates, J. 1996, *Women Talk: Conversation between Women Friends*, Blackwell Publishers, Oxford.

Coates, J. 2003, *Men Talk*, Blackwell, Oxford.

Coehlo, P. 1993, *The Alchemist: A Fable about Following Your Dream*, HarperCollins Publishing, San Francisco.

Cohen, L. 1992, "Dance me to the end of love," *More Best of Leonard Cohen* [sound recording], Columbia Records.

Cohler, B.J. 1994, "The human sciences, the life story, and clinical research," in *Qualitative Research in Social Work*, ed. E. Sherman & W.J. Reid, Columbia University Press, New York.

Collins, J.K. & Harper, J.F. 1978, *The Adolescent Girl: An Australian Analysis*, Cassell Australia, Melbourne.

Coney, S. 1996, "The last post for feminism," in *Radically Speaking: Feminism Reclaimed*, ed. D. Bell & R. Klein, Spinifex, Melbourne.

Connell, R.W. 1995, *Masculinities*, Allen & Unwin, St. Leonards.

Cotterill, P. & Letherby, G. 1993, "Weaving stories: Personal auto/biographies in feminist research," *Sociology*, vol. 27, no. 1, pp. 67–80.

Cowan, G. & Warren, L.W. 1994, "Codependency and gender-stereotyped traits," *Sex Roles*, vol. 30, no. 9/10, pp. 631–645.

Cranny-Francis, A. 1994, *Popular Culture*, Deakin University Press, Geelong.

Currie, D. 1999, *Girl Talk: Adolescent Magazines and Their Readers*, University of Toronto Press, Toronto.

Daly, M. 1973, *Beyond God the Father: Toward a Philosophy of Women's Liberation*, Beacon Press, Boston.

Daly, M. 1978, *Gyn/ecology: The Metaethics of Radical Feminism*, Beacon Press, Boston.

Daly, M. 1996, "The witches return: Patriarchy on trial," in *Radically Speaking: Feminism Reclaimed*, ed. D. Bell & R. Klein, Spinifex, Melbourne.

Davidson, C. 1992, *The Book of Love: Writers and Their Love Letters*, Pocket Books, New York.

de Beauvoir, S. [1949] 1973, *The Second Sex*, Vintage Press, New York.

de Beauvoir, S. 1963, *Memoirs of a Dutiful Daughter*, Penguin Books, London.

de Certeau, M. 1984, *The Practice of Everyday Life*, trans. Steven Rendall, University of California Press, Berkeley.

Deangelis, B. 2001, *What Women Want Men to Know*, Hyperion, New York.

Delmar, R. 1972, "What is feminism?" in *The Body Politic*, ed. J. Mitchell & A. Oakley, Basil Blackwell Ltd., Oxford.

Denzin, N.K. 1991, *Images of Postmodern Society, Social Theory, and Contemporary Cinema*, Sage, London.

Denzin, N.K. 1995, *The Cinematic Society: The Voyeur's Gaze*, Sage, London.

Department of Justice Canada 2007, *Family Violence: A fact sheet from the Department of Justice Canada*, http://www.justice.gc.ca/en/ps/fm/familyvfs.html.

Dion, C. 1998, *Let's Talk about Love* [sound recording], Sony.

Domestic Violence and Incest Resource Centre (DVIRC) 2006, "When love hurts," *Working to Prevent Domestic Violence in Victoria*, http://www.dvirc.org.au/index.htm.

Donovan, P. 2000, "On the pills with Gen Ecstasy," *The Age*, February 19, 1, 6.

Dowling, E. 1995, *Love, Passion, Action: The Meaning of Love and Its Place in Life*, Australian Scholarly Publishing, Melbourne.

Dowrick, S. 1993, *Intimacy and Solitude*, Mandarin Books, Melbourne.

Dowrick, S. 1997, *Forgiveness and Other Acts of Love: Finding True Value in Your Life*, Viking, Penguin Books, Ringwood.

Dowrick, S. 2003, *The Universal Heart: Bring out the Best in Yourself and All Your Relationships*, Penguin, Melbourne.

Dowrick, S. 2005, *Choosing Happiness: Life and Soul Essentials*, Allen & Unwin, St. Leonards.

Dowrick, S. 2007, *The Almost-Perfect Marriage: One-Minute Relationship Skills*, Allen & Unwin, St. Leonards.

Doyle, C. 1990, *Working with Abused Children*, MacMillan Education, London.

Doyle, L. 2000, *The Surrendered Wife: A Woman's Spiritual Guide to True Intimacy with a Man*, Simon & Schuster, Sydney.

Drewery, W. & Winslade, J. 1997, "The theoretical story of narrative therapy," in *Narrative Therapy in Practice: The Archaelogy of Hope*, ed. G. Monk, J. Winslade, K. Cricket & D. Epston, Jossey Bass, San Francisco.

DuBois, E. 1975, "The radicalism of the women suffrage movement: Notes toward the reconstruction of nineteenth-century feminism," *Feminist Studies*, vol. 3, no. 1/2, pp. 63–71.

Duncombe, J. & Marsden, D. 1993, "Love and intimacy: The gender division of emotion and 'emotion work': A neglected aspect of sociological discussion of heterosexual relationships," *Sociology*, no. 27, pp. 221–241.

Dworetzky, J.P. 1982, *Psychology*, West Publishing Company, New York.

Dworkin, A. [1978] 1996, "Biological superiority: The world's most dangerous and deadly idea" in *Feminism and Sexuality: A Reader*, ed. S. Jackson & S. Scott, Edinburgh University Press, Edinburgh.

Dworkin, A. 1981, *Pornography: Men Possessing Women*, The Women's Press, London.

Dworkin, A. 1997, *Life and Death: Unapologetic Writings on the Continuing War against Women*, Virago Press, New York.

Easton, D. & Liszt, A. 2002, *The Ethical Slut: A Guide to Infinite Sexual Possibilities*, Greenery Press, Oakland.

Ebert, T. 1996, *Ludic Feminism and After: Postmodernism, Desire, and Labor in Late Capitalism*, University of Michigan Press, Ann Arbor.

Ehrenreich, B. & English, D. 1978, *For Her Own Good: 150 Years of the Experts' Advice to Women*, Doubleday, New York.

Ehrenreich, B. & Hochschild, A. (eds.) 2003, *Global Women: Nannies, Maids, and Sex Workers in the New Economy*, Granta Books, New York.

Eisikovits, Z., Buchbinder, E. & Mor, M. 1998, "What it was won't be anymore: Reaching the turning point in coping with intimate violence," *Affilia Journal of Women and Social Work*, vol. 13, no. 4, pp. 411–424.

Ellis, B. 1998, *First Abolish the Customer: 202 Arguments against Economic Rationalism*, Penguin Books, Melbourne.

Ellis, B. 1999, "The dangerous game we loosely call love," *The Age*, May 23, p. 24.

Ellerman, A. 1998, "Can discourse analysis enable reflective social work practice?" in *Social Work Education*, vol. 17, no. 1, pp 35–44.

Ellwood, R.S. 1996, "The origin of romantic love and human family life," *National Forum*, vol. 76, no. 1, pp. 31–35.

Engels, F. 1978, "The origin of the family, private property, and the state," *Feminist Frameworks*, ed. A.M. Jaggar & P. Rothenberg Struhl, McGraw-Hill, New York.

England, H. 1986, *Social Work as Art: Making Sense for Good Practice*, Allen & Unwin, London.

Evans, M. 1998, "Falling in love with love is falling for make believe: Ideologies of romance in post-enlightenment culture," *Theory, Culture, and Society: Explorations in Critical Social Science*, vol. 15, no. 3–4, pp. 265–275.

Faludi, S. 1992, *Backlash: The Undeclared War against Women*, Vintage, London.

Faust, B. 1994, *Backlash? Balderdash: Where Feminism Is Going Right*, University of New South Wales Press, Sydney.

Featherstone, M. 1998, "Love and eroticism: An introduction," *Theory, Culture, and Society: Explorations in Critical Social Science*, vol. 15, no. 3–4, pp. 1–18.

Feeney, J.A. & Noller, P. 1990, "Attachment style as a predictor of adult romantic relationships," *Journal of Personality and Social Psychology*, vol. 48, no. 2, pp. 281–291.

Fein, E. & Schneider, S. 1995, *The Rules: Time-Tested Secrets For Capturing the Heart of Mr. Right*, HarperCollins, London.

Fein, E. & Schneider, S. 2002, *The Rules for Online Dating: Capturing the Heart of Mr. Right in Cyberspace*, Pocket Books, New York.

Ferguson, K. 1993, *The Man Question: Visions of Subjectivity in Feminist Theory*, University of California Press, Berkeley.

Firestone, S. 1970, *The Dialectic of Sex: The Case for Feminist Revolution*, Jonathan Cape, London.

Fisher, A. 2004, "Narrative possibilities for unpacking 'homophobia': Responding to the complexities of men's life journeys," keynote presented at the International Summer School of Narrative Practice, Dulwich Centre, Adelaide.

Fisher, A. 2005, "The Power and Promise of Innocent Places," *Narrative Network News*, Issue 34, Sydney, http://www.yaletownfamilytherapy.com/tcpapers/artfisher02.pdf.

Fisher, H. 1995, "The nature and evolution of romantic love," in *Romantic Passion: A Universal Experience*, ed. W. Jankowiak, Columbia University Press, New York.

Fonow, M. & Cook, J. (eds.) 1991, *Beyond Methodology: Feminist Scholarship as Lived Research*, Indiana University Press, Bloomington.

Fook, J. (ed.) 1996, *The Reflective Researcher*, Allen & Unwin, St. Leonards.

Foucault, M. 1984, *The History of Sexuality, Vol. 2: The Use of Pleasure*, Penguin Books, London.

Franklin, M. 1902, *My Brilliant Career*, William Blackwood & Sons, Edinburgh.

Franzosi, R. 1998, "Narrative analysis—or why (and how) sociologists should be interested in narrative," *Annual Review of Sociology*, vol. 24, no. 1, pp. 517–555.

Fraser, H. 1998, "Young women and substitute care: One case study," *Women in Welfare Education*, vol. 2, no. 2, pp. 23–34.

Fraser, H. 1999, "She makes love just like a woman: Romantic love narratives and young women in state care," *Australian Social Work*, vol. 54, no. 4, pp. 17–23.

Fraser, H. 2000, "Considering the needs of children who are exposed to domestic violence: A feminist perspective for practitioners," *Women against Violence: An Australian Feminist Journal*, issue 6, pp. 34–40.

Fraser, H. 2002, "Narrating love and abuse in social work: A critical post-modern feminist perspective," PhD thesis, Monash University, Victoria.

Fraser, H. 2003, "Narrating love and abuse in intimate relationships," *British Journal of Social Work*, vol. 33, pp. 273–290.

Fraser, H. 2004, "Doing narrative research: Analysing personal stories line by line," *Qualitative Social Work*, vol. 3, no. 2, pp. 179–201.

Fraser, H. 2005, "Women, love, and intimacy 'gone wrong': Fire, wind, and ice," *Affilia: Women and Social Work*, pp. 10–20.

French, M. 1978, *The Women's Room*, Sphere Books, London.

French, M. 1985, *Beyond Power: On Women, Men, and Morals*, Ballantine Books, New York.

French, M. 1993, *The War against Women*, Ballantine Books, New York.

Freud, S. [1908] 1990, "Hysterical phantasies and their relation to bisexuality," in *Freud on Women*, ed. E. Young-Bruehl, The Hogarth Press, London.

Freud, S. [1915] 1990, "Three essays on the theory of sexuality" in *Freud on Women*, ed. E. Young-Bruehl, The Hogarth Press, London.

Freud, S. [1931] 1990, "Femininity" in *Freud on Women*, ed. E. Young-Bruehl, The Hogarth Press, London.

Freud, S. 1986, *The Essentials of Psycho-Analysis: The Definitive Collection of Sigmund Freud's Writing*, Penguin Books, London.

Friday, N. 1996, *The Power of Beauty*, Hutchinson, London.

Friedan, B. 1963, *The Feminine Mystique*, Penguin Books, Ringwood.

Friedan, B. 1997, *Beyond Gender: The New Politics of Work and Family*, John Hopkins University Press, Baltimore.

Frith, H. & Kitzinger, C. 1998, "Emotion work as participant resource: A feminist analysis of young women's talk-in-interaction," *Sociology*, vol. 32, no. 2, pp. 299–321.

Fuery, P. 1995, *Theories of Desire*, Melbourne University Press, Melbourne.

Gagnon, J.H. & Simon, W. 1974, *Sexual Conduct*, Hutchinson, London.

Galper, J. 1975, *The Politics of Social Services*, Prentice-Hall, Clifton Hills.

Garner, H. 1995, *The First Stone: Some Questions About Sex and Power*, Pan Macmillan, Sydney.

Gergen, K. & Gergen, M. 1988. "It's a love story," *Psychology Today*, vol. 22, no. 12, pp. 48–50.

Gerhard, J. 2005, "'Sex and the City': Carrie Bradshaw's queer postfeminism," *Feminist Media Studies*, vol. 5, no. 1, pp. 37–49.

Gibson-Graham, J.K. 1995, "Beyond patriarchy and capitalism: Reflections on political subjectivity," in *Transitions: New Australian Feminisms*, ed. B. Caine & R. Pringle, Allen & Unwin, St. Leonards.

Giddens, A. 1992, *The Transformation of Intimacy: Sexuality, Love and Eroticism in Modern Societies*, Polity Press, Cambridge.

Gilbert, P. & Taylor, S. 1991, *Fashioning the Feminine: Girls, Popular Culture, and Schooling*, Allen & Unwin, Sydney.

Gilligan, C. 1982, *In a Different Voice: Psychological Theory and Women's Development*, Harvard University Press, Cambridge.

Gillis, S. & Munford, R. 2004, "Generations and genealogies: The policies and praxis of third wave feminism," *Women's History Review*, vol. 13, no. 2, pp. 165–182.

Glass, J.M. 1993, *Shattered Selves: Multiple Personality in a Postmodern World*, Cornell University Press, London.

Goddard, C. 1996, *Child Abuse and Child Protection: A Guide for Health, Education, and Welfare Workers*, Churchill Livingstone, Melbourne.

Goddard, C. & Carew, R. 1993, *Responding to Children: Child Welfare Practice*, Longman Cheshire, Melbourne.

Goffman, E. 1959, *The Presentation of Self in Everyday Life*, Penguin Books, New York.

Goffman, E. 1963, *Stigma: Notes on the Management of Spoiled Identity*, Penguin Books, Harmondsworth.

Goldman, E. [1908] 1992, "Marriage and love" in *Feminism: The Essential Historical Writings*, ed. M. Schneir, Vintage Books, New York, pp. 318–324.

Goldrick Jones, A. 2002, *Men Who Believe in Feminism*, Praeger, Westport.

Goodison, L. 1983, "Really being in love means wanting to live in a different world," in *Sex and Love: New thoughts on Old Contradictions*, ed. S. Cartledge & J. Ryan, The Women's Press, London.

Gornick, V. 1997, "Closing the book of love," *The Australian*, October 8, pp. 30–31.

Gray, J. 1993, *Men Are from Mars, Women Are from Venus: A Practical Guide for Improving Communication and Getting What You Want in Your Relationships*, Thorsons, an Imprint of HarperCollins Publishers, London.

Gray, J. 1996, *Mars and Venus in Love*, Hodder Headline Australia, Rydalmere.

Gray, P. 1993, "What is love?" *Time*, February 15, pp. 47–48.

Greer, G. 1972, *The Female Eunuch*, Paladin, London.

Greer, G. 1999, *The Whole Woman*, Doubleday, London.

Griffin, S. 1981, *Pornography and Silence: Culture's Revenge against Nature*, The Women's Press, London.

Grimm Brothers 1958, *Cinderella*, Heinemann, London.

Grosz, E. 1987, "Notes towards a corporeal feminism," *Australian Feminist Studies*, no. 5, pp. 2–15.

Grosz, E. 1990, "Contemporary theories of power and subjectivity," in *Feminist Knowledge, Critique, and Construct*, ed. S. Gunew, Routledge, London.

Grosz, E. 1991, "Part 2: Male theories of power: Introduction," in *A Reader in Feminist Knowledge*, ed. S. Gunew, Routledge, London.

Grosz, E. 1994, *Volatile Bodies: Towards a Corporeal Feminism*, Allen & Unwin, Sydney.

Gubrium, J.F. & Holstein, J.A. 1995, "Individual agency, the ordinary and postmodern life," *Sociological Quarterly*, vol. 36, no. 3, pp. 555–570.

Hall, J.M. & Kondora, L.L. 1997, "Beyond 'true' and 'false' memories: Remembering and recovery in the survival of childhood sexual abuse," *Advances in Nursing Science*, vol. 19, no. 4, pp. 37–55.

Hamblin, A. 1983, "Is a feminist heterosexuality possible?" in *Sex and Love: New Thoughts on Old Contradictions*, ed. S. Cartledge & J. Ryan, The Women's Press, London.

Harris, H. 1995, "Rethinking Polynesian heterosexual relationships: A case study on Mangaia, Cook Islands" in *Romantic Passion: A Universal Experience?*, ed. W. Jankowiak, Columbia University Press, New York.

Haule, J.R. 1990, *Divine Madness: Archetypes of Romantic Love*, Shambhala Publications, Boston.

Hawley, J. 2000a, "A life in parts," *The Age Magazine, Good Weekend*, Melbourne, pp. 16–21d.

Hawley, J. 2000b, "Our foolish hearts," *The Age Magazine, Good Weekend*, Melbourne, pp. 26–32.

Heimel, C. 1993, "Shutting up shop," *Cosmopolitan*, March, pp. 49, 167.

Herman, J. 1992, *Trauma and Recovery: From Domestic Abuse to Political Terror*, Pandora, London.

Hey, V. 1997, *The Company She Keeps: An Ethnography of Girls' Friendships*, Open University Press, Buckingham.

Hite, S. 1991, *The Hite Report on Love, Passion, and Emotional Violence*, Macdonald Optima, London.

Hochschild, A.R. 1983, *The Managed Heart: Commercialization of Human Feeling*, University of California Press, Berkeley.

Hoff, J. 1996, "The Pernicious effect of post-structuralism on women's history," in *Radically Speaking: Feminism Reclaimed*, ed. D. Bell & R. Klein, Spinifex, Melbourne.

Hollibaugh, A. [1989] 1996, "Desire for the future, radical hope in passion and pleasure" in *Feminism and Sexuality: A Reader*, ed. S. Jackson & S. Scott, Edinburgh University Press, Edinburgh.

Hollway, W. 1983, "Heterosexual sex: Power and desire for the other" in *Sex and Love: New Thoughts on Old Contradictions*, ed. S. Cartledge & J. Ryan, The Women's Press, London.

Hollway, W. [1984] 1996, "Gender difference and the production of subjectivity" in *Feminism and Sexuality: A Reader*, ed. S. Jackson & S. Scott, Edinburgh University Press, Edinburgh.

Hollway, W. & Jefferson, T. 2000, *Doing Qualitative Research Differently: Free Association, Narrative, and the Interview Method*, Sage, London.

Hones, D.F. 1998, "Known in part: The transformational power of narrative inquiry," *Qualitative Inquiry*, vol. 4, no. 2, pp. 225–249.

hooks, b. [1986] 1991, "Sisterhood" in *A Reader in Feminist Knowledge,* ed. S. Gunew, Routledge, London.

hooks, b. 2000, *All about Love: New Visions,* William Morrow and Co. Inc., New York.

Howe, D. 1995, *Attachment Theory for Social Work Practice,* MacMillan, London.

Hudson, B. 1984, "Femininity and adolescence," in *Gender and Generation,* ed. A. McRobbie & M. Nava, Macmillan Publishers, Houndmills, pp 31–53.

Human Rights and Equal Opportunity Commission 1997, *Bringing Them Home: Report of the National Inquiry into the Separation of Aboriginal and Torres Strait Islander Children from Their Families,* ACT, AUS, http://www.austlii.edu.au/au/special/rsjproject/rsjlibrary/hreoc/stolen/.

Hyden, M. 1994, "Women battering as a marital act: Interviewing and analysis in context," in *Qualitative Studies in Social Work Research,* ed. C.K. Riessman, Sage Publications, Thousand Oaks.

Ife, J. 1997, *Rethinking Social Work: Towards Critical Practice,* Longman, Melbourne.

Ife, J. 2001, *Human Rights and Social Work: Towards Rights-Based Practice,* Cambridge University Press, Cambridge.

Illouz, E. 1998, "The lost innocence of love: Romance as a postmodern condition," *Theory, Culture, and Society: Explorations in Critical Social Science,* vol. 15, no. 3–4, pp. 161–186.

Indian Residential Schools Resolution Canada 2007, *Indian Residential Schools in Canada— Historical Chronology,* http://www.irsr-rqpi.gc.ca/english/historical_events.html.

Ireland, W. 1988, "Eros, agape, amor, libido: Concepts in the history of love" in *Love: Psychoanalytic Perspectives,* ed. J.F. Lasky & H.W. Silverman, New York University Press, New York.

Irigaray, L. 1985, *This Sex Which Is Not One,* trans. Catherine Porter, Cornell University Publishing, New York.

Irigaray, L. 1992, *Elemental Passions,* trans. J. Collie & J. Still, The Athlone Press, London.

Jackson, S. 1996, "Heterosexuality and feminist theory," in *Theorising Heterosexuality: Telling It Straight,* ed. D. Richardson, Open University Press, Buckingham.

Jackson, S. 1998, "Telling stories: Memory, narrative, and experience in feminist research and theory" in *Standpoints and Differences: Essays in the Practice of Feminist Psychology,* ed. K. Henwood, C. Griffin & A. Phoenix, Sage Publications, London.

Jackson, S. 1999, *Heterosexuality in Question,* Sage, London.

Jackson, S. & Scott, S. 1996, "Sexual skirmishes and feminist factions" in *Feminism and Sexuality: A Reader,* ed. S. Jackson & S. Scott, Edinburgh University Press, Edinburgh.

Jagger, E. 1998, "Marketing the self, buying an other: Dating in a postmodern, consumer society," *Sociology,* vol. 32, no. 4, pp. 795–809.

Jamieson, L. 1998, *Intimacy: Personal Relationships in Modern Societies,* Polity Press, Cambridge.

Jankowiak, W. (ed) 1995, *Romantic Passion: A Universal Experience?* Columbia University Press, New York.

Jeffreys, S. [1985] 1997, *The Spinster and Her Enemies: Feminism and Sexuality 1880–1930,* Spinifex, Melbourne.

Jeffreys, S. 1990, *Anticlimax: A feminist perspective on the sexual revolution,* Women's Press, London.

Jenkins, A. 1990, *Invitations to Responsibility: The Therapeutic Engagement of Men Who Are Violent and Abusive,* Dulwich Centre Publications, Adelaide.

Johnson, A.K. 1999, "Working and nonworking women: Onset of homelessness within the context of their lives," *Affilia Journal of Women and Social Work,* vol. 14, no. 1, pp. 42–61.

Johnson, L. 1993, *The Modern Girl, Girlhood, and Growing up,* Allen and Unwin, St. Leonards.

Johnson, M.P. & Ferraro, K.J. 2000, "Research on domestic violence in the 1990s: Making distinctions," *Journal of Marriage and Family,* vol. 62, no. 4, pp. 948–963.

Johnson, S. (ed.) 1992, *Women Love Sex*, Vintage, Sydney.

Jong, E. 1974, *Fear of Flying*, Granada Publishing Ltd., Panther Books, London.

Jordan, B. & Jordan, C. 2000, *Social Work and the Third Way: Tough Love Policy*, Sage, London.

Julius-Mathews, J. 1984, *Good and Mad Women: The Historical Construction of Femininity in Twentieth-Century Australia*, Allen and Unwin, Sydney.

Kamen, P. 2000, *Her Way: Young Women Remake the Sexual Revolution*, Broadway Books, New York.

Kaplan, B. 1979, *Growing Up in Care*, Basil Blackwell Publisher, Oxford.

Kaplan, L. 1995, *Lost Children: Separation and Loss between Children and Parents*, HarperCollins, London.

Kearney, M. 2001, "Enduring love: A grounded formal theory of women's experience of domestic violence," *Research in Nursing and Health*, vol. 24, no. 4, pp. 270–282.

Kipnis, L. 2003, *Against Love: A Polemic*, Random House, New York.

Kingston, A. 2004, *The Meaning of Wife*, Harper Collins, Toronto

Koedt, A. 1970, "Myths about women: The myth of the vaginal orgasm," in *Voices from Women's Liberation*, ed. L. Tanner, Signet, New York.

Kollantai, A. [1919] 1972, *Sexual Relations and the Class Struggle: Love and the New Morality*, trans. and introduced by A. Holt, Falling Wall Press, Bristol.

Kramer, P. 1998, "Women first: 'Titanic' (1997) action-adventure films and Hollywood's female audience" in *Historical Journal of Film, Radio, and Television*, vol. 18, no. 6, pp. 599–614.

Kristeva, J. 1984, *Revolution in Poetic Language*, trans. Margaret Waller, Columbia University Press, New York.

Lacan, J. 1986, *The Four Fundamental Concepts of Psychoanalysis*, trans. A. Sheridan, Penguin Books, Harmondsworth.

Laird, J. 1994, "'Thick description' revisited: Family therapist as anthropologist-constructivist," in *Qualitative Studies in Social Work Research*, ed. C.K. Reissman, Sage, Thousand Oaks.

Langford, W. 1999, *Revolutions of the Heart: Gender, Power and the Delusions of Love*, Routledge, London.

Lasky, J.F & Silverman, H.W. (eds.) 1988, *Love: Psychoanalytic Perspectives*, New York University Press, New York.

Lawler, S. 2002, "Narrative in social research" in *Qualitative Research in Action*, ed. T. May, Sage, London.

Laws, J.L. & Schwartz, P. 1977, *Sexual Scripts: The Social Construction of Female Sexuality*, Dryden Press, Hinsdale.

Lee, J.A. 1998, "Ideologies of lovestyle and sexstyle," in *Romantic Love and Sexual Behaviour*, ed. V.C. De Munck, Praeger, London.

Lees, S. 1986, *Losing out: Sexuality and Adolescent Girls*, Hutchinson, London.

Lees, S. 1989, "Learning to love: Sexual reputation, morality, and the social control of girls," in *Growing up Good*, ed. M. Cain, Sage, London.

Leonard, P. 1997, *Postmodern Welfare: Reconstructing an Emancipatory Project*, Sage, London.

Leros, G. 1998, "The science of love," *The Sunday Age Magazine: The Love Issue*, February 8, p. 13.

Lewis, C.S. 1963, *The Four Loves: Affection, Friendship, Eros, and Charity*, Fontana Books, London.

Lindholm, C. 1995, "Love as an experience of transcendence" in *Romantic Passion: A Universal Experience*, ed. W. Jankowiak, Columbia University Press, New York.

Lindholm, C. 1998, "Love and structure," *Theory, Culture, and Society: Explorations in Critical Social Science*, vol. 15, no. 3–4, pp. 243–263.

Livermore, B. 1993, "The lessons of love," *Psychology Today*, vol. 26, no. 2, pp. 30–40.

Luhmann, N. 1986, *Love as Passion: The Codification of Intimacy*, trans. J. Gaines & D.L. Jones, Polity Press, Cambridge.

Lumby, C. 1997, *Bad Girls: The Media, Sex, and Feminism in the '90's*, Allen & Unwin, St. Leonards.

Lupton, D. 1998, *The Emotional Self*, Sage Publications, London.

Lyne, A. (director) 1997, *Lolita* [motion picture], Guild/Pathé.

Lyotard, J.F. 1979, *The Postmodern Condition: A Report on Knowledge*, Manchester University Press, Manchester.

MacCannell, D. & Flower-MacCannell, J. 1987, "The beauty system" in *The Ideology of Conduct: Essays in Literature and the History of Sexuality*, ed. N. Armstrong & L. Tennenhouse, Methuen & Co., New York.

MacDonald, K. 1996, "The uncertain family," *Arena*, no. 23, pp. 32–34.

Mackay, H. 1999, "Amid the haste, love thy neighbour," *The Age*, December 31, p. 2.

MacKinnon, A. 1997, *Love and Freedom: Professional Women and the Reshaping of Personal Life*, Cambridge University Press, Cambridge.

Mackinnon, C. [1982] 1996, "Feminism, Marxism, method, and the state: An agenda for theory," in *Feminism and Sexuality: A Reader*, ed. S. Jackson & S. Scott, Edinburgh University Press, Edinburgh.

Madigan, S. & Law, I. (eds.) 1998, *Praxis: Situating Discourse, Feminism and Politics in Narrative Therapies*, Yaletown Family Therapy, Vancouver.

Maeve, M.K. 1999, "The social construction of love and sexuality in a women's prison," *Advances in Nursing Science*, vol. 21, no. 13, pp. 46–59.

Mahony, P. & Zmroczek, C. 1996, "Working-class radical feminism: Lives beyond the text," in *Radically Speaking: Feminism Reclaimed*, ed. D. Bell & R. Klein, Spinifex, Melbourne.

Mann, P. 1994, *Micro-Politics: Agency in a Post Feminist Era*, University of Minnesota Press, Minneapolis.

Mann, P. 1996, "Girls' own story: The search for a sexual identity in times of family change," in *Sex, Sensibility, and the Gendered Body*, ed. J. Holland & L. Adkin, St. Martin's Press, New York.

Margolin, L. 1997, *Under the Cover of Kindness*, University Press of Virginia, Charlottesville.

Marx, K. [1848] 1988, *The Communist Manifesto*, W.W. Norton, New York.

Maushart, S. 2001, *Wifework: What Marriage Really Means for Women*, Text Publishing, Melbourne.

McCabe, A. & Bliss, L. 2003, *Patterns of Narrative Discourse: A Multicultural, Life Span Approach*, Pearson Education, Boston.

McCabe, M.P. 1999, "The interrelationship between intimacy, relationship functioning, and sexuality among men and women in committed relationships," *The Canadian Journal of Human Sexuality*, vol. 8, no. 1, pp. 31–41.

McKenzie, M. 2006, "Figuring violence: The personal safety survey 2005," *DVIRC Quarterly*, vol. 3, pp. 19–20.

McLean-Taylor, J., Gilligan, C. & Sullivan, A. 1995, *Between Voice and Silence: Women and Girls, Race and Relationship*, Harvard University Press, Cambridge.

McRobbie, A. 1984, "Dance and social fantasy," in *Gender and Generation*, ed. A. McRobbie & M. Nava, McMillan Education, London.

Mead, M. 1935, *Sex and Temperament in Three Primitive Societies*, Morrow, New York.

Melucci, A. 1996, *The Playing Self: Person and Meaning in the Planetary Society*, Cambridge University Press, Cambridge.

Memmott, P., Stacy, R., Chambers, C. & Keys, C. 2001, *Violence in Indigenous Communities*, Attorney-General's Department, Canberra.

Mendes, S. (director) 1999, *American Beauty* [motion picture], DreamWorks SKG.

Mill, J.S. 1970, *J.S Mill and H.T Hill: Essays of Sex Equality*, University of Chicago Press, Chicago.

Miller, M.V. 1995, *Intimate Terrorism: The Deterioration of Erotic Life*, Norton, New York.

Millett, K. 1971, *Sexual Politics*, Avon Publishing, New York.

Milner, J. 2001, *Women and Social Work: Narrative Approaches*, Palgrave, New York.

Minichiello, V., Aroni, R., Timewell, E. & Alexander, L. 1995, *In-Depth Interviewing: Principles, Techniques, Analysis*, 2nd ed., Longman, Melbourne.

Mishler, E.G. 1991, "Representing discourse: The rhetoric of transcription," *Journal of Narrative and Life History*, vol. 1, no. 4, pp. 255–280.

Mitchell, J. 1971, *Women's Estate*, Penguin Books, London.

Moeller, T.P. & Bachman, G.A. 1993, "The combined effects of physical, sexual, and emotional abuse during childhood: Long-term health consequences for women," *Child Abuse and Neglect*, vol. 17, pp. 623–640.

Moi, T. 1986, *The Kristeva Reader*, Basil Blackwell, Oxford.

Monk, G., Winslade, J., Crocket, K. & Epston, D. (eds.) 1997, *Narrative Therapy in Practice: The Archaeology of Hope*, Jossey-Bass Publishers, San Francisco.

Moore, D. 2000, "Man who beat prostitute to death granted parole," *The Toronto Star*, November 11, p. A19.

Morgan, R. [1970] 1971, "Goodbye to all that," in *Voices from Women's Liberation*, ed. L.B. Tanner, Signet Books, New York.

Morgan, R. 1996, "Light bulbs, radishes, and the politics of the 21st century," in *Radically Speaking: Feminism Reclaimed*, ed. D. Bell & R. Klein, Spinifex, Melbourne.

Mullaly, B. 1997, *Structural Social Work: Ideology, Theory, and Practice*, Oxford University Press, Toronto.

Mullaly, B. 2002, *Challenging Oppression: A Critical Social Work Approach*, Oxford University Press, Toronto.

Mullaly, B. 2007, *The New Structural Social Work*, Oxford University Press, Toronto.

Mulroney, J. & Chan, C. 2005, "Men as victims of domestic violence," *Australian Domestic and Family Violence Clearinghouse*, Sydney, http://www.austdvclearinghouse.unsw.edu.au/topics/topics_pdf_files/Men_as_Victims.pdf.

Myerhoff, B. & Ruby, J. 1992, "A crack in the mirror: Reflexive perspectives in anthropology," in *Remembered Lives: The Work of Ritual, Storytelling, and Growing Older*, ed. B. Myerhoff with D. Metzger, J. Ruby & V. Tufte, University of Michigan Press, Ann Arbor.

New Zealand Police 2007, "Hard truths," in *Protection and Domestic Violence Orders*, http://www.police.govt.nz/safety/home.domesticviolence.html.

Newton, K.M. 1990, *Interpreting the Text: A Critical Introduction to the Theory and Practice of Literary Interpretation*, Harvester Wheatsheaf, New York.

Nies, J. 1977, *Seven Women*, Penguin Books, New York.

Nietzsche, F. 1977, *A Nietzsche Reader*, Penguin Books, London.

Norwood, R. 1976, *Women Who Love Too Much: How to Avoid the Pain of Loving Men Who Cannot Love Back*, St. Martin's Press, New York.

Oakley, A. 1972, *Sex, Gender, and Society*, Sun Books, South Melbourne.

Oakley, A. 1981, *Subject Women*, Fontana Paperbacks, Oxford.

Oakley, A. 1982, "The politics of 'sex differences' research," in *Subject Women*, ed. M. Robertson, London.

Olson, K. & Shopes, L. 1991, "Crossing boundaries, building bridges: Doing oral history among working-class women and men," in *Women's Words: The Feminist Practice of Oral History*, ed. S. Berger Gluck & D. Patai, Routledge, New York.

Orenstein, P. 2000, *Flux: Women on Sex, Work, Love, Kids, and Life in a Half-Changed World*, Hodder Headline Australia, Sydney.

Overall, C. 1998, "Monogamy, nonmonogamy, and identity," *Hypatia*, vol. 13, no. 4, pp. 1–10.

Owen, J. 1996, *Every Childhood Lasts a Lifetime: Personal Stories from the Frontline of Family Breakdown*, Australian Association of Young People in Care, Brisbane.

Owen, U. (ed.) 1985, *Fathers: Reflections by Daughters*, Pantheon Books, New York.

Page, R. 1984, *Stigma*, Routledge and Kegan Paul, London.

Parliament of Australia, Senate 2001, *Lost Innocents: Righting the Record—Report on Child Migration*, http://www.aph.gov.au/SEnate/committee/clac_ctte/completed_inquiries/1999-02/child_migrat/report/index.htm.

Parton, N. & Byrne, P. 2000, *Constructive Social Work: Towards a New Practice*, Macmillan, Basingstoke.

Parv, V. 1997, *I'll Have What She's Having: How to Hook Your Hero and Keep Him Yours Forever*, Mandarin Books, Melbourne.

Patai, D. 1991, "U.S. academics and Third World women: Is ethical research possible?" in *Women's Words: The Feminist Practice of Oral History*, ed. S. Berger Gluck & D. Patai, Routledge, New York.

Pateman, C. 1988, *The Sexual Contract*, Polity Press, Cambridge.

Peacock, G. & Collins, S. 1988, *Social Work and Received Ideas*, Routledge, London.

Pease, B. 1996, "Naming violence as a gender issue: Victimisation, blame, and responsibility," *Women against Violence*, no. 1, November, pp. 33–39.

Peplau, L.A. & Garnets, L.D. 2000, "A new paradigm for understanding women's sexuality and sexual orientation," *Journal of Social Issues*, vol. 56, no. 2, pp. 329–350.

Perkin, C. 1999, "Sex, minus the rose-colored glasses," *The Sunday Age Review*, February 14, p. 16.

Peterson, C.C. 1984, *Looking Forward through the Life Span: Developmental Psychology*, Prentice Hall, Sydney.

Pilcher, J. 1999, *Women in Contemporary Britain: An Introduction*, Routledge, London.

Pipher, M. 1995, *Reviving Ophelia: Saving the Selves of Adolescent Girls*, Random House, Toronto.

Pithouse, A. 1987, *Social Work: The Social Organisation of an Invisible Trade*, Gower Publishing Co., London.

Pittman, F. 1997, "Just in love," *Journal of Marital and Family Therapy*, vol. 23, no. 3, pp. 309–312.

Plummer, K. 1995, *Telling Sexual Stories: Power, Change, and Social Worlds*, Routledge, London.

Plummer, K. 2001, *Documents of Life 2, An Invitation to Critical Humanism*, Sage, London.

Plummer, K. 2003, *Intimate Citizenship: Private Decisions and Public Dialogues*, University of Washington Press, Seattle.

Pringle, R. 1995, "Destabilising patriarchy," in *Transitions: New Australian Feminisms*, ed. B. Caine & R. Pringle, Allen & Unwin, St. Leonards.

Probert, B. 1995, "A restructuring world?" in *Women in a Restructuring Australia: Work and Welfare*, Allen & Unwin, St. Leonards.

Radway, J. 1991, *Reading the Romance: Women, Patriarchy, and Popular Literature*, University of North Carolina Press, Chapel Hill.

Ravenhill, M. 1996, *Shopping and F***ing*, Methuen, Random House, London.

Razer, H. 1996, *In Pursuit of Hygiene*, Random House, Sydney

"Red Stocking Manifesto" [1970] 1971, in *Voices From Women's Liberation*, ed. L.B. Tanner, Signet Books, New York.

Reinharz, S. 1992, *Feminist Methods in Social Research*, Oxford University Press, Oxford.

Reissman, C.K. 1990, *Divorce Talk: Women and Men Make Sense of Personal Relationships*, Rutgers University Press, New Brunswick.

Reissman, C.K. 1993, *Narrative Analysis*, Sage, Newbury.

Reissman, C.K. 1994, "Making sense of marital violence: One woman's narrative," in *Qualitative Studies in Social Work Research*, ed. C.K. Reissman, Sage Publications, Thousand Oaks.

Reissman, C.K. 2002, "Illness narratives; positioned identities," paper presented at Invited Annual Lecture, Health Communication Research Centre, Cardiff University, Wales, May, http://www.cf.ac.uk/encap/hcrc/comet/prog/narratives.pdf.

Reissman, C.K. 2003, "Performing identities in illness narrative," *Qualitative Research*, vol. 3. no.1, pp 5–34.

Rich, A. 1980, "Compulsory heterosexuality and lesbian existence," *Signs*, vol. 5, no. 4, pp. 631–660.

Ricketts, W. & Gochros, H.L. (eds.) 1987, *Intimate Relationships: Some Social Work Perspectives on Love*, Haworth Press Inc., New York.

Ristock, J. 2002, *No More Secrets: Violence in Lesbian Relationships*, Routledge, London.

Rose, S. 2000, "Heterosexism and the study of women's romantic and friend relationships," *Journal of Social Issues*, vol. 56, no. 2, pp. 315–328.

Rossiter, A.B. 1996, "A perspective on critical social work," *Journal of Progressive Human Services*, vol. 7, no. 2, pp. 23–41.

Rowbotham, S. 1972, *Women, Resistance, and Revolution*, Allen Lane, London.

Rowland, R. 1996, "Politics of intimacy: Heterosexuality, love, and power," in *Radically Speaking: Feminism Reclaimed*, ed. D. Bell & R. Klein, Spinifex, Melbourne.

Rubin, Z. 1970, "Measurement of romantic love," *Journal of Personality and Social Psychology*, vol. 16, pp. 265–273.

Ryan, W. 1976, *Blaming the Victim*, Vintage, New York.

Saakvitne, K.W., Tennen, H. & Affleck, G. 1998, "Exploring thriving in the context of clinical trauma theory: Constructivist self development theory," *Journal of Social Issues*, vol. 54, no. 2, pp. 279–292.

Salecl, R. 1998, *(Per)versions of Love and Hate*, Verso, London.

Saraga, E. 1993, "The abuse of children," in *Social Problems and the Family*, ed. R. Dallos and E. McLaughlin, Sage, London, pp. 47–82.

Schaef, A.W. 1989, *Escape from Intimacy: Untangling the "Love" Addictions: Sex, Romance, Relationships*, Harper & Row, San Francisco.

Schneir, M. (ed) 1994, *Feminism: The Essential Historical Writings*, Vintage Books, New York.

Schultz, L.G. 1987, "A note on brief intimate encounters," in *Intimate Relationships: Some Social Work Perspectives on Love*, ed. W. Ricketts & H.L. Gochros, Haworth Press, New York.

Scott-Peck, M. 1978, *The Road Less Travelled: A New Psychology of Love, Traditional Values and Spiritual Growth*, Simon & Schuster, New York.

Scutt, J. 1990, *Even in the Best of Homes: Violence in the Family*, McCulloch Publishing, Melbourne.

Segal, L. 1999, *Why Feminism?* Polity Press, Cambridge.

Seidman, S. 1994, *Contested Knowledge: Social Theory in the Postmodern Era*, Blackwell, Cambridge.

Setzman, E.J. 1988, "Falling in love and being in love: A developmental and object-relations approach," in *Love: Psychoanalytic Perspectives*, ed. J.F. Lasky & H.W. Silverman, New York University Press, New York.

Simon, W. 1996, *Postmodern Sexualities*, Routledge, London.

Simon, W. & Gagnon, J. 1998, "Psychosexual development," *Society*, vol. 35, no. 2, pp. 60–68.

Skeggs, B. 2002, "Techniques for telling the reflexive self," in *Qualitative Research in Action*, ed. T. May, Sage, London, pp. 349–374.

Smith, D. 1999a, *Writing the Social: Critique, Theory, and Investigations*, University of Toronto Press, Toronto.

Smith, D. 1999b, "The family pill: A new way to make love last," *The Age*, December 13, p. 3.

Snyder, S. 1992, "Interviewing college students about their constructions of love," in *Qualitative Methods in Family Research*, ed. J. Gilgun, K. Daly & G. Handel, Springer, New York.

Solas, J. 1995, "Recovering and reconstructing the client's story in social work," *Australian Social Work*, vol. 48, no. 3, pp. 33–36.

Spence, S. 1996, "'Lo cop mortal': The evil eye and the origins of courtly love," *The Romanic Review*, vol. 87, no. 3, pp. 307–319.

Sprecher, S. & Regan, P.C. 1998, "Passionate and companionate love in courting and young married couples," *Sociological Inquiry*, vol. 68, no. 2, pp. 163–185.

Steinem, G. 1992, *Revolution from Within: A Book of Self-Esteem*, Bloomsbury, London.

Sternberg, R. 1998, *Love Is a Story: A New Theory of Relationships*, Oxford University Press, New York.

Summers, A. 1993, "The future of feminism: A letter to the next generation," *Refractory Girl*, Autumn, pp. 192–197.

Summers, A. 1994, *Damned Whores and God's Police*, 2nd ed., Penguin Books, Melbourne.

Tarnas, R. 1991, *The Passion of the Western Mind*, Pimlico, London.

Taylor, J.M., Gilligan, C. & Sullivan, A.M. 1995, *Between Voice and Silence: Women and Girls, Race and Relationship*, Harvard University Press, Cambridge.

Tennov, D. 1979, *Love and Limerence: The Experience of Being in Love*, Stein and Day, New York.

Thompson, N. 1998, *Promoting Equality: Challenging Discrimination and Oppression in the Human Services*, MacMillan Press, London.

Thorpe, R. & Irwin, J. (eds.) 1996, *Women and Violence: Working for Change*, Hale and Iremonger, Sydney.

Tucker, J.S. & Anders, S.L. 1999, "Attachment style, interpersonal perception accuracy, and relationship satisfaction in dating couples," *Personality and Social Psychology Bulletin*, vol. 25, no. 4, pp. 403–412.

Ussher, J. 1997, *Fantasies of Femininity: Reframing the Boundaries of Sex*, Penguin Books, London.

Valverde, M. 1985, *Sex, Power, and Pleasure*, Women's Press, Toronto.

Vellerman, D. 1999, "Love as a moral emotion," *Ethics*, vol. 109, no. 12, pp. 338–363.

Vika and Linda 1994, "Gone again," in *Vika and Linda* [sound recording], Mushroom Records.

Walker, L. 1989, *Terrifying Love: Why Battered Women Kill and How Society Responds*, Harper & Row Publishers, New York.

Walkerdine, V. 1984, "Some day my prince will come," in *Gender and Generation*, ed. A. McRobbie & M. Nava, Macmillan Publishers, Houndmills.

Wallace, C. 1997, *Greer: Untamed Shrew*, Pan Macmillan, Sydney.

Waring, M. 1999, *Counting for Nothing: What Men Value and What Women Are Worth*, 2nd ed., University of Toronto Press, Toronto.

Waters, K. 1996, "(Re)turning to the modern: radical feminism and the post-modern turn," in *Radically Speaking: Feminism Reclaimed*, ed. D. Bell & R. Klein, Spinifex, Melbourne.

Wearing, B. 1996, *Gender: The Pain and Pleasure of Difference*, Longman, Melbourne.

Weedon, C. 1987, *Feminist Practice and Poststructuralist Theory*, Basil Blackwell, Oxford.

Weeks, J. 1998, "The sexual citizen," *Theory, Culture, and Society: Explorations in Critical Social Science*, vol. 15, no. 3–4, pp. 35–52.

Weeks, W. 1995, "Women's work, the gendered division of labour, and community services," in *Issues Facing Australian Families: Human Services Respond*, 2nd ed., ed. W. Weeks & J. Wilson, Pearson Education Australia, French Forrest.

Weeks, W. 2000, "Towards the prevention of violence and the creation of safe and supportive gender relations," in *Issues Facing Australian Families: Human Services Respond*, 3rd ed., ed. W. Weeks & M. Quinn, Pearson Education Australia, French Forrest.

Weir, A. 1996, *Sacrificial Logics: Feminist Theory and the Critique of Identity*, Routledge, New York.

Westlund, A.C. 1999, "Pre-modern and modern power: Foucault and the case of domestic violence," *Signs*, vol. 24, no. 4, pp. 1045–1059.

Wetherell, M. 1995, "Romantic discourse and feminist analysis: Interrogating investment, power, and desire," in *Feminism and Discourse: Psychological Perspectives*, ed. S. Wilkinson & C. Kitzinger, Sage, London.

White, C. & Denborough, D. (eds.) 1998, *Introducing Narrative Therapy: A Collection of Practice-Based Writings*, Dulwich Centre Publications, Adelaide.

Wilkinson, S. & Kitzinger, C. 1996, "The queer backlash," in *Radically Speaking: Feminism Reclaimed*, ed. D. Bell & R. Klein, Spinifex, Melbourne.

Williams, N. 1997, *Four Letters of Love*, McMillan, London.

Williams, S. 1998, "Modernity and the emotions: Corporeal reflections on the (ir)rational," *Sociology*, vol. 32, no. 4, pp. 747–749.

Willis, E. 1992, *No More Nice Girls: Counter-cultural Essays*, University Press of New England, Hanover.

Wilson, E. 1998, "Bohemian love," *Theory, Culture, and Society: Explorations in Critical Social Science*, vol. 15, no. 3–4, pp. 111–127.

Winterson, J. 1989, *Sexing the Cherry*, Vintage, London.

Winterson, J. 1992, *Written on the Body*, Great Moments, London.

Winterson, J. 1996, *Art Objects: Essays on Ecstasy and Effrontery*, Vintage, London.

Winterson, J. 1997, *Gut Symmetries*, Granta, London.

Wolf, N. 1990, *The Beauty Myth*, Vintage, London.

Wolf, N. 1993, *Fire with Fire: The New Female Power and How It Will Change the 21st Century*, Random House, London.

Wolf, N. 1997, *Promiscuities: A Secret History of Female Desire*, Random House, London.

Wollstonecraft, M. [1792] 1975, *Vindication of the Rights of Woman*, Penguin Books, London.

Women's Aid, Until Women and Children Are Safe (UK) 2005, *About Domestic Violence*, http://www.womensaid.org.uk/landing_page.asp?section=000100010005.

Wood, J.T. 2001, "The normalization of violence in heterosexual romantic relationships: Women's narrative of love and violence," *Journal of Social and Personal Relationships*, vol. 18, no. 2, pp. 239–254.

Wood, M. 2000, *Just a Prostitute*, University of Queensland Press, St. Lucia.

Wurtzel, E. 1998, *Bitch*, Quartet Books, London.

Yeatman, A. 1994, *Postmodern Revisionings of the Political*, Routledge, London.

Young, I.M. 1990, *Justice and the Politics of Difference*, Princeton University Press, Princeton.

Young, I.M. 1997, *Intersecting Voices: Dilemmas of Gender, Political Philosophy, and Policy*, Princeton University Press, Princeton.

Zetzel Lambert, E. 1995, *The Face of Love, Feminism, and the Beauty Question*, Beacon Press, Boston.